God's Providence in American History

From the Pilgrims to the Present

Teachers Edition

A Scripture-Based Teaching Manual

"Blessed is the nation whose God is the LORD;
and the people whom he hath chosen for his own inheritance."

Psalm 33:12

Russell Vance McFall

This book is a Scripture-based exploration of history and spiritual truth. While every effort has been made to present Scripture accurately and respectfully, it is not intended to function as a formal commentary or academic theological work.

Published by Ordained Path Books
For permissions or inquiries, contact: ordainedpathbooks@gmail.com
Cover illustration and interior artwork were generated with the assistance of artificial intelligence under the direction of the author.

First Edition -- Version 1.03 — January 2026

Scripture Note
Scripture quotations are taken from the King James Version. The King James Version is in the public domain.

"Thy word is a lamp unto my feet, and a light unto my path."
—Psalm 119:105

Ordained Path Books is dedicated to stories that reflect timeless truth, courage, and the quiet strength of faith—guided by purpose and written to inspire the next generation.

ISBN (Paperback): 9798243377577

Printed in the United States of America.

DEDICATION

This book is dedicated to **Steve Cole** and **Janet Cole**, with gratitude for their faithful service, steady encouragement, and years of labor in teaching and strengthening others through God's Word.

ACKNOWLEDGMENTS

This project would not exist without the shared labor and prayer that stand behind it. I am deeply grateful to my brother-in-law, **Steve Cole**, and his wife **Janet Cole** (my sister), whose time, diligence, and faithful commitment are evident throughout this work. Their efforts reflect a true labor of love, offered for God's glory.

Steve has served as a teacher in his church for decades—first with youth, and now with an adult class. For many years, he has carried a desire to develop teaching material that highlights the guiding hand of God in the history of America. He has researched this subject thoughtfully and patiently over a long period of time. Janet has faithfully supported that work by helping organize teaching notes, offering wise suggestions, and giving careful attention to editing and layout.

As we gathered resources and shaped the lessons, Steve continued to bring forward ideas and refinements that strengthened each chapter. It has been a joy to work together in bringing this material into its present form.

This book has been prepared so that Steve may teach it in his home church, and it is our prayer that it will help others recognize our nation's dependence on God in the past—and our continuing need for His help today, not only nationally, but personally in each of our lives.

With sincere gratitude,
Russell McFall

PREFACE

Why Study Providence in History?

This book was not written to glorify a nation, defend a political system, or declare America exceptional in a biblical covenant sense. Scripture reserves covenant election uniquely for the nation of Israel—God's covenant people in the past, present, and future.
Rather, this book exists to answer a simpler—and more sobering—question:

Does God still govern the affairs of nations?
The Bible answers that question clearly.

"The LORD hath prepared his throne in the heavens;
and his kingdom ruleth over all."
— Psalm 103:19

History is not random.
Nations do not rise and fall by accident.
Power does not operate outside God's authority.
At the same time, providence must be handled with care.
God's involvement does not mean His approval of every action.
Preservation does not imply righteousness.
Mercy does not cancel accountability.
This study approaches American history through a **biblical lens**, not a nationalistic one—observing where God restrained, preserved, corrected, and guided events **despite human weakness**.

The goal is not pride.
The goal is humility.

How to Use This Book

This book may be used in several ways:

- As a **personal study**, read devotionally alongside Scripture
- As a **classroom or small-group resource**
- As a **historical reflection** grounded in biblical truth

Each lesson is designed to:

- Begin with Scripture
- Examine historical reality honestly
- Identify providential patterns without speculation
- End with reflection and application

This book does not attempt to explain every event.
It seeks instead to **recognize God's hand where Scripture allows us to observe it**—and to remain silent where God has not spoken.

Important Clarifications

This book:

- Does **not** declare America (or any modern nation) to be "chosen" in the biblical covenant sense uniquely given to the nation of Israel—God's covenant people in the past, present, and future (Genesis 12:1–3; Deuteronomy 7:6–8; Romans 9:4–5).
- Does **not** equate national success with divine favor.
- Does **not** excuse national sin under the banner of providence.
- Does not presume to explain God's specific purposes where Scripture has not spoken.

Providence is not entitlement.
It is accountability.

INTRODUCTION

God's Providence in American History
From the Pilgrims to the Present

"The LORD hath done great things for us; whereof we are glad."
— *Psalm 126:3*

Why This Study Exists

History is often taught as a sequence of dates, decisions, and personalities. Scripture, however, reveals something deeper: **God is actively at work in the affairs of nations**.

This study was written to help believers examine American history through a **biblical lens of providence**—not nostalgia, not political ideology, and not triumphalism, but **humble recognition of God's sovereign hand**.

The Bible teaches that:

"He removeth kings, and setteth up kings."
— *Daniel 2:21*

Nations rise and fall not by chance, but under God's authority.

What This Study Is — and Is Not

This curriculum **does not claim** that America is a chosen nation like Israel.

It **does not declare** that every historical outcome proves righteousness.

It **does not attempt** to explain every tragedy or assign motives God has not revealed.

Instead, this study seeks to:

- Observe **patterns of providence**
- Recognize **mercy and restraint**
- Acknowledge **judgment and correction**
- Call God's people to **humility and responsibility**

Providence is not always dramatic. Often, it is seen most clearly in **what did not happen**, in disasters restrained, in survival against odds, and in mercy extended despite failure.

Why History Matters Spiritually

Scripture repeatedly calls God's people to **remember**:

"Remember the days of old, consider the years of many generations."

— *Deuteronomy 32:7*

Memory guards against pride.

Forgetfulness invites repetition of error.

By studying history alongside Scripture, believers learn that:

- Blessing follows humility
- Pride invites correction
- Repentance precedes restoration

These truths apply to individuals **and** nations.

How This Study Is Structured

This curriculum contains **32 lessons**, organized into six sections:

1. **Foundations** — God's rule before America existed
2. **Survival & Covenant** — Preservation against impossibility
3. **The American Revolution** — Deliverance against odds
4. **The Early Republic** — Wisdom and restraint
5. **Civil War & National Testing** — Judgment tempered with mercy
6. **Modern Preservation** — Restraint in an age of power

Each lesson includes:

- Scripture
- Historical context
- Providential observations
- Discussion questions
- Personal and national application

Lessons are designed for **40 minutes**, adaptable for church classes, small groups, or homeschool settings.

A Final Word Before You Begin

This study invites reflection—not certainty.

Humility—not conclusions.

Gratitude—not presumption.

As you begin, let Scripture guide interpretation, and let history instruct the heart.

"Blessed is the nation whose God is the LORD."

— *Psalm 33:12*

Contents

SECTION I - FOUNDATIONS

God's Hand Before America Existed

"Known unto God are all his works from the beginning of the world."
— **Acts 15:18**

Section Purpose

Before America was founded,
before colonies were planted,
before documents were written,
God was already at work.

This section establishes the biblical truth that history does not begin with nations—it begins with **God's purposes**. Long before the Pilgrims crossed the Atlantic, the Lord was shaping events, preparing hearts, restoring truth, and guiding conscience.

These lessons lay the foundation for understanding providence not as coincidence, but as **God's sovereign hand working across generations**.

Lessons in This Section

- **Lesson 1:** Providence Defined — God Governs Nations
- **Lesson 2:** The Reformation Roots of Liberty
- **Lesson 3:** The Pilgrims' Escape from Tyranny
- **Lesson 4:** The Mayflower Crossing (1620)

Guiding Truth

God does not respond to history —
He authors it.

(Optional Closing Line for Print or Teaching)

"The foundations of nations are laid long before their flags are raised."

Lesson 1 — Providence Defined: God Governs Nations

Series Title

God's Providence in American History: From the Pilgrims to the Present

---

Theme Verse

"Blessed is the nation whose God is the LORD; and the people whom he hath chosen for his own inheritance."

— *Psalm 33:12*

Lesson Aim (For the Teacher)

To establish a biblical understanding of **providence** before studying history—so events are interpreted through Scripture rather than assumed to be coincidence, luck, or human achievement alone.

This lesson lays the **theological foundation** for the entire series.

If providence is misunderstood here, history will be misread everywhere else.

Time Flow (Minimum 40 Minutes)

- Opening Scripture & Prayer – **4 minutes**
- Core Biblical Teaching – **18 minutes**
- Historical Framing & Examples – **12 minutes**
- Discussion & Application – **6 minutes**

---

1. Opening Scripture Reading

Read aloud together:

"And hath made of one blood all nations of men for to dwell on all the face of the earth, and hath determined the times before appointed, and the bounds of their habitation."

— *Acts 17:26*

Teaching Note:

Pause briefly after reading. Emphasize *determined*, *appointed*, and *bounds.*

2. Core Truth Statement

Providence is God actively governing the affairs of nations—
often quietly, sometimes remarkably, always purposefully.
Providence is not chance.
Providence is not luck.
Providence is not history "working itself out."
Providence is the steady, sovereign rule of God over what He has made.
Scripture does not present God as distant or reactive—
but as reigning.
"The LORD reigneth; let the earth rejoice."
— **Psalm 97:1**
God's rule does not fluctuate with human strength or weakness.
It does not depend on moral perfection.
It is not limited by geography, culture, or era.
Providence means that events unfold under God's authority even when His hand is unseen, His purposes are misunderstood, and His timing is resisted.
"The LORD hath prepared his throne in the heavens; and his kingdom ruleth over all."
— **Psalm 103:19**
This study begins with that conviction.

---

3. What the Bible Means by Providence

Although the word *providence* does not appear frequently in Scripture, the **reality of providence appears everywhere**.
The Bible consistently affirms that God is not merely aware of world events—
He governs them.

Key Scriptures

"The king's heart is in the hand of the LORD, as the rivers of water: he turneth it whithersoever he will."
— **Proverbs 21:1**
Human rulers may believe they act independently, but Scripture teaches that even their decisions operate within God's sovereign allowance and restraint.
"This matter is by the decree of the watchers… to the intent that the living may know that the most High ruleth in the kingdom of men."
— **Daniel 4:17**
Here, God's purpose is stated plainly:
that nations might *know* He rules.

"He removeth kings, and setteth up kings."
— **Daniel 2:21**
Authority is neither accidental nor permanent.
God grants it, limits it, and removes it according to His purposes.

Teaching Point (Scripture-Anchored)
God does not merely observe history—He directs it.

This truth is affirmed throughout Scripture:
• **God Governs Rulers —**
"The king's heart is in the hand of the LORD, as the rivers of water: he turneth it whithersoever he will."
— Proverbs 21:1
• **God Assigns Authority —**
"And he changeth the times and the seasons: he removeth kings, and setteth up kings: he giveth wisdom unto the wise, and knowledge to them that know understanding."
— Daniel 2:21
• **God Overrules Pride —**
"This matter is by the decree of the watchers, and the demand by the word of the holy ones: to the intent that the living may know that the most High ruleth in the kingdom of men, and giveth it to whomsoever he will, and setteth up over it the basest of men."
— Daniel 4:17
• **God Establishes Boundaries —**
"And hath made of one blood all nations of men for to dwell on all the face of the earth, and hath determined the times before appointed, and the bounds of their habitation."
— Acts 17:26

This does **not** mean:
• **Nations Are Not Always Righteous —**
"O Assyrian, the rod of mine anger, and the staff in their hand is mine indignation…
Howbeit he meaneth not so, neither doth his heart think so; but it is in his heart to destroy and cut off nations not a few."
— Isaiah 10:5–7

• Leaders Are Not Always Godly —
"Thus saith the LORD to his anointed, to Cyrus… I have surnamed thee, though thou hast not known me."
— Isaiah 45:1–4
• Outcomes Are Not Always Pleasant —
"For, lo, I raise up the Chaldeans, that bitter and hasty nation…"
— Habakkuk 1:5–6

It **does** mean:
Nothing unfolds outside God's authority.
No nation rises without His allowance.
No power continues beyond His restraint.
"The LORD reigneth."
— **Psalm 103:19**

---

4. What Providence Is — and What It Is Not
Providence IS:

- **God restraining evil** —

"Surely the wrath of man shall praise thee: the remainder of wrath shalt thou restrain."
— *Psalm 76:10*

- **God timing events** —

"To every thing there is a season."
— *Ecclesiastes 3:1*

- **God preserving people** —

"He that keepeth Israel shall neither slumber nor sleep."
— *Psalm 121:4*

- **God working through imperfect leaders** —

"But as for you, ye thought evil against me; but God meant it unto good."
— *Genesis 50:20*

- **God accomplishing purposes over generations** —

"He hath remembered his covenant for ever."
— *Psalm 105:8*

Providence Is NOT:

- **God approving every action** —

"Thou art of purer eyes than to behold evil."
— *Habakkuk 1:13*

- **God excusing national sin** —

"Righteousness exalteth a nation: but sin is a reproach to any people."
— *Proverbs 14:34*

- **God promising permanent blessing** —

Jeremiah 18:7–10

- **God guaranteeing success** —

"Not by might, nor by power, but by my spirit."
— *Zechariah 4:6*

Providence governs **both blessing and discipline**.
It preserves purpose—not comfort.

---

5. Why This Matters Before Studying American History

Before examining Pilgrims, wars, revivals, or founding documents, **one foundational question must be settled**:

Does God deal with nations at all?

Scripture answers clearly.
"Righteousness exalteth a nation: but sin is a reproach to any people."
— **Proverbs 14:34**
"The LORD bringeth the counsel of the heathen to nought."
— **Psalm 33:10**

Teaching Insight

If God governs *all* nations, then America is:

- **Not exempt from His care** — *Psalm 33:12*
  "Blessed is the nation whose God is the LORD; and the people whom he hath chosen for his own inheritance."
- **Not exempt from His correction** — *Hebrews 12:6*
  "For whom the Lord loveth he chasteneth, and scourgeth every son whom he receiveth."
- **Not exempt from His judgment** — *Psalm 9:17*
  "The wicked shall be turned into hell, and all the nations that forget God."

This series is **not** about national pride.
It is about national accountability before God.
"Shall not the Judge of all the earth do right?"
— **Genesis 18:25**

6. Historical Framing — Early Providential Patterns

Without debate or conclusions, history records moments where outcomes:

- Defied human odds
- Aligned at improbable times
- Preserved people unexpectedly
- Redirected events suddenly

Examples we will examine later include:

- Small colonies surviving conditions that should have erased them
- Armies preserved when defeat seemed certain
- Unity emerging after widespread repentance
- Catastrophe narrowly avoided through restraint

Scripture affirms that such patterns are not unknown to God:

"Known unto God are all his works from the beginning of the world."

— **Acts 15:18**

The question is not:

"Was America perfect?"

The real question is:

"Did God restrain, preserve, and guide events despite human weakness?"

That is the biblical lens this study will use.

---

7. Avoiding Common Errors When Studying Providence

When studying God's providence in history, several common errors must be carefully avoided.

Scripture warns us not only about *what* to believe, but *how* to discern rightly.

This lesson intentionally avoids the following mistakes:

Error #1 — Declaring Any Nation "Chosen" Like Israel

Scripture is clear that covenant status belongs uniquely to Israel.

"The LORD hath chosen Zion; he hath desired it for his habitation."

— **Psalm 132:13**

No modern nation inherits Israel's covenant promises.

God may bless, restrain, or correct nations—but Scripture alone defines covenant election.

Providence must never be confused with covenant.

Error #2 — Assuming Providence Equals Approval

God's involvement does not imply endorsement.

Scripture repeatedly shows God using nations and leaders **without approving their sin**.

"O Assyrian, the rod of mine anger… howbeit he meaneth not so."

— **Isaiah 10:5–7**

God may accomplish His purposes through flawed people while still holding them accountable.

Providence governs outcomes—

righteousness governs judgment.

Error #3 — Reading Modern Politics Back into Scripture

This series does not interpret Scripture through political outcomes.

Instead, it interprets history **through Scripture**.

"For my thoughts are not your thoughts, neither are your ways my ways."

— **Isaiah 55:8**

Biblical providence calls believers to humility, not certainty—

discernment, not triumphalism.

Error #4 — Treating History as Proof of Moral Superiority

Scripture warns that blessing can lead to pride if not accompanied by gratitude and obedience.

"Beware lest thou forget the LORD."

— **Deuteronomy 8:11**

History should humble us—not flatter us.

Providence remembered without repentance becomes presumption.

Error #5 — Ignoring Human Responsibility

God's sovereignty does not cancel human accountability.

"The soul that sinneth, it shall die."

— **Ezekiel 18:4**

Providence does not excuse sin.

It exposes it, restrains it, judges it, and—when hearts respond—redeems it.

Teacher's Doctrinal Summary Box — Lesson 1

Purpose:

This box is designed to help teachers summarize the doctrinal framework of Lesson 1 before moving forward.

Core Doctrinal Affirmations

- God sovereignly governs nations (*Psalm 103:19*)
  "The LORD hath prepared his throne in the heavens; and his kingdom ruleth over all."
- God restrains evil and sets boundaries.
  "Surely the wrath of man shall praise thee: the remainder of wrath shalt thou restrain." - *Psalm 76:10*
  "And hath made of one blood all nations of men for to dwell on all the face of the earth, and hath determined the times before appointed, and the bounds of their habitation;" - *Acts 17:26*
- God uses imperfect leaders without approving sin (*Genesis 50:20*)
  "But as for you, ye thought evil against me; but God meant it unto good, to bring to pass, as it is this day, to save much people alive."
- God blesses righteousness and reproaches sin (*Proverbs 14:34*)
  "Righteousness exalteth a nation: but sin is a reproach to any people."
- God disciplines nations without abandoning His purposes (*Jeremiah 18:7–10*)
  "7. At what instant I shall speak concerning a nation, and concerning a kingdom, to pluck up, and to pull down, and to destroy it;"
  "8. If that nation, against whom I have pronounced, turn from their evil, I will repent of the evil that I thought to do unto them."
  "9. And at what instant I shall speak concerning a nation, and concerning a kingdom, to build and to plant it;"
  "10. If it do evil in my sight, that it obey not my voice, then I will repent of the good, wherewith I said I would benefit them."

Key Guardrails for Interpretation

- Providence ≠ Covenant
- Providence ≠ Moral Approval
- Providence ≠ Guaranteed Blessing
- Providence ≠ Political Certainty

Teaching Emphasis

This lesson is not about:

- National exceptionalism
- Political validation
- Historical nostalgia

It **is** about:

- God's sovereignty
- Human accountability
- Humility before history
- Discernment rooted in Scripture

"The secret things belong unto the LORD our God: but those things which are revealed belong unto us."

— **Deuteronomy 29:29**

Suggested Teaching Transition (Optional)

Before moving to Lesson 2, teachers may ask:

- *If God governs nations, how does He prepare people long before deliverance occurs?*
- *What does obedience look like when liberty has not yet been secured?*

Lesson 2 answers those questions by tracing **the spiritual soil from which liberty grew**.

---

8. Discussion Questions (Choose 2–3)

1. Why are people often more comfortable crediting luck than providence?
2. What biblical examples show God using ungodly leaders for His purposes?

(Isaiah 45:1–4; Romans 13:1)

3. How does believing God governs nations affect how we view current events?
4. What dangers arise when God is removed from history?

(Allow brief, guided responses. Avoid debate.)

---

9. Personal & National Application

Personal

- **Humility:** God does not need us — *Job 41:11*

"Who hath prevented me, that I should repay him? whatsoever is under the whole heaven is mine."

- **Gratitude:** Preservation is mercy, not entitlement — *Lamentations 3:22*

"It is of the LORD'S mercies that we are not consumed, because his compassions fail not."

- **Soberness:** Blessing can be withdrawn — *Jeremiah 18:10*

"If it do evil in my sight, that it obey not my voice, then I will repent of the good, wherewith I said I would benefit them."

National

- Nations rise when they acknowledge God — *Psalm 33:12*

"Blessed is the nation whose God is the LORD; and the people whom he hath chosen for his own inheritance."

- Nations fall when they forget Him — *Psalm 9:17*

"The wicked shall be turned into hell, and all the nations that forget God."

- History warns before it celebrates — *1 Corinthians 10:11*

"Now all these things happened unto them for ensamples: and they are written for our admonition, upon whom the ends of the world are come."

---

10. Closing Reflection

This series will trace God's hand across history—not as sentiment, but as sovereignty. Again and again, Scripture affirms that God works **before events are visible**, preparing outcomes long before human eyes recognize the need.

"Declaring the end from the beginning, and from ancient times the things that are not yet done."

— *Isaiah 46:10*

As we study history, we will see God arranging timing, restraining destruction, and preserving people in ways that only become clear when we look back. Deliverance is often prepared quietly, patiently, and far in advance of crisis.

We will also encounter moments when preservation came at the edge of loss—when survival itself seemed unlikely, when prayer rose not from confidence but from desperation.

"Then they cried unto the LORD in their trouble, and he saved them out of their distresses."

— *Psalm 107:19*

In those moments, God did not act because nations were righteous, nor because leaders were flawless. He acted because He is faithful to His purposes and merciful beyond human deserving.

Yet providence is not merely protective.

Scripture is equally clear that God allows hardship to correct pride, permits discipline to expose false confidence, and calls nations to repentance when they forget Him.

"Before I was afflicted I went astray: but now have I kept thy word."

— *Psalm 119:67*

Preservation does not mean approval.
Deliverance does not erase accountability.
God's providence governs both mercy and correction.
"For whom the LORD loveth he correcteth; even as a father the son in whom he delighteth."
— *Proverbs 3:12*
This series will therefore show God allowing difficulty—not to destroy, but to humble; not to abandon, but to awaken conscience and restore perspective.
Providence is not indulgent.
It is holy in its standards, patient in its timing, and purposeful in its outcomes.
"The LORD is righteous in all his ways, and holy in all his works."
— *Psalm 145:17*
As we study American history through this lens, we are not invited to celebrate ourselves, nor to excuse our failures. We are called instead to recognize the mercy of God, the limits of human wisdom, and the serious responsibility that comes with blessing.
"Unto whomsoever much is given, of him shall be much required."
— *Luke 12:48*
History, viewed rightly, becomes more than a record of events.
It becomes a witness—calling each generation to humility, gratitude, repentance, and faithfulness under the hand of God.

Optional Teaching Pause (Adult Class)
You might ask:

- *Why does Scripture present both mercy and discipline as acts of God's faithfulness?*
- *How does this reflection change the way we read national success or survival?*
- *What responsibility accompanies preservation?*

---

11. Closing Scripture & Prayer Prompt
Read aloud:
"Blessed is the nation whose God is the LORD."
— *Psalm 33:12*
Prayer Prompt:
"Lord, give us eyes to see Your hand in history, hearts humble enough to learn from it, and wisdom to walk faithfully in our own generation."

Lesson 2 — The Reformation Roots of Liberty

Series Title
God's Providence in American History: From the Pilgrims to the Present

---

Theme Verse
"And ye shall know the truth, and the truth shall make you free."
— *John 8:32*

Lesson Aim (For the Teacher)
To show how God prepared the way for liberty in America **long before America existed**—by restoring access to Scripture, awakening conscience, and breaking spiritual monopolies during the Reformation.
This lesson establishes that **political liberty followed spiritual liberty**, not the other way around.

Time Flow (Minimum 40 Minutes)

- Opening Scripture & Prayer – **4 minutes**
- Core Biblical Teaching – **18 minutes**
- Historical Narrative & Providential Examples – **12 minutes**
- Discussion & Application – **6 minutes**

---

1. Opening Scripture Reading
Read aloud together:
"Stand fast therefore in the liberty wherewith Christ hath made us free, and be not entangled again with the yoke of bondage."
— *Galatians 5:1*
Teaching Note:
Emphasize that this verse speaks of **spiritual liberty first**, not political independence.

---

2. Core Truth Statement

Liberty begins when God's Word is restored to God's people and truth is allowed to speak to conscience.

Political freedom is fragile without spiritual freedom.
Where Scripture is silenced, tyranny soon follows.
"If the Son therefore shall make you free, ye shall be free indeed."
— *John 8:36*

---

3. The Biblical Connection Between Truth and Liberty

Key Scriptures

"The entrance of thy words giveth light; it giveth understanding unto the simple."
— *Psalm 119:130*
"Where the Spirit of the Lord is, there is liberty."
— *2 Corinthians 3:17*
"Sanctify them through thy truth: thy word is truth."
— *John 17:17*

Teaching Point (Now Scripture-Anchored)

The Bible presents liberty not as rebellion, but as freedom of the soul under God's authority.

True liberty, according to Scripture:

- **Frees the conscience**
  "22. Hast thou faith? have it to thyself before God. Happy is he that condemneth not himself in that thing which he alloweth."
  "23. And he that doubteth is damned if he eat, because he eateth not of faith: for whatsoever is not of faith is sin." -- Romans 14:22–23
- **Submits to truth**
  "Whoso looketh into the perfect law of liberty, and continueth therein, he being not a forgetful hearer, but a doer of the work, this man shall be blessed in his deed."
  — James 1:25
- **Produces responsibility, not chaos**
  "As free, and not using your liberty for a cloke of maliciousness, but as the servants of God." — 1 Peter 2:16

Biblical liberty is never lawlessness.
It is **obedience without coercion**.
"I will walk at liberty: for I seek thy precepts."
— *Psalm 119:45*

---

4. What Changed During the Reformation

For centuries across much of Europe, spiritual life was shaped by distance rather than access. Scripture existed—but it was largely inaccessible. The Bible was written and preserved in languages the common people could not read. Worshippers depended almost entirely on clergy to hear, interpret, and apply God's Word:
"For the time will come when they will not endure sound doctrine."
— *2 Timothy 4:3*
Literacy among ordinary people was limited, not merely by circumstance, but by design. Reading Scripture independently was often discouraged, restricted, or even punished. Conscience was regulated not by personal engagement with God's Word, but by institutional authority that claimed exclusive interpretive power:
"They bind heavy burdens and grievous to be borne, and lay them on men's shoulders."
— *Matthew 23:4*
Faith, for many, became mediated rather than personal. Obedience was measured by compliance, not conviction. Truth was received secondhand.
The Reformation altered this landscape profoundly.
As Scripture was translated into common languages, God's Word crossed boundaries it had long been kept behind. For the first time in generations, ordinary men and women could read the Bible in their own homes, with their own eyes, and hear God's voice directly through His Word:
"The entrance of thy words giveth light; it giveth understanding unto the simple."
— *Psalm 119:130*
Reading Scripture began to awaken conscience. Authority was no longer assumed—it was measured. Teachings were examined in light of the written Word. Belief shifted from inherited custom to personal conviction:
"Search the scriptures; for in them ye think ye have eternal life."
— *John 5:39*
This change did not produce instant harmony. It produced questions. It challenged long-standing assumptions. It disrupted systems built on control rather than truth.
What changed was not merely theology—it was worldview.

When Scripture moved from locked pulpits to open homes, faith moved from obligation to responsibility. People began to understand that they stood accountable before God Himself—not merely before institutions:

"So then every one of us shall give account of himself to God."

— *Romans 14:12*

This shift quietly prepared generations to value conscience, responsibility, and moral restraint. It did not create rebellion—it cultivated accountability. It did not demand freedom—it learned it under truth:

"Stand fast therefore in the liberty wherewith Christ hath made us free."

— *Galatians 5:1*

The Reformation was not merely a religious shift.

It was a worldview earthquake.

God's Word moved from locked pulpits to open homes—and history would never be the same.

---

5. Concrete Providential Examples (Quiet but Powerful)

Providential Example #1 — Scripture and Language

One of the quietest yet most far-reaching developments of the Reformation era was the restoration of Scripture to the common people—not only in content, but in **language**.

For centuries, the Bible existed largely outside the reach of ordinary households. It was read aloud, interpreted by authorities, and preserved in forms inaccessible to most people. Literacy was limited, and Scripture remained distant—heard occasionally, but rarely examined personally.

At precisely the moment when reformers began emphasizing the authority of God's Word, something remarkable occurred.

Bible translation accelerated.

Scripture began appearing in the **common languages of the people**, not only in Latin or scholarly forms, but in words spoken at home, in the marketplace, and within families. This shift did more than make Scripture available—it **stabilized language itself**. As people learned to read, they often did so using the Bible. Vocabulary, grammar, and written forms took shape around Scripture.

In countless homes, God's Word became the first substantial book read aloud, studied carefully, and passed from one generation to the next.

This development was not accidental.

Scripture affirms that God's Word is not bound by circumstance:

"For ever, O LORD, thy word is settled in heaven."

— *Psalm 119:89*

Yet what is settled in heaven was now being **anchored on earth**—in living language, accessible to ordinary people. God ensured that His Word could be **read**, not merely heard or filtered through others.

The effect was profound.

As Scripture entered homes, conscience awakened. Truth was no longer mediated exclusively by institutions; it was encountered personally. People began measuring beliefs, traditions, and authority against what they could now read for themselves. Faith became something examined, not inherited blindly.

This quiet shift reshaped how individuals understood responsibility before God.

The Bible did not teach rebellion.

It taught accountability.

And accountability, once awakened, does not remain confined to private devotion. It influences how people think about authority, obligation, and liberty.

Providence here did not announce itself through dramatic events. It worked slowly—through ink, paper, and language—preparing hearts and minds long before political consequences appeared. By the time questions of liberty arose, the foundation had already been laid in Scripture-formed conscience.

God's hand was not only restoring truth.

He was restoring **access**.

Theological Reflection (Optional Transition Sentence)

When God gives His Word to a people in their own language, He prepares more than devotion—He prepares discernment.

Providential Example #2 — Printing and Preservation

As Scripture was translated into the common languages of Europe, another development quietly ensured that it would not be confined, controlled, or easily silenced.

Printed Scripture began to spread.

The emergence of the printing press did not create the Reformation, nor did it cause spiritual renewal on its own. But in God's providence, it **served the moment perfectly**. What had once required years of hand copying could now be reproduced rapidly and accurately.

Scripture moved faster than authorities could restrain it.

Attempts to suppress the Bible continued.

Books were banned. Printers were threatened. Copies were seized and destroyed. Yet the very nature of printing made complete censorship impossible. Once Scripture entered circulation, it crossed borders, passed from hand to hand, and reappeared wherever people were willing to read.

Truth proved difficult to confine.

Scripture describes God's Word as active and purposeful:

"So shall my word be that goeth forth out of my mouth: it shall not return unto me void, but it shall accomplish that which I please."

— *Isaiah 55:11*

Printing became one of the means by which that promise unfolded in history.

Where a single manuscript could be burned, dozens of printed copies survived. Where one city suppressed Scripture, another preserved it. The Word moved quietly, often unnoticed, shaping thought and conscience far from centers of control.

This preservation mattered deeply.

Ideas that survive suppression tend to harden into ideology. But Scripture, preserved through printing, remained **available, examinable, and corrective**. People could compare teachings, test claims, and return repeatedly to the text itself. Truth did not depend on memory alone—it was **fixed in print**.

Providence here was not dramatic.

It was persistent.

God did not remove opposition.

He rendered it ineffective.

Printing did not cause reform—but it **protected** it. It ensured that Scripture could outlast opposition, cross generations, and remain accessible long after the initial wave of renewal passed.

By the time questions of conscience, authority, and liberty arose in later centuries, the Bible had already been secured—not by force, but by faithful preservation.

God's Word endured not because it was defended perfectly, but because it was **distributed widely**.

Theological Reflection (Optional Transition Sentence)

God often preserves truth not by shielding it from resistance, but by giving it the means to outlast resistance.

Providential Example #3 — Conscience Before Authority

As Scripture spread into the homes and hands of ordinary people, a profound transformation occurred—one that reached far beyond personal devotion.

Conscience awakened.

For generations, obedience had often been shaped primarily by **fear**: fear of punishment, fear of exclusion, fear of authority. Moral responsibility was frequently mediated through institutions and enforced externally. Right and wrong were defined largely by what was permitted or forbidden by those in power.

But when individuals began reading Scripture for themselves, obedience took on a different character.

Truth was no longer distant.

Authority was no longer unquestioned.

Responsibility became **personal**.

Men and women encountered commands not merely issued by leaders, but spoken by God Himself. Obedience began to flow not from fear of consequences, but from conviction of conscience. Scripture placed each individual directly before God—accountable not only for actions, but for faithfulness.

This shift is deeply biblical.

"We ought to obey God rather than men."

— *Acts 5:29*

That declaration did not call for rebellion. It called for **rightly ordered allegiance**. God was not being removed from authority structures; He was being placed **above** them.

Conscience, informed by Scripture, did not eliminate submission. It redefined it. Authority was to be respected—but measured. Obedience was to be rendered—but never at the expense of faithfulness to God.

This development carried lasting implications.

When moral accountability becomes personal, tyranny loses its strongest tool: unquestioned compliance. People shaped by conscience do not resist authority impulsively or violently. They resist it **morally**—by refusing to surrender obedience where it belongs only to God.

Providence here worked quietly, reshaping the inner life of individuals long before it reshaped societies.

This was not political ideology.

It was theological clarity.

By the time later generations faced oppressive systems, the groundwork had already been laid. Resistance, when it came, would not be rooted in lawlessness, but in conviction—measured, principled, and restrained.

Conscience before God does not produce chaos.
It produces responsibility.
And responsibility, once awakened, does not remain private. It influences families, communities, and eventually the way authority itself is understood.

Theological Reflection (Optional Transition Sentence)
When conscience is shaped by Scripture, authority is neither idolized nor despised—it is weighed.

---

6. Important Clarifications About Providence
The Reformation was a work of God—but it was **not a flawless movement led by flawless people**.

- **Reformers were flawed**
  They carried personal weaknesses, blind spots, and inconsistencies.
  Courage and conviction often coexisted with fear and limitation.
- **Conflict occurred**
  Disagreements arose not only between reformers and established authorities, but among reformers themselves.
  Unity was often hard-won and sometimes absent.
- **Errors remained**
  Not every theological conclusion was fully mature.
  Not every action reflected Christlike restraint.

History reminds us that **God's providence does not depend on human perfection**.
"But we have this treasure in earthen vessels, that the excellency of the power may be of God, and not of us."
— *2 Corinthians 4:7*
Providence works through:

- Obedience mixed with weakness
- Faith marked by imperfection
- Progress that unfolds unevenly over time

"For he knoweth our frame; he remembereth that we are dust."
— *Psalm 103:14*
God did not wait for perfect reformers.
He worked through willing ones.
This clarification matters because it guards against two errors:

- **Romanticizing history** as if God only works through ideal circumstances
- **Dismissing history** because its instruments were imperfect

Providence does not require spotless vessels.
It requires surrendered ones.

---

7. Why This Matters for America

The influence of the Reformation reached far beyond Europe's borders.
Those who later crossed the Atlantic carried with them **deeply formed convictions**, shaped by generations of Scripture-centered faith.
They:

- **Came from Bible-reading cultures**
  Scripture had become accessible, personal, and authoritative in daily life.
- **Valued conscience before God**
  Individuals understood themselves as morally accountable first to God, not merely to institutions.
- **Expected authority to be limited**
  Power was viewed with caution, recognizing the fallibility of all human rulers.
- **Understood liberty as stewardship, not license**
  Freedom was seen as a responsibility to live rightly, not permission to do as one pleased.

"Whether it be right in the sight of God to hearken unto you more than unto God, judge ye."
— *Acts 4:19*

By the time colonists arrived in the New World, the conviction that:
"No man stands between a believer and God"
was already firmly planted.
This belief reshaped how authority, law, and liberty were understood.
America did not **invent** liberty.
It **inherited** it—at great cost and with great responsibility.
"Stand fast therefore in the liberty wherewith Christ hath made us free, and be not entangled again with the yoke of bondage."
— *Galatians 5:1*

Liberty rooted in Scripture produced:

- Self-governance under God
- Accountability without tyranny
- Freedom restrained by conscience

This inheritance would later shape institutions, laws, and expectations—but only as long as the spiritual roots remained intact.

Providence prepared liberty long before it was declared.

What remained was whether it would be **guarded faithfully** once received.

---

8. Discussion Questions (Choose 2–3)

1. Why is access to Scripture essential for true liberty?

(Psalm 119:130)

2. What happens when conscience is controlled rather than informed?

(Romans 14:12)

3. Can liberty survive without truth? Why or why not?

(John 17:17)

4. Why does Bible literacy often threaten tyranny?

(Keep responses brief and Scripture-focused.)

---

9. Personal & National Application

Personal

- Do I allow Scripture to shape my conscience?
  "For the word of God is quick, and powerful, and sharper than any twoedged sword, piercing even to the dividing asunder of soul and spirit, and of the joints and marrow, and is a discerner of the thoughts and intents of the heart." — Hebrews 4:12
- Am I using liberty to serve God or self?
  "For, brethren, ye have been called unto liberty; only use not liberty for an occasion to the flesh, but by love serve one another." — Galatians 5:13

National

- Liberty must be guarded by truth
  "Blessed is the nation whose God is the LORD; and the people whom he hath chosen for his own inheritance." — Psalm 33:12
- Freedom without moral grounding collapses
  "In those days there was no king in Israel: every man did that which was right in his own eyes." — Judges 21:25
- Forgetting Scripture erodes conscience

"My people are destroyed for lack of knowledge: because thou hast rejected knowledge, I will also reject thee, that thou shalt be no priest to me: seeing thou hast forgotten the law of thy God, I will also forget thy children."— Hosea 4:6

---

10. Closing Reflection

God did not wait until 1776 to prepare liberty.

Long before declarations were written or nations were formed, He was already at work—quietly, patiently, and deliberately—shaping hearts, ideas, and consciences across generations:

"Known unto God are all his works from the beginning of the world."

— *Acts 15:18*

Liberty was not an accident of politics. It was the fruit of truth patiently restored.

God worked through **translation**, ensuring that His Word could be read rather than mediated:

"The entrance of thy words giveth light; it giveth understanding unto the simple."

— *Psalm 119:130*

He worked through **printing**, allowing Scripture to spread beyond borders and beyond control:

"So shall my word be that goeth forth out of my mouth: it shall not return unto me void."

— *Isaiah 55:11*

He worked through **conscience**, awakening individuals to stand before God rather than merely submit to institutions:

"For when the Gentiles… shew the work of the law written in their hearts, their conscience also bearing witness."

— *Romans 2:15*

And He worked through **generations willing to suffer for truth**—men and women who obeyed without seeing the outcome, trusting God with what they could not yet understand:

"These all died in faith, not having received the promises, but having seen them afar off."

— *Hebrews 11:13*

Providence rarely moves quickly. It works across lifetimes, cultures, and centuries. What seems slow to man is deliberate to God:

"Though it tarry, wait for it; because it will surely come."

— *Habakkuk 2:3*

Liberty, rightly understood, was not seized—it was prepared. Not demanded—it was entrusted. And it came at great cost to those who valued truth more than comfort:

"Ye shall know the truth, and the truth shall make you free."

— *John 8:32*

Providence often works slowly—but it works surely.

What God begins, He completes—according to His timing, not ours:

"The counsel of the LORD standeth for ever, the thoughts of his heart to all generations."
— *Psalm 33:11*

---

11. Closing Scripture & Prayer Prompt

Read aloud:

"Thy word is a lamp unto my feet, and a light unto my path."
— *Psalm 119:105*

Prayer Prompt:

"Lord, thank You for Your Word. Guard our hearts, our homes, and our nation by truth. Help us never take liberty lightly."

Lesson 3 — The Pilgrims' Escape from Tyranny

Series Title
God's Providence in American History: From the Pilgrims to the Present

---

Theme Verse
"Many are the afflictions of the righteous: but the LORD delivereth him out of them all."
— *Psalm 34:19*

Lesson Aim (For the Teacher)
To show how God preserved a small, faithful group through persecution and danger—guiding them **step by step** toward freedom long before they understood where the journey would lead.
This lesson emphasizes **obedient faith under pressure**, not national ambition or political strategy.

Time Flow (Minimum 40 Minutes)
- Opening Scripture & Prayer – **4 minutes**
- Core Biblical Teaching – **16 minutes**
- Historical Narrative & Providential Examples – **14 minutes**
- Discussion & Application – **6 minutes**

---

1. Opening Scripture Reading
Read aloud together:
"When thou passest through the waters, I will be with thee; and through the rivers, they shall not overflow thee."
— *Isaiah 43:2*
Teaching Note:
Emphasize *when*, not *if*. God promises presence, not exemption from hardship.

2. Core Truth Statement

God often delivers His people in stages—calling them to trust Him step by step, not all at once.

Deliverance is rarely immediate.
Obedience often comes **before** understanding.
"Thy word is a lamp unto my feet, and a light unto my path."
— *Psalm 119:105*
(A lamp shows the next step, not the whole road.)

---

3. The Biblical Pattern of Escape and Preservation

Key Scriptures

"The LORD also will be a refuge for the oppressed, a refuge in times of trouble."
— *Psalm 9:9*
"Fear thou not; for I am with thee."
— *Isaiah 41:10*
"By faith he forsook Egypt, not fearing the wrath of the king."
— *Hebrews 11:27*

Teaching Point (Now Scripture-Anchored)

Throughout Scripture, God repeatedly calls His people to:

- **Leave oppressive systems**
  "7. And the LORD said, I have surely seen the affliction of my people which are in Egypt, and have heard their cry by reason of their taskmasters; for I know their sorrows;" "8. And I am come down to deliver them out of the hand of the Egyptians, and to bring them up out of that land unto a good land and a large, unto a land flowing with milk and honey; unto the place of the Canaanites, and the Hittites, and the Amorites, and the Perizzites, and the Hivites, and the Jebusites." — Exodus 3:7–8.
  "And I heard another voice from heaven, saying, Come out of her, my people, that ye be not partakers of her sins, and that ye receive not of her plagues." — Revelation 18:4
- **Trust Him in uncertainty**
  "5. Trust in the LORD with all thine heart; and lean not unto thine own understanding." "6. In all thy ways acknowledge him, and he shall direct thy paths."
  — Proverbs 3:5–6

- **Obey without full visibility**

"By faith Abraham, when he was called to go out into a place which he should after receive for an inheritance, obeyed; and he went out, not knowing whither he went." — Hebrews 11:8

God rarely reveals the destination before obedience begins.
"The steps of a good man are ordered by the LORD."
— *Psalm 37:23*
The Pilgrims followed this same **biblical pattern of faith**.

---

4. The Pressure They Faced

In early 1600s England, faith was not merely a private matter—it was regulated by law. Scripture reading outside state control was restricted, not because the Bible was rejected outright, but because its independent reading threatened uniformity. Worship was required to conform to the established church, and gatherings outside approved forms were viewed as acts of defiance rather than devotion:
"They profess that they know God; but in works they deny him."
— *Titus 1:16*
For believers whose consciences were shaped by Scripture rather than ceremony, this created constant tension. To worship according to conviction was to risk punishment. Attendance at unauthorized services could result in fines that accumulated week after week. Refusal to comply could lead to imprisonment, public shame, or loss of livelihood:
"Yea, and all that will live godly in Christ Jesus shall suffer persecution."
— *2 Timothy 3:12*
These pressures were not momentary. They were sustained and exhausting. Families lived under surveillance. Neighbors were encouraged to report one another. Faithful believers faced the slow erosion of stability—jobs lost, homes threatened, futures uncertain.
Yet these men and women did not seek conflict.
They did not organize rebellion.
They did not demand power.
They sought faithful obedience.
They desired to worship God according to Scripture, teach their children in truth, and live quietly under God's authority. Their resistance was moral, not violent. It was rooted in conscience, not ambition:
"Whether it be right in the sight of God to hearken unto you more than unto God, judge ye."
— *Acts 4:19*
As pressure increased, neutrality disappeared. Faith could no longer remain private. Obedience now carried a cost, and every believer faced a clear and unavoidable choice:

- **Conform and survive**
- **Or obey and suffer**

This moment revealed a timeless truth: when law claims authority over conscience, faith is tested. What had once been theoretical belief became lived conviction:
"We ought to obey God rather than men."
— *Acts 5:29*
The pressure they faced did not weaken their faith—it clarified it. And that clarity would shape decisions that carried them far beyond England's shores.

---

5. Concrete Providential Example #1 — Failed Escapes

Providence did not remove hardship immediately.
When the group that would later be known as the Pilgrims first sought to leave England, their path toward freedom did not open smoothly. Obedience did not bring instant relief. Instead, it led into a season marked by frustration, fear, and apparent failure.
Their early attempts to escape were **unsuccessful**.
Plans were made carefully and quietly, yet they unraveled. Some who had promised assistance proved unreliable. In one attempt, those arranging passage betrayed the group to authorities. Men were arrested. Women and children were left behind in confusion and distress. Families were separated, unsure when—or if—they would be reunited.
For believers seeking only the freedom to worship according to conscience, these moments were deeply discouraging.
Humanly speaking, these setbacks looked like failure.
From the outside, it appeared that obedience had led not to deliverance, but to loss: loss of security, loss of dignity, and loss of hope. The cost of faith became visible not in distant sacrifice, but in immediate pain.
Yet Scripture speaks directly to such moments:
"Though he fall, he shall not be utterly cast down: for the LORD upholdeth him with his hand."
— *Psalm 37:24*
The failed escapes did not mean God had abandoned them. They meant the journey was not yet complete.
These delays served a quiet but important purpose. They tested resolve. They clarified commitment. They revealed who was willing to endure hardship for the sake of obedience—and who was not. Faith that survives betrayal, imprisonment, and disappointment emerges tempered, not weakened.
God often works this way.

Before delivering His people, He prepares them—sometimes by stripping away expectations of ease, sometimes by teaching patience through waiting, and sometimes by allowing plans to fail so reliance may shift fully to Him.

The setbacks forced these believers to confront a hard truth: following God's call did not guarantee safety, speed, or success as the world defines it. What it guaranteed was His presence—sustaining them even when progress seemed reversed.

Providence here was not seen in success.

It was seen in **preservation through disappointment**.

The failed escapes did not end the story.

They shaped it.

Theological Reflection (Optional Transition Sentence)

Delay is not denial.

In God's economy, waiting often prepares the way for endurance.

---

6. Concrete Providential Example #2 — Safe Arrival in Holland

After repeated setbacks, arrests, betrayals, and the emotional toll of separation, deliverance finally came—but not in the form the group may have expected.

Eventually, the believers who sought freedom of worship **reached Holland**.

The journey itself was dangerous, undertaken quietly and without assurance of success. But this time, the passage held. The authorities did not intercept them. The sea did not claim them. Families were reunited. Lives were preserved.

For the first time in years, they were able to worship **openly and without fear**.

This moment of arrival was not dramatic. There were no celebrations recorded, no proclamations of triumph. What there was, however, was **relief**—the quiet relief of being allowed to obey God without punishment.

Scripture speaks to this kind of deliverance:

"He shall deliver thee in six troubles: yea, in seven there shall no evil touch thee."

— *Job 5:19*

The timing mattered.

Holland was one of the few places in Europe where religious tolerance was practiced to any meaningful degree. That such a refuge existed—and that these believers reached it after years of danger—was not insignificant. It represented a **pause in affliction**, a season where persecution ceased and wounds could begin to heal.

But Holland was never meant to be the final chapter.

Though worship was free, life was not easy. Economic hardship followed them. Work was demanding and poorly paid. Cultural pressures pressed in on their families. Their children began adopting customs and language that threatened to slowly erode the convictions their parents had sacrificed so much to preserve.

What Holland offered was **safety**, not fulfillment.

And this distinction is important.

Providence had not yet led them to settlement, but it had provided **shelter**. God had not completed the journey, but He had granted rest along the way. In Scripture, this pattern appears often: God brings His people to places of refuge—not to end the calling, but to sustain them until the next step becomes clear.

"The LORD also will be a refuge for the oppressed, a refuge in times of trouble."
— *Psalm 9:9*

Holland was that refuge.

It allowed faith to breathe again.

It preserved lives that might otherwise have been lost.

It created space for prayer, reflection, and discernment.

Providence here was not about arrival—it was about **preservation between trials**.

God often works this way. Before asking His people to move forward, He first allows them to recover. Before leading them onward, He gives them a place to stand.

Holland was not the destination.

But it was exactly where they needed to be—for a time.

Theological Reflection (Optional Transition Sentence)

God's providence does not always bring us home immediately.

Sometimes it brings us somewhere safe, so we are able to continue.

---

7. Why Holland Was Not the End

Holland provided something the Pilgrims had long sought—**safety**.

There, they could worship freely without fear of imprisonment or persecution.

Yet safety alone did not resolve every danger.

Over time, new challenges emerged:

- **Economic hardship continued**
  Many Pilgrims labored long hours in difficult trades.
  Poverty was persistent, leaving little margin for stability or growth.
- **Cultural pressure threatened their children**
  Dutch society, while tolerant, differed sharply in values and customs.
  Parents grew concerned that their children were absorbing beliefs and behaviors that weakened their spiritual identity.

- **Language and customs eroded identity**
  Children increasingly spoke Dutch more fluently than English.
  Cultural assimilation slowly diluted the distinctiveness the community had sought to preserve.
- **Convictions slowly weakened**
  What persecution could not destroy, comfort began to soften.
  Urgency gave way to accommodation.

Comfort became a **new danger**.
"Woe to them that are at ease in Zion."
— *Amos 6:1*
The Pilgrims faced a difficult realization:
freedom from oppression did not guarantee faithfulness.
"Beware that thou forget not the LORD thy God."
— *Deuteronomy 8:11*
Remaining in Holland meant safety—but also slow spiritual erosion.
Leaving meant danger—but also the opportunity to preserve conviction.
Providence, in this moment, did not offer the easiest path.
It offered the **right one**.
"Arise ye, and depart; for this is not your rest."
— *Micah 2:10*
God sometimes leads His people **out of safety and into calling**.
Not because safety is wrong—but because comfort can quietly undermine purpose.
The Pilgrims did not leave Holland seeking prosperity.
They left seeking faithfulness.
Providence guided them not toward ease—but toward obedience.

8. Concrete Providential Example #3 — A Second Call to Trust

After arriving safely in Holland, the believers who had fled England entered a season of relative peace. For the first time in years, they could worship freely. Fear of arrest lifted. The immediate threat to their lives receded.

In many ways, this was the answer they had prayed for.

Yet over time, another realization began to take shape.

Safety, while welcome, came at a cost. The pressures they faced were no longer violent, but subtle. Economic hardship persisted, requiring long hours of demanding labor. Cultural influences pressed steadily upon their families. Their children began to grow more comfortable in a society that did not share their convictions or values. The danger was no longer persecution—it was **slow erosion.**

They now faced a second decision, one far more difficult than the first.

They could remain where they were:

- Safe from punishment
- Free to worship
- Secure from immediate danger

But in doing so, they risked watching their identity quietly fade.

Or they could take another step—one filled with uncertainty and risk—toward a place they had never seen and a future they could not fully imagine.

Scripture reveals that this kind of decision is not unusual in God's dealings with His people. Often, obedience is not completed in a single act, but renewed after relief.

Abraham experienced this pattern. After leaving Ur, he settled for a time in Haran. There, life stabilized. But God's call did not end with safety:

"Now the LORD had said unto Abram, Get thee out of thy country… unto a land that I will shew thee."

— *Genesis 12:1*

Israel experienced something similar. After deliverance from Egypt, they were sustained in the wilderness. Protection was given, provision supplied. Yet only those willing to trust God again—beyond the safety of what was familiar—were allowed to move forward:

"My servant Caleb… hath followed me fully, him will I bring into the land."

— *Numbers 14:24*

The believers in Holland stood at such a moment.

God had preserved them.

God had sheltered them.

But the calling was not complete.

Providence now asked not for escape, but for **renewed trust.**

This second call required more faith than the first. Leaving England meant fleeing danger. Leaving Holland meant **choosing obedience over comfort**. It meant risking safety for the sake of conviction, and trusting that God's provision would extend beyond refuge into the unknown.

Providence here did not remove fear.

It revealed responsibility.

God's call often intensifies after protection—not because He is unkind, but because faith, once sustained, is meant to move forward.

Holland had been a place of rest.

Now it was time for decision.

Theological Reflection (Optional Transition Sentence)

Obedience does not always end with safety.

Sometimes it begins again, precisely because safety has been granted.

---

9. Discussion Questions (Choose 2–3)

The questions below are not intended to invite quick answers, but thoughtful consideration. Scripture shows that God often works through **process**, **waiting**, and **obedient response**, rather than immediate resolution. These questions are meant to help us examine our own hearts through that same lens.

1. Why does God often deliver in stages rather than all at once?

Scripture frequently reveals God guiding His people step by step, rather than revealing the entire path at once.

"Thy word is a lamp unto my feet, and a light unto my path."

— *Psalm 119:105*

God's guidance often illuminates only the next step, requiring trust rather than certainty. Staged deliverance teaches dependence, patience, and obedience before understanding. It guards against pride and trains faith to walk forward without full visibility.

2. What spiritual dangers can long-term comfort bring?

Comfort, while a blessing, can quietly weaken spiritual alertness.

"Beware lest thou forget the LORD… when thou hast eaten and art full… and thine heart be lifted up, and thou forget the LORD thy God."

— *Deuteronomy 8:11–14*

Scripture warns that prolonged ease can dull gratitude, soften conviction, and replace dependence on God with self-sufficiency. Comfort is not sinful—but unexamined comfort can become spiritually dangerous.

3. How do you discern when God is calling you to stay versus move?
God's calling is not always dramatic. Sometimes He leads through circumstances, counsel, and conviction rather than clear commands.
Scripture encourages wisdom, prayer, and humility in such discernment:
"Trust in the LORD with all thine heart; and lean not unto thine own understanding."
— *Proverbs 3:5*
Discernment requires listening—not only to opportunity, but to conscience shaped by God's Word. God may call some to remain faithful where they are, and others to step forward into uncertainty.
4. Why is freedom of worship worth sacrifice?
Throughout Scripture, obedience to God has often carried cost.
"We ought to obey God rather than men."
— *Acts 5:29*
Freedom of worship is not merely a personal preference—it is the freedom to honor God according to conscience. History shows that such freedom has frequently been preserved through sacrifice, endurance, and faithful obedience rather than comfort or ease.
As these questions are discussed, the focus should remain on **faith**, **obedience**, and **trust in God's leading**, not political argument or personal ideology.

Teaching Guidance (Optional for Instructor)

- Allow silence before answers
- Encourage Scripture-based responses
- Gently redirect discussion if it drifts into political debate
- Emphasize humility rather than certainty

These questions are intended to **form the heart**, not to win arguments.

---

10. Personal & National Application
Personal

- Am I willing to obey God when obedience costs comfort?
  "And he said to them all, If any man will come after me, let him deny himself, and take up his cross daily, and follow me." — Luke 9:23
- Do I trust God's leading without full clarity?
  "A man's heart deviseth his way: but the LORD directeth his steps."
  — Proverbs 16:9

National

- Religious liberty was born from sacrifice
- Comfort can dull conviction

- Freedom must be protected, not assumed

"If the Son therefore shall make you free, ye shall be free indeed."
— *John 8:36*

---

11. Closing Reflection

The Pilgrims did not leave England to build a nation.
They left because obedience to God had become costly—and conscience would no longer allow compromise.
Their desire was not political freedom, but the freedom to worship God faithfully according to His Word.
Scripture has always placed obedience above ambition:
"To obey is better than sacrifice, and to hearken than the fat of rams."
— *1 Samuel 15:22*
America was not their vision.
Faithfulness was.
They did not possess a clear map of the future, nor did they understand the full consequences of their decision. They stepped forward with limited knowledge, trusting God for what lay ahead.
This reflects a consistent biblical pattern.
God often calls His people to move before outcomes are visible, asking for trust rather than foresight.
"By faith Abraham, when he was called to go out into a place which he should after receive for an inheritance, obeyed; and he went out, not knowing whither he went."
— *Hebrews 11:8*
The Pilgrims' journey followed this same pattern of faith. Their obedience preceded understanding. Their faithfulness came before fruit.
Providence did not unfold because they predicted the future accurately.
It unfolded because they obeyed God faithfully in the present.
Scripture reminds us:
"The steps of a good man are ordered by the LORD: and he delighteth in his way."
— *Psalm 37:23*
God's providence often moves quietly through ordinary obedience—through men and women who seek faithfulness rather than legacy.
What followed their obedience was not guaranteed success, comfort, or ease. It was hardship, uncertainty, and sacrifice. Yet God honored their faith by preserving them and using their obedience as part of a far larger story than they could have imagined.
Providence moved not through their foresight, but through their faith.

And in this, the Pilgrims stand not as national heroes first—but as believers who trusted God when obedience demanded courage.

Optional Teaching Pause (Adult Class)

You might ask:

- *Why does God often call obedience before revealing outcomes?*
- *How does this reflection challenge modern ideas of success or planning?*
- *Where might God be asking for faithfulness rather than foresight in our own lives?*

---

12. Closing Scripture & Prayer Prompt

Read aloud:

"Commit thy way unto the LORD; trust also in him; and he shall bring it to pass."
— *Psalm 37:5*

Prayer Prompt:

"Lord, help us trust You when the path is uncertain. Give us courage to obey and patience to wait."

Lesson 4 — The Mayflower Crossing (1620)

Series Title
God's Providence in American History: From the Pilgrims to the Present

---

Theme Verse
"They that go down to the sea in ships, that do business in great waters;
These see the works of the LORD, and his wonders in the deep."
— *Psalm 107:23–24*

Lesson Aim (For the Teacher)
To show how God preserved a small, largely unprepared group through natural danger and human uncertainty—demonstrating that **providence often becomes most visible when human control is lost.**
This lesson emphasizes **dependence**, not daring or expertise.

Time Flow (Minimum 40 Minutes)

- Opening Scripture & Prayer – **4 minutes**
- Core Biblical Teaching – **16 minutes**
- Historical Narrative & Providential Examples – **14 minutes**
- Discussion & Application – **6 minutes**

---

1. Opening Scripture Reading
Read aloud together:
"For he commandeth, and raiseth the stormy wind, which lifteth up the waves thereof."
— *Psalm 107:25*
Teaching Note:
Pause briefly. Emphasize that storms are not outside God's command—they occur *under* it.

---

2. Core Truth Statement

When human control ends, God's providence becomes most visible.

The sea strips away certainty.

Planning reaches its limit.

Dependence becomes unavoidable.

"Without me ye can do nothing."

— *John 15:5*

---

3. The Biblical Pattern of Deliverance at Sea

Key Scriptures

"He maketh the storm a calm, so that the waves thereof are still."

— *Psalm 107:29*

"Thou rulest the raging of the sea: when the waves thereof arise, thou stillest them."

— *Psalm 89:9*

"Then they cry unto the LORD in their trouble, and he bringeth them out of their distresses."

— *Psalm 107:28*

Teaching Point (Now Scripture-Anchored)

Throughout Scripture, the sea represents:

- **Human helplessness**

  "12. And he said unto them, Take me up, and cast me forth into the sea; so shall the sea be calm unto you: for I know that for my sake this great tempest is upon you."

  "13. Nevertheless the men rowed hard to bring it to the land; but they could not: for the sea wrought, and was tempestuous against them."

  "14. Wherefore they cried unto the LORD, and said, We beseech thee, O LORD, we beseech thee, let us not perish for this man's life, and lay not upon us innocent blood: for thou, O LORD, hast done as it pleased thee."

  "15. So they took up Jonah, and cast him forth into the sea: and the sea ceased from her raging." — Jonah 1:12–15
- **God's uncontested authority**

  "8. Or who shut up the sea with doors, when it brake forth, as if it had issued out of the womb?" "9. When I made the cloud the garment thereof, and thick darkness a swaddlingband for it," "10. And brake up for it my decreed place, and set bars and doors," "11. And said, Hitherto shalt thou come, but no further: and here shall thy proud waves be stayed?" — Job 38:8–11

- **Deliverance beyond human strength**

  "26. And he saith unto them, Why are ye fearful, O ye of little faith? Then he arose, and rebuked the winds and the sea; and there was a great calm." "27. But the men marvelled, saying, What manner of man is this, that even the winds and the sea obey him!"
  — Matthew 8:26–27

Deliverance at sea consistently follows this pattern:

1. Human effort fails
2. Fear exposes weakness
3. God demonstrates authority

The Mayflower voyage fits this **biblical pattern of dependence**.

---

4. The Reality of the Voyage

The Mayflower was not a vessel designed for long Atlantic crossings. By ocean-going standards, it was small, sturdy enough for coastal trade but ill-suited for transporting families across a winter sea:

"They that go down to the sea in ships… these see the works of the LORD, and his wonders in the deep."
— *Psalm 107:23–24*

The ship was heavily overcrowded. More than one hundred passengers were confined below deck in dark, damp conditions with limited ventilation. Space was scarce. Privacy was nonexistent. Food was rationed. Fresh water was carefully guarded. Seasickness, exhaustion, and illness spread quickly:

"My soul is cast down within me."
— *Psalm 42:6*

The voyage was delayed well into the Atlantic storm season. What was originally intended as a late-summer journey became a late-autumn crossing—one of the most dangerous times to sail. Storms battered the ship, forcing passengers below deck for weeks at a time as violent waves crashed overhead:

"For he commandeth, and raiseth the stormy wind, which lifteth up the waves thereof."
— *Psalm 107:25*

Those aboard were not hardened sailors. The passengers included families with small children, the elderly and infirm, and many individuals with no maritime experience whatsoever. There was no naval escort. No rescue fleet. No guarantee of assistance if disaster struck:

"When my spirit was overwhelmed within me, then thou knewest my path."
— *Psalm 142:3*

Life aboard the Mayflower demanded endurance. Cold, hunger, fear, and uncertainty tested resolve daily. Yet this was not a voyage marked by bravado or ambition. It was marked by quiet submission:

They sailed not in comfort.

They sailed not in confidence.

They sailed in obedience and trust.

Their decision rested not on favorable conditions, but on conviction. They committed themselves to God's care when human preparation could not secure the outcome:

"Commit thy works unto the LORD, and thy thoughts shall be established."

— *Proverbs 16:3*

The reality of the voyage stripped away illusion. What remained was dependence. And in that dependence, providence would soon make itself known.

---

5. Concrete Providential Example #1 — Relentless Storms

From the moment the Mayflower left England, the voyage unfolded under nearly constant strain. The ship did not encounter a single dramatic storm and then pass into calm waters. Instead, it faced **weeks of persistent, violent weather**, testing both the vessel and the people aboard.

The North Atlantic in late autumn was unforgiving.

Winds howled across the open sea. Waves rose and crashed against the hull with relentless force. The ship pitched violently, rolling from side to side and plunging into troughs that left passengers bracing for impact. For most of those aboard—unaccustomed to the sea—each surge brought fear, disorientation, and helplessness.

As the storms intensified, passengers were forced to remain **below deck for extended periods**. Fresh air was scarce. Darkness and dampness surrounded them. The smell of seawater, sickness, and unwashed bodies filled the confined space. Seasickness became common. Weakness followed quickly.

Illness spread easily under such conditions.

Children cried. The elderly struggled. The already weary grew more exhausted by the day. Sleep was interrupted constantly as the ship lurched without warning. Morale declined as fear compounded physical suffering.

From a human standpoint, the voyage bordered on disaster.

There were moments when the passengers could do nothing but endure—unable to influence the weather, unable to hasten their arrival, unable to escape the danger pressing in on every side. Control was stripped away, leaving only dependence.

Scripture gives language to such moments:

"When my spirit was overwhelmed within me, then thou knewest my path."
— *Psalm 142:3*
The storms did not cease at the first prayer.
They did not relent quickly.
They were not removed.
And yet, they were **endured**.
God did not prevent the storm.
He preserved them **through** it.
The ship remained afloat.
The passengers survived day after day.
Strength, though strained, was sustained.

Providence here was not visible in calm seas, but in **continuance**. Each sunrise after a night of terror bore quiet testimony that the storm had not exceeded its bounds. The waves rose—but only so far. The wind raged—but not without limit.

This pattern reflects a consistent biblical truth: God's authority over creation does not always manifest in immediate deliverance, but in **measured restraint**.

"Thus far shalt thou come, but no further: and here shall thy proud waves be stayed."
— *Job 38:11*

The relentless storms revealed the fragility of the ship and the vulnerability of its passengers. But they also revealed something deeper—that survival did not depend on strength, skill, or resolve, but on a sustaining hand that governed even the chaos of the sea.

Theological Reflection (Optional Transition Sentence)

Providence is often seen not when danger disappears, but when it does not destroy.

---

6. Concrete Providential Example #2 — The Broken Main Beam

Among the many dangers faced during the Mayflower's crossing, few were as threatening—or as quietly revealing—as the failure of the ship's main structural beam.

The Mayflower was not designed for the violent winter seas of the North Atlantic. As storms battered the vessel day after day, the constant strain of wind and waves placed tremendous pressure on the ship's frame. At some point during the voyage, a **primary support beam amidships cracked**, compromising the ship's integrity.

This was not a minor problem.

The beam was essential to holding the hull together. If it failed completely, the ship could twist, leak, or break apart under the force of the sea. In open ocean, far from any port, such damage would have meant disaster—not only for the ship, but for every life aboard.

Humanly speaking, the voyage should have ended there.

The passengers and crew faced an unavoidable reality: no amount of courage or determination could repair a broken ship in the middle of the Atlantic. They lacked tools, materials, and expertise for such a repair. The danger could not be outrun, and there was nowhere to turn back.

Yet providence again appeared—not in the removal of danger, but in the **means of restraint**.

Among the ship's supplies was a **large iron screw**, from a printing press, a piece of equipment not intended for ship repair, but carried for other practical uses. Using this simple device, the crew was able to brace the damaged beam, stabilizing the structure enough to withstand the remaining journey.

The repair was imperfect.

The danger remained.

But the ship held.

William Bradford later noted that without this provision, the voyage could not have continued.

The beam did not miraculously heal itself. The storm did not cease. Instead, God provided **just enough** to preserve life and allow the journey to proceed.

Scripture often describes God's care in precisely these terms:

"Except the LORD keep the city, the watchman waketh but in vain."

— *Psalm 127:1*

The preservation of the Mayflower did not come through superior planning or exceptional skill. It came through a provision that, at the moment of greatest need, proved sufficient.

Providence here was not dramatic.

It was practical.

And it was timely.

This pattern appears repeatedly throughout Scripture: God supplying what is necessary—not always in advance, and rarely in abundance, but faithfully at the moment when failure seems inevitable.

The cracked beam remained a reminder for the remainder of the voyage: the ship was fragile, the passengers were vulnerable, and their survival depended not on strength or design, but on a sustaining hand beyond their control.

Theological Reflection (Optional Transition Sentence)

Providence does not guarantee ideal conditions.

It ensures that **what must hold, holds—until God's purpose is complete**.

7. Concrete Providential Example #3 — Preservation of Life

The dangers of the Mayflower voyage were not limited to storms or damaged timbers. The conditions aboard the ship placed every passenger at continual risk—physically, emotionally, and spiritually.

For more than two months, over one hundred passengers and crew were confined to a small, crowded vessel. Space was scarce. Ventilation was poor. Sanitation was primitive. The air below deck was damp and foul, and illness spread easily in such an environment. Seasickness, exhaustion, and anxiety weakened bodies already strained by uncertainty and fear.

Added to this were the constant storms.

The ship pitched violently, throwing passengers against walls and bunks. Water leaked below deck. Sleep was scarce. For families traveling with children and the elderly, every day carried the threat of serious injury or death.

Humanly speaking, loss of life should have been expected.

And yet, remarkably, **no passenger died during the crossing**.

This fact stands out precisely because it was so unlikely. Ships of that era frequently lost lives on long Atlantic voyages, especially under far better conditions than those endured by the Mayflower. Disease alone often proved fatal before landfall was reached.

Yet life was preserved.

Even more striking, during the voyage **a child was born**—a small but profound sign of life continuing amid danger. The birth did not remove hardship, but it testified that God's care extended not only to survival, but to the future.

"Lo, children are an heritage of the LORD."

— *Psalm 127:3*

Despite overcrowding, structural damage, illness, and relentless storms, the ship arrived intact.

Fragile, worn, and weathered—but whole.

Scripture often speaks of God's preservation in precisely this way:

"He preserveth the souls of his saints."

— *Psalm 97:10*

The preservation of life aboard the Mayflower does not suggest the absence of danger. It highlights its **limitation**. Harm was possible. Death was near. But destruction was restrained.

Providence here was not dramatic intervention.

It was **measured mercy**.

God did not calm every storm.

He did not remove every hardship.

He did not make the voyage safe.

He made it **endurable**.

The survival of every passenger serves as a quiet reminder that providence often works not by erasing threats, but by setting their boundaries. Life continues—not because conditions improve, but because God sustains.

Theological Reflection (Optional Transition Sentence)
Providence does not promise ease.
It promises that danger will not exceed God's purpose.

---

8. Concrete Providential Example #4 — John Howland: Preserved from the Deep
Among the passengers aboard the Mayflower was a young man named **John Howland**, a servant in the household of Governor John Carver. Like many aboard, he was not a sailor and had little experience with the open sea. The voyage itself had already proven exhausting and dangerous, marked by violent storms and weeks of confinement below deck.

At one point during the crossing, as the ship pitched violently in heavy seas, John Howland went up on deck. Whether he was attempting to assist or simply seeking fresh air, the record does not say. What is known is that a sudden lurch of the ship threw him overboard and into the freezing Atlantic.

In such conditions, falling into the sea was usually a **death sentence**.

The Mayflower was moving forward through storm-driven waves. The water was rough, the air cold, and a man in heavy clothing would have been quickly pulled under. To fall overboard meant not only drowning, but being lost beyond any reasonable hope of recovery.

Yet as Howland was swept away from the ship, he managed—by what eyewitnesses later described as remarkable timing—to grasp a **rope trailing from the vessel**. Though repeatedly pulled under by the waves and nearly exhausted, he held on long enough for the crew to notice and haul him back aboard.

William Bradford later recorded that Howland was "taken up with much ado," having "sunk many times" before being rescued. By all human expectation, he should not have survived.

But he did.

Howland recovered from the incident and went on to live a long life in the New World. He became a respected member of the Plymouth Colony, married Elizabeth Tilley, and raised a large family. He lived into old age—his life preserved at the very moment it seemed most certainly lost.

Over time, John Howland's descendants became woven deeply into American history. Through his children and grandchildren came individuals who would shape culture, leadership, and public life in later generations. Among his well-documented descendants are figures such as **Presidents Franklin D. Roosevelt and George H. W. Bush**, poets like **Henry**

Wadsworth Longfellow, reformers such as **Ralph Waldo Emerson**, and countless others who influenced the nation in quieter but lasting ways.

The significance of this is not that greatness was guaranteed, nor that one man's survival ensured national success. Scripture does not teach that preservation always leads to prominence. Rather, it reminds us that **a single spared life may touch generations unseen.**

The account does not describe a calm sea.

It does not describe heroic strength.

It does not describe perfect conditions.

It describes **preservation in chaos.**

Scripture often speaks of God's authority over the deep—not by eliminating danger, but by restraining it:

"They cried unto the LORD in their trouble, and he bringeth them out of their distresses."

— *Psalm 107:28*

John Howland's rescue did not still the storm, nor did it guarantee the safety of the voyage. But it stands as a quiet testimony that even in moments of apparent randomness, life is not beyond God's reach.

Providence does not always announce itself.

Sometimes it is seen only afterward—

in the simple fact that someone lived who, by all natural expectation, should not have.

---

9. Order Preserved in Chaos — The Mayflower Compact

As the voyage dragged on and conditions worsened, **strain within the small community increased.**

The crossing had been longer and harsher than expected.

Fatigue, fear, and uncertainty tested patience.

- **Disagreements arose**
  Passengers came from different backgrounds and motivations.
  Stress exposed fault lines that had been manageable on land.
- **Authority structures were unclear**
  The ship had sailed outside the original patent's jurisdiction.
  Some argued that once ashore, no binding authority would exist.
- **Survival depended on cooperation**
  Without shared order, the settlement could collapse before it began.
  Disorder threatened survival as much as storms or disease.

In this fragile moment, **a remarkable decision was made.**

Rather than allowing confusion to harden into conflict, the passengers formed **a voluntary covenant**—not imposed by force, but agreed upon by consent.

They committed themselves to:

- **Mutual submission under agreed authority**
- **Shared responsibility for governance**
- **Obedience to laws formed for the common good**

The Mayflower Compact emphasized:

- **Accountability**
  No individual was above the rules.
  Authority was limited and purposeful.
- **Community responsibility**
  Personal freedom was balanced by obligation to others.
  Survival required cooperation, not independence.
- **God-conscious language**
  The agreement explicitly acknowledged God's authority and purpose.
  Governance was framed as stewardship under Him.

"Let all things be done decently and in order."
— *1 Corinthians 14:40*

This moment was not revolutionary in tone.
It was **practical, restrained, and humble**.
Order was not demanded—it was chosen.
Authority was not seized—it was entrusted.
Providence, in this instance, did more than preserve life.
It **shaped order**.
Out of uncertainty came structure.
Out of vulnerability came responsibility.
Out of chaos came covenant.
The Mayflower Compact stands as an early example of a crucial principle:
self-government requires moral restraint before it can succeed politically.
Providence guided not only where the Pilgrims landed—but how they chose to live together once they arrived.

---

10. Discussion Questions (Choose 2–3)

1. Why does God often reveal His authority most clearly in helpless situations?
(Psalm 107:28–29)
2. How does adversity expose what truly holds a community together?
(Proverbs 11:14)
3. Why is order essential during crisis?
(1 Corinthians 14:33)
4. What does the Mayflower Compact reveal about responsibility under God?

---

11. Personal & National Application

Personal

- Do I trust God when circumstances feel uncontrollable?
 "God is our refuge and strength, a very present help in trouble." — Psalm 46:1
- Am I willing to submit to order for the good of others?
 "3. Let nothing be done through strife or vainglory; but in lowliness of mind let each esteem other better than themselves." "4. Look not every man on his own things, but every man also on the things of others." — Philippians 2:3–4
- **National**
- Unity often forms under pressure
- Covenant precedes survival
- Self-governance requires moral restraint

"Except the LORD build the house, they labour in vain that build it."
— *Psalm 127:1*

---

12. Closing Reflection

The Mayflower crossing was not heroic.
It was fragile.
The journey was not marked by bold confidence or careful planning, but by vulnerability. The ship was small, the season was late, the passengers were unprepared for the dangers they faced. Human strength, foresight, and skill were insufficient.
Scripture reminds us how often God allows His people to reach the end of themselves:
"For when I am weak, then am I strong."
— *2 Corinthians 12:10*
The crossing was not a triumph of planning.
It was a lesson in dependence.

Again and again, Scripture teaches that God's work is not accomplished by human control, but by trust in His sustaining power.

"Not by might, nor by power, but by my spirit, saith the LORD of hosts."

— *Zechariah 4:6*

The sea stripped away illusion. It exposed human limitation. Storms, uncertainty, and fear left no room for self-reliance. In that place, dependence was no longer optional—it was unavoidable.

Yet it was there, in weakness, that providence became visible.

"God is our refuge and strength, a very present help in trouble."

— *Psalm 46:1*

Providence did not remove danger.

It carried them through it.

The ship held together when it should not have. Lives were preserved when loss seemed likely. Each day at sea was not a guarantee—but a mercy.

This reflects a deeper biblical truth: God often carries His people **where preparation cannot take them**.

"Commit thy way unto the LORD; trust also in him; and he shall bring it to pass."

— *Psalm 37:5*

The Mayflower did not arrive because the passengers were capable.

It arrived because God was faithful.

Their survival was not a testimony to human planning, but to divine preservation. Providence sustained them not because they were strong—but because they were dependent.

And in that dependence, God carried them farther than preparation ever could.

Optional Teaching Pause (Adult Class)

You might ask:

- *Why does God often lead His people into situations where self-reliance fails?*
- *How does dependence reshape our understanding of success?*
- *Where might God be calling us to trust Him beyond our preparation?*

---

13. Closing Scripture & Prayer Prompt

Read aloud:

"Commit thy way unto the LORD; trust also in him; and he shall bring it to pass."

— *Psalm 37:5*

Prayer Prompt:

"Lord, when we are beyond our strength, teach us to depend fully on You."

SECTION II - SURVIVAL & COVENANT

Faith Tested in a New Land (1620–1700)

"And thou shalt remember all the way which the LORD thy God led thee these forty years in the wilderness, to humble thee, and to prove thee, to know what was in thine heart."
— **Deuteronomy 8:2**

Section Purpose
Arrival did not mean security.
Freedom did not mean ease.
This section explores the early years when faith was **tested by hunger, disease, isolation, and loss**. Survival depended not on strength or preparation alone, but on **daily dependence upon God** and commitment to one another.
Here, covenant moves from theory to practice.

Lessons in This Section

- **Lesson 5:** Plymouth — Survival Against All Odds
- **Lesson 6:** Squanto and Divine Timing
- **Lesson 7:** The First Thanksgiving
- **Lesson 8:** The Great Awakening
- **Lesson 9:** Unity Through Revival

Guiding Truth
God often uses hardship to form a people before He blesses a nation.

(Optional Closing Line for Print or Teaching)
"Before a nation could stand, a people had to learn how to depend."
Teaching Orientation (Optional – Leader Use)
Encourage the class to view this section not as heroic legend, but as:

- Shared suffering
- Quiet endurance
- Faith refined through loss

Remind them:
Survival itself can be an act of providence.

Lesson 5 — Plymouth: Survival Against All Odds

Series Title

God's Providence in American History: From the Pilgrims to the Present

Theme Verse

"Thou shalt remember all the way which the LORD thy God led thee… to humble thee, and to prove thee."

— *Deuteronomy 8:2*

Lesson Aim (For the Teacher)

To show how God preserved a fragile settlement through extreme loss, limited resources, and human weakness—demonstrating that **survival itself can be an act of divine providence**. This lesson emphasizes **daily dependence**, not strength or strategy.

Time Flow (Minimum 40 Minutes)

- Opening Scripture & Prayer – 4 minutes
- Biblical Framework – 10 minutes
- Historical Narrative & Providential Examples – 16 minutes
- Discussion – 6 minutes
- Application & Closing Reflection – 4 minutes

---

1. Opening Scripture Reading

Read aloud together:

"I have been young, and now am old; yet have I not seen the righteous forsaken, nor his seed begging bread."

— *Psalm 37:25*

---

2. Core Truth Statement

God often preserves His people not by abundance, but by sustaining them one day at a time.

Survival does not require comfort.

It requires faith, obedience, and endurance.

---

3. Biblical Pattern: God Sustains Through Scarcity

Key Scriptures

"And he humbled thee, and suffered thee to hunger, and fed thee with manna… that man doth not live by bread only."

— *Deuteronomy 8:3*

"My God shall supply all your need according to his riches in glory by Christ Jesus."

— *Philippians 4:19*

"Bread shall be given him; his waters shall be sure."

— *Isaiah 33:16*

Teaching Point (Scripture-Anchored)

God often allows **lack** in order to teach **dependence**.

4. He sustains life not always by removing hardship, but by **providing just enough**.

"Thy raiment waxed not old upon thee, neither did thy foot swell, these forty years."

— Deuteronomy 8:4

"31. Therefore take no thought, saying, What shall we eat? or, What shall we drink? or, Wherewithal shall we be clothed?" "32. (For after all these things do the Gentiles seek:) for your heavenly Father knoweth that ye have need of all these things." "33. But seek ye first the kingdom of God, and his righteousness; and all these things shall be added unto you."

— Matthew 6:31–33

---

4. The Reality of Plymouth's First Winter

By the winter of 1620–1621, the reality of settlement set in with sobering force.

Shelter was incomplete. Many of the settlers were still living aboard the Mayflower or in hastily constructed dwellings that offered little protection from cold, wind, and damp. The New England winter arrived early and harshly, bringing freezing temperatures and relentless exposure:

"Thou hast covered thyself with anger, and persecuted us."

— *Lamentations 3:43*

Food supplies dwindled rapidly. What little had survived the voyage was rationed carefully, yet scarcity became unavoidable. Hunger weakened bodies already exhausted from months at sea and weeks of labor in unfamiliar terrain:

"Our flesh was as the flesh of our brethren… and, lo, we bring into bondage our sons and our daughters."

— *Nehemiah 5:5*

(the language captures desperation rather than identical circumstance)

Illness spread quickly. Scurvy, pneumonia, and tuberculosis took hold in cramped, unsanitary conditions. With limited medical knowledge and few remedies, sickness often progressed unchecked. Fever and weakness became common companions, and recovery was uncertain:

"My days are swifter than a weaver's shuttle, and are spent without hope."

— *Job 7:6*

Historical records testify to the severity of the suffering. Roughly half of the settlers died during that first winter. At the lowest point, only six or seven individuals were well enough to care for the sick, prepare food, and maintain what order they could. The healthy labored beyond endurance, nursing the dying while trying to preserve the living:

"As thy days, so shall thy strength be."

— *Deuteronomy 33:25*

Burials were done quietly, often at night. Graves were leveled and disguised so that nearby tribes would not perceive the colony's weakness. Even mourning had to be restrained. Survival demanded vigilance as well as endurance:

"In weariness and painfulness, in watchings often."

— *2 Corinthians 11:27*

By every human calculation, the settlement should have failed.

There were too few people.

Too little food.

Too much sickness.

Too much exposure.

Yet collapse did not come.

Providence did not appear as sudden relief. It did not remove hardship or reverse loss. Instead, it sustained a remnant—just enough strength, just enough resolve, just enough life to carry the colony through its most vulnerable season:

"It is of the LORD's mercies that we are not consumed, because his compassions fail not."

— *Lamentations 3:22*

The first winter at Plymouth was not a story of success.

It was a story of survival.

And survival itself bore witness that God's hand was at work—quietly preserving where human effort could not.

5. Specific Providential Preservations A. Survival of Leadership

The first winter at Plymouth was devastating.

Exposure, disease, malnutrition, and exhaustion took a heavy toll. Nearly half of the colonists died before spring arrived. Graves were dug quietly. Strength faded. Hope was tested daily.

Humanly speaking, the colony stood on the edge of collapse.

Yet in the midst of this suffering, one quiet pattern stands out.

Key leadership survived.

The loss of certain individuals would likely have ended the colony altogether. Organization, discipline, and morale were already strained to the breaking point. Without steady leadership, disorder, despair, or abandonment could have followed quickly.

But God preserved just enough.

Those responsible for governance, order, and spiritual guidance remained. They were weakened, grieving, and burdened—but present. Decisions could still be made. Unity could still be maintained. The community did not fracture.

This kind of preservation is deeply biblical.

In the wilderness, when Israel's survival depended on Moses' endurance, Scripture records that God sustained leadership through support:

"But Moses' hands were heavy; and they took a stone, and put it under him, and he sat thereon; and Aaron and Hur stayed up his hands… and his hands were steady until the going down of the sun."

— *Exodus 17:12*

The victory did not come through strength alone.

It came through **preserved leadership** sustained by God.

Similarly, Scripture speaks of survival not through abundance, but through restraint:

"Except the LORD of hosts had left unto us a very small remnant, we should have been as Sodom."

— *Isaiah 1:9*

Plymouth survived not because many lived—but because **enough** did.

Providence here was not dramatic rescue. It was selective preservation. God did not spare everyone. He did not remove suffering. He did not reverse loss. But He ensured that leadership necessary for continuity endured.

This mattered deeply.

Leadership provided structure when despair threatened to overwhelm. It preserved order when fear could have turned inward. It maintained purpose when grief made the future uncertain. Without it, the colony's story would likely have ended in its first year.

Providence often works this way.

God does not always preserve all strength.

He preserves **sufficient strength**.

He does not remove loss.

He limits its reach.

The survival of leadership at Plymouth reminds us that God's purposes frequently advance not through abundance, but through endurance—carried forward by those He sustains when others fall.

Theological Reflection (Optional Transition Sentence)

God often preserves just enough to continue His work, even when circumstances appear nearly undone.

B. Specific Providential Preservation — Strength Given to the Few

The survival of Plymouth through its first winter required more than leadership alone. It required **endurance**—the kind that does not come naturally to bodies already weakened by hunger, cold, and grief.

Of those who survived the early months, only a small number remained healthy enough to function consistently. These few bore responsibilities far beyond what would normally be expected.

They worked relentlessly.

The able-bodied labored to secure food, repair shelters, and protect the settlement. They nursed the sick, tending to those too weak to rise. They buried the dead quietly, often at night, to conceal the colony's losses from potential threats. They maintained order when despair could easily have led to collapse.

Humanly speaking, the workload was impossible.

Exhaustion should have overtaken them. Illness should have spread unchecked. Discipline should have broken down under the weight of grief and fear. Yet the work continued—day after day.

Scripture speaks directly to such sustaining strength:

"As thy days, so shall thy strength be."

— *Deuteronomy 33:25*

This promise does not suggest abundance of ease. It speaks of **sufficiency for the moment**—strength matched precisely to the demands of each day.

Providence here was not visible in physical vitality. It was visible in **continuance**. Strength was given not in advance, but as needed. Each day brought its own burden—and with it, enough ability to endure.

This pattern appears repeatedly in Scripture. God often does not remove the weight; He supplies the strength to carry it.

At Plymouth, the survival of the colony rested not on many hands, but on faithful ones. Those few who remained capable did not falter under the load placed upon them. Their endurance became a means through which the entire community was preserved.

Providence did not multiply workers.

It multiplied **capacity**.

The strength given to the few was not for their own sake. It was for the survival of all.

Through them, God sustained a people who could not sustain themselves.

Theological Reflection (Optional Transition Sentence)

When resources are few, God often supplies strength rather than relief.

C. Specific Providential Preservation — Protection From Hostile Threats

The Plymouth settlement entered its first winter in a position of extreme vulnerability.

The colonists were few in number, weakened by illness, and struggling to survive the cold.

Their defenses were minimal. Supplies were scarce. From a human perspective, the settlement presented an easy target.

Nearby tribes were aware of their presence.

The settlers were observed. Movements were noticed. At times, signs of nearby activity were unmistakable. Under different circumstances, such vulnerability could have led to swift and overwhelming conflict.

Yet **no major attack occurred**.

This absence of violence is striking not because conflict was impossible, but because it was **plausible**. The colonists lacked the strength to defend themselves effectively. Any sustained aggression would likely have ended the settlement entirely.

Scripture speaks to moments like this:

"When a man's ways please the LORD, he maketh even his enemies to be at peace with him."

— *Proverbs 16:7*

This verse does not promise permanent harmony, nor does it deny the reality of conflict. It acknowledges that God, in His providence, can **restrain hostility** when circumstances would otherwise invite it.

Providence here did not erase danger.

It held it at bay.

Protection took the form of **restraint**, not force. Potential threats were delayed. Observations did not become assaults. Time was granted—time for recovery, organization, and survival.

This restraint mattered deeply.

Without it, leadership and strength would have been irrelevant. The colony's fragile existence depended not only on endurance within, but on peace without. God preserved the settlement by limiting what others chose—or were allowed—to do.

It is important to note what this does *not* imply.

Protection does not mean moral superiority.

Restraint does not imply innocence or entitlement.

Providence does not guarantee perpetual peace.

It means that, for a time, God governed circumstances so that destruction did not occur.

In Scripture, God often works through what does **not** happen as much as through what does. Unfought battles and unspoken attacks are just as much under His authority as victories and deliverance.

At Plymouth, the absence of attack was itself a form of preservation—quiet, unseen, and easily overlooked, yet absolutely essential.

Theological Reflection (Optional Transition Sentence)

God's providence is often revealed not in conflict avoided by strength, but in danger restrained by His hand.

---

6. Daily Provision, Not Excess

In the earliest months at Plymouth, survival depended on careful stewardship rather than abundance.

Food was scarce, and every decision carried weight.

- **Food was measured carefully**
  Rations were planned with restraint.
  Waste could mean hunger later.
- **Shared communally**
  What little was available was distributed for the good of all.
  Survival depended on cooperation, not individual stockpiling.
- **Never plentiful**
  There were no reserves to fall back on.
  Each day brought uncertainty about the next.

Yet despite these limitations, **the colony did not collapse**.

There was no sudden abundance.

No overflowing storehouses.

No escape from daily dependence.

Instead, provision came **just in time**.

"Give us this day our daily bread."
— *Matthew 6:11*
God's providence often supplies **what is needed**, not what is desired.
"It is of the LORD's mercies that we are not consumed, because his compassions fail not. They are new every morning."
— *Lamentations 3:22–23*
This pattern mirrors Scripture repeatedly:
God trains His people to trust Him daily rather than rely on stored confidence.
Like Israel in the wilderness, excess was withheld—not as punishment, but as instruction.
"Man doth not live by bread only, but by every word that proceedeth out of the mouth of the LORD."
— *Deuteronomy 8:3*
Plymouth survived not through surplus, but through **sustained mercy**.
Providence did not remove hardship.
It prevented despair.
Each measured meal became a reminder:
life was being preserved by God's hand, one day at a time.
In this season, the colony learned a truth that history often forgets:
dependence is not weakness—it is preparation.

---

7. Discussion Questions (Choose 2–3)

1. Why does God sometimes allow His people to face extreme hardship?
2. How does scarcity reveal what we truly trust in?
3. Why is survival itself sometimes the miracle?
4. What parallels do you see between Israel's wilderness experience and Plymouth?

---

8. Personal & National Application

Personal

- Am I faithful when God provides just enough?
- Do I trust God daily or only when resources are abundant?

National

- Prosperity can cause forgetfulness
- Hardship often clarifies dependence
- Survival precedes blessing

"It is of the LORD's mercies that we are not consumed."
— *Lamentations 3:22*

---

9. Closing Reflection

Plymouth survived not because conditions improved quickly,
but because God sustained them slowly.
The winter did not break suddenly.
Hunger did not vanish.
Disease did not retreat all at once.
Day after day, weakness lingered. Loss accumulated. Hope was tested not by a single crisis, but by endurance.
Scripture prepares us for this kind of providence:
"It is of the LORD's mercies that we are not consumed, because his compassions fail not.
They are new every morning: great is thy faithfulness."
— *Lamentations 3:22–23*
God's mercy was not dramatic.
It was daily.
Providence did not arrive with rescue fleets or sudden abundance. It appeared in breath preserved, strength renewed just enough for the next task, and life sustained one day at a time.
This, too, is a biblical pattern.
God often chooses **gradual preservation** over immediate relief, teaching His people dependence not on outcomes, but on Himself.
"Give us this day our daily bread."
— *Matthew 6:11*
Daily bread is not excess.
It is sufficiency.
Providence does not always shout.
Sometimes it whispers—through survival, through restraint, through the quiet continuation of life when collapse seems likely.
Scripture reminds us that preservation itself is an act of God:
"Thou hast holden me by my right hand."
— *Psalm 73:23*

Plymouth endured because God held them—not because circumstances improved quickly, but because mercy remained constant.

Slow preservation requires patience.

It humbles pride.

It trains gratitude.

And when deliverance finally comes, it is recognized not as entitlement, but as grace.

Providence did not eliminate suffering.

It limited destruction.

God did not remove hardship.

He sustained life within it.

Sometimes God's greatest work is not seen in sudden change—but in the quiet miracle of endurance.

Optional Teaching Pause (Adult Class)

You might ask:

- *Why does God often preserve through endurance rather than immediate relief?*
- *How does slow provision deepen faith?*
- *Where have we mistaken survival itself for insignificance rather than mercy?*

---

10. Closing Scripture & Prayer Prompt

Read aloud:

"Except the LORD keep the city, the watchman waketh but in vain."

— *Psalm 127:1*

Prayer Prompt:

"Lord, teach us to trust You daily, to endure faithfully, and to recognize Your hand even in hardship."

Lesson 6 — Squanto and Divine Timing

Series Title

God's Providence in American History: From the Pilgrims to the Present

Theme Verse

"But as for you, ye thought evil against me; but God meant it unto good."
— *Genesis 50:20*

Lesson Aim (For the Teacher)

To show how God can redeem suffering, loss, and injustice across years—and even generations—to provide help at the exact moment it is needed.

This lesson emphasizes **timing**, not coincidence.

Time Flow (Minimum 40 Minutes)

- Opening Scripture & Prayer – 4 minutes
- Biblical Framework – 10 minutes
- Historical Narrative & Providential Examples – 18 minutes
- Discussion – 5 minutes
- Application & Closing Reflection – 3 minutes

---

1. Opening Scripture Reading

Read aloud together:

"To every thing there is a season, and a time to every purpose under the heaven."
— *Ecclesiastes 3:1*

---

2. Core Truth Statement

God often prepares provision years in advance—long before His people realize they will need it.

What appears tragic at one moment may become essential later.

---

3. Biblical Pattern: God Uses Suffering to Prepare Deliverance

Key Scriptures

"He sent a man before them, even Joseph, who was sold for a servant."
— *Psalm 105:17*
"And we know that all things work together for good to them that love God."
— *Romans 8:28*
"The LORD maketh poor, and maketh rich: he bringeth low, and lifteth up."
— *1 Samuel 2:7*

Teaching Point (Scripture-Anchored)

God often **allows hardship** in order to **position people** for future deliverance—both for themselves and for others.

"5. Now therefore be not grieved, nor angry with yourselves, that ye sold me hither: for God did send me before you to preserve life." "6. For these two years hath the famine been in the land: and yet there are five years, in the which there shall neither be earing nor harvest." "7. And God sent me before you to preserve you a posterity in the earth, and to save your lives by a great deliverance." "8. So now it was not you that sent me hither, but God: and he hath made me a father to Pharaoh, and lord of all his house, and a ruler throughout all the land of Egypt." — Genesis 45:5–8

"10. For thou, O God, hast proved us: thou hast tried us, as silver is tried." "11. Thou broughtest us into the net; thou laidst affliction upon our loins." "12. Thou hast caused men to ride over our heads; we went through fire and through water: but thou broughtest us out into a wealthy place." — Psalm 66:10–12

This does not make suffering good, but it shows that **God is never absent from it.**

---

4. Who Was Squanto? (Tisquantum)

Squanto, also known as Tisquantum, was a member of the Patuxet tribe, whose people lived along the coast of what would later become Plymouth. His life was marked not by planning or advantage, but by loss layered upon loss:

"The LORD killeth, and maketh alive: he bringeth down to the grave, and bringeth up."
— *1 Samuel 2:6*

Years before the Pilgrims arrived, Squanto was captured by English explorers and taken across the Atlantic against his will. What began as a violent disruption became a defining turning point. He was sold into slavery and removed entirely from the land, language, and people that had shaped his identity:

"They took Joseph, and sold him… and Joseph was brought down to Egypt."
— *Genesis 37:28*

(The comparison highlights providential pattern, not identical circumstance.)

In England, Squanto was exposed to a foreign world—learning the English language, observing European customs, and encountering a culture entirely unlike his own. His captivity was unjust. His suffering was real. Yet God was quietly preparing him in ways he could not have imagined:

"For my thoughts are not your thoughts, neither are your ways my ways, saith the LORD."
— *Isaiah 55:8*

Eventually, Squanto found his way back across the Atlantic. When he returned to his homeland, the loss deepened. Disease had swept through the coastal tribes, devastating entire communities. The Patuxet village stood empty. His people were gone. His land was silent:

"I am become a stranger unto my brethren, and an alien unto my mother's children."
— *Psalm 69:8*

By the time the Pilgrims landed, Squanto stood alone. He belonged fully to neither world. He was one of the very few natives who spoke English, yet he had no surviving tribe to return to. His suffering had stripped him of home, family, and identity—everything that normally gives a man place and purpose:

"When my father and my mother forsake me, then the LORD will take me up."
— *Psalm 27:10*

Humanly speaking, Squanto had lost everything.

Yet providence was at work where loss seemed final. What appeared as wasted years of suffering had quietly prepared a man uniquely positioned for a moment no one could have foreseen:

"And we know that all things work together for good to them that love God."
— *Romans 8:28*

Squanto's story reminds us that providence often works through pain long before it reveals purpose. His life was not spared hardship—but it was preserved for a moment when survival itself would depend on what God had been preparing all along.

---

5. The Exactness of Divine Timing — Providential Example #1: Language

When the settlers at Plymouth encountered Squanto, they did not simply meet a native inhabitant willing to help. They encountered a man whose life had been shaped—painfully and unexpectedly—by events that occurred **years before their arrival**.

Squanto's earlier captivity was not brief, nor was it gentle.

He had been taken against his will, removed from his homeland, and carried across the Atlantic. He endured displacement, hardship, and the loss of family and familiarity. Nothing about his experience could be described as good in itself.

And yet, through that suffering, something unlikely occurred.

Squanto learned English.

Not only the language, but elements of European customs, expectations, and methods of communication. He learned how Europeans thought, how they negotiated, and how they understood agreements. These skills were acquired long before the Mayflower set sail—and without any visible connection to its future arrival.

Years later, when the settlers arrived weakened, ill, and unable to communicate effectively with the surrounding tribes, Squanto stood at a singular intersection of two worlds.

He could speak to both.

This was not a general ability shared by many. It was **exactly what was needed**, precisely when it was needed.

Scripture reveals that God often works this way—preparing understanding long before the moment of encounter:

"And how hear we every man in our own tongue, wherein we were born?"

— *Acts 2:8*

"So they read in the book in the law of God distinctly, and gave the sense, and caused them to understand the reading."

— *Nehemiah 8:8*

In both cases, language served as a bridge—allowing truth, instruction, and cooperation to occur where confusion would otherwise have prevailed.

Providence here did not erase pain.

It **redeemed preparation**.

Squanto's suffering did not suddenly become good. But it became **useful**—not by human planning, but by divine timing. What had once seemed meaningless hardship became a means through which lives were preserved.

God prepared a translator before the settlers arrived.

Not after they landed.

Not once danger had escalated.

But years earlier, through events no one at Plymouth could have anticipated.

This is the precision of providence.

God did not merely provide help.

He prepared help **in advance**, shaping circumstances across time and cultures to meet a need before it was visible.

Theological Reflection (Optional Transition Sentence)

God's providence often prepares answers long before the questions are asked.

Providential Example #2 — Agricultural Knowledge

The settlers at Plymouth faced a problem that prayer alone could not immediately solve: they did not know how to survive in the land they had entered.

The soil was unfamiliar.

The climate was harsher than expected.

European farming methods failed in New England conditions.

Even if peace had been secured, survival would have remained uncertain without knowledge—practical, specific, and local.

Squanto provided that knowledge.

He taught the settlers how to plant corn in a way suited to the land, using fish as fertilizer to enrich the soil. He showed them which crops could survive the region's short growing season and which would not. He helped them locate food sources unfamiliar to Europeans—shellfish beds, native plants, and fishing areas essential for survival.

This instruction did not merely supplement their efforts.

It **made survival possible**.

Without this guidance, starvation was not a remote risk—it was the most likely outcome. The settlers lacked both the experience and the time required to experiment through failure. Another winter without sufficient harvest would almost certainly have ended the colony.

Scripture reminds us that provision does not always arrive in the form we expect:

"The earth is the LORD's, and the fulness thereof."

— *Psalm 24:1*

God's provision here did not come as food delivered directly to the table. It came as **understanding**—knowledge that unlocked the land's capacity to sustain life.

Providence supplied not merely what was needed for the moment, but what would enable ongoing survival. Instead of continual dependence on emergency relief, the settlers were given tools for stewardship—wisdom that could be applied season after season.

This pattern is consistent throughout Scripture. God often provides not by bypassing effort, but by equipping His people to work wisely within what He has created.

Providence here was not passive.

It was instructive.

God did not simply feed the settlers.

He taught them **how to live** in the land.

Theological Reflection (Optional Transition Sentence)

God's provision often arrives as wisdom that unlocks what He has already placed before us.

Providential Example #3 — Mediation and Peace

The survival of Plymouth depended on more than food and shelter. It depended on **peace**—not as an ideal, but as a necessity.

The settlers were few. They were weakened by disease and loss. Any prolonged conflict with surrounding tribes would have overwhelmed them. Without understanding and restraint on both sides, violence was not just possible—it was likely.

Squanto served as a mediator.

He did more than translate words. He explained **customs, expectations, and intentions**. He helped each side understand what the other meant—not merely what was said. This role was essential in an environment where misunderstanding could quickly turn into hostility.

Through his mediation, peace was established with neighboring tribes. Agreements were formed. Boundaries were understood. Communication replaced suspicion.

This peace did not erase all tension.

It did not guarantee permanent harmony.

But it created **time**.

Time to recover.

Time to plant and harvest.

Time to strengthen the settlement.

Scripture recognizes the unique role of those who stand between opposing sides:

"Blessed are the peacemakers: for they shall be called the children of God."

— *Matthew 5:9*

Peacemaking in Scripture is not passive. It requires discernment, humility, and courage. It involves explaining, listening, and restraining escalation.

Providence here did not remove the potential for conflict.

It restrained it through understanding.

Squanto's presence reduced misunderstanding at the most fragile moment in the colony's existence. His ability to move between cultures transformed fear into cooperation and allowed survival to become possible.

This peace mattered more than comfort.

It mattered more than prosperity.

It mattered more than success.

Without it, the colony would not have lasted long enough for any future to take shape.

Providence sometimes works not by strengthening defenses, but by **lowering swords**—granting peace where conflict would otherwise have destroyed what weakness could not endure.

Theological Reflection (Optional Transition Sentence)
Peace, when granted by God, often serves as the quiet space in which survival becomes possible.

---

6. Redemption Without Erasing Pain
Squanto's story is often told as one of remarkable usefulness—but it must first be understood as one of **real suffering**.
Providence does not ask us to minimize pain in order to recognize purpose.
Important clarification:

- **Squanto's suffering was real**
  He was taken violently from his homeland.
  His freedom was stolen, and his future was uncertain.
- **His captivity was unjust**
  He was treated as property rather than as a person made in the image of God.
  No providential outcome makes injustice acceptable.
- **His losses were permanent**
  When Squanto returned, his people were gone.
  His village lay empty, erased by disease.

Providence does not erase scars.
It does not rewind history.
It does not pretend suffering never occurred.
"The LORD is nigh unto them that are of a broken heart; and saveth such as be of a contrite spirit."
— *Psalm 34:18*
What providence does is **redeem purpose from pain**.
God did not cause Squanto's suffering—but He did not waste it.
"And we know that all things work together for good to them that love God."
— *Romans 8:28*
Squanto's knowledge, language, and experience—gained through trauma—became instruments of preservation for others.
This redemption did not cancel his grief.
It gave his suffering meaning.
"Thou hast turned for me my mourning into dancing."
— *Psalm 30:11*
This does not suggest celebration of pain.
It acknowledges transformation beyond it.

Squanto's life teaches a sobering truth:

God's providence does not always deliver us from suffering, but it can deliver purpose through it.

Pain is not denied.

Loss is not dismissed.

But neither is it final.

Providence works not by erasing what was broken—but by bringing something life-giving from it.

---

7. Discussion Questions (Choose 2–3)

1. Why do you think God sometimes prepares provision far in advance?
2. How does Squanto's story compare to Joseph's in Scripture?
3. Can suffering still have purpose even if it is never explained?
4. Why is timing such a strong indicator of providence?

---

8. Personal & National Application

Personal

- Do I trust God with seasons that do not yet make sense?
- Am I open to God using my experiences to help others?

National

- Survival often depends on unexpected cooperation
- Humility opens the door to help
- God often uses unlikely individuals

"God hath chosen the foolish things of the world to confound the wise."

— *1 Corinthians 1:27*

---

9. Closing Reflection

Squanto did not plan his role.

His life unfolded through hardship, captivity, loss, and displacement—events that, at the time, appeared tragic and purposeless. He did not choose his suffering, nor could he have imagined how it would one day be used.

The Pilgrims did not anticipate him.

They arrived with no expectation that a single man would hold the knowledge, language, and relationships necessary for their survival. From their perspective, help did not exist.

Yet when survival required assistance, God had already prepared a man.

Scripture consistently reveals this pattern: God often prepares His provision **long before the need is visible.**

"And we know that all things work together for good to them that love God, to them who are the called according to his purpose."

— *Romans 8:28*

Squanto's suffering was not wasted. His years of hardship produced exactly what was required—fluency in language, understanding of culture, knowledge of the land, and the ability to mediate peace. None of this was accidental. None of it was rushed.

Providence does not scramble to respond.

It arranges.

"The LORD shall guide thee continually."

— *Isaiah 58:11*

What appeared to be delay was preparation. What seemed like misfortune became provision. God had already positioned help before the Pilgrims fully understood their need.

This truth echoes throughout Scripture.

Joseph could not see the purpose of his betrayal until famine arrived.

"But as for you, ye thought evil against me; but God meant it unto good."

— *Genesis 50:20*

Providence is often recognized only in hindsight—when necessity reveals that God has already gone ahead.

Squanto's presence reminds us that God's care is not reactive. He does not wait for crisis to begin His work. He prepares quietly, patiently, and precisely.

Help often arrives not when we expect it—but exactly when we need it.

Providence is not always visible in advance.

It is often revealed only after the need becomes clear.

And when it is seen, it humbles us—reminding us that survival, provision, and guidance are not products of foresight, but gifts of God's sovereign care.

Optional Teaching Pause (Adult Class)

You might ask:

- *Why does God so often prepare provision long before we recognize the need?*
- *How does hindsight change our understanding of suffering?*
- *Where might God already be preparing answers we have not yet asked for?*

10. Closing Scripture & Prayer Prompt

Read aloud:

"My times are in thy hand."

— *Psalm 31:15*

Prayer Prompt:

"Lord, help us trust Your timing, even when we do not understand Your ways."

Lesson 7 — The First Thanksgiving

Series Title

God's Providence in American History: From the Pilgrims to the Present

Theme Verse

"O give thanks unto the LORD; for he is good: for his mercy endureth for ever."
— *Psalm 107:1*

Lesson Aim (For the Teacher)

To show that thanksgiving was not a response to abundance or ease, but a **deliberate act of faith**, offered in recognition of God's mercy after loss, hardship, and preservation.
This lesson emphasizes **gratitude rooted in faith**, not circumstance.

Time Flow (Minimum 40 Minutes)

- Opening Scripture & Prayer – 4 minutes
- Biblical Framework – 10 minutes
- Historical Narrative & Providential Examples – 18 minutes
- Discussion – 5 minutes
- Application & Closing Reflection – 3 minutes

---

1. Opening Scripture Reading

Read aloud together:
"In every thing give thanks: for this is the will of God in Christ Jesus concerning you."
— *1 Thessalonians 5:18*

---

2. Core Truth Statement

True thanksgiving flows from recognizing God's mercy, not from enjoying prosperity.
Gratitude is an act of worship before it is an emotion.

---

3. Biblical Pattern: Thanksgiving Before Abundance

Key Scriptures

"Offer unto God thanksgiving; and pay thy vows unto the most High."
— *Psalm 50:14*
"Enter into his gates with thanksgiving, and into his courts with praise."
— *Psalm 100:4*
"By him therefore let us offer the sacrifice of praise to God continually."
— *Hebrews 13:15*

Teaching Point (Scripture-Anchored)

Thanksgiving in Scripture is often commanded **during hardship**, not after deliverance is complete.
"17. Although the fig tree shall not blossom, neither shall fruit be in the vines; the labour of the olive shall fail, and the fields shall yield no meat; the flock shall be cut off from the fold, and there shall be no herd in the stalls:" "18. Yet I will rejoice in the LORD, I will joy in the God of my salvation." — Habakkuk 3:17–18
"1. I will bless the LORD at all times: his praise shall continually be in my mouth." — Psalm 34:1
Gratitude declares trust in God's character even when outcomes remain uncertain.

---

4. The Historical Reality Behind the First Thanksgiving

The gathering traditionally called "The First Thanksgiving" took place in the autumn of 1621—but it bears little resemblance to later national celebrations or modern imagery.
It followed a devastating year marked by suffering and loss. The settlers had endured a brutal winter that claimed roughly half their number. Hunger, illness, and exhaustion were not distant memories—they were recent wounds:
"It is good for a man that he bear the yoke in his youth."
— *Lamentations 3:27*
Food security remained uncertain. The harvest was modest and hard-won, dependent on knowledge the settlers had not possessed months earlier. Every meal served as a reminder that survival had come not through abundance, but through mercy:
"Give us this day our daily bread."
— *Matthew 6:11*
This gathering was not proclaimed by government.
It was not marked by speeches of success.
It was not framed as a celebration of achievement.
It was a communal act of worship.

Those who gathered had buried spouses, children, and friends. They had lived months unsure whether the colony would survive another season. Gratitude was offered not because the future was secure, but because God had sustained them through the past:

"O give thanks unto the LORD; for he is good: for his mercy endureth for ever."

— *Psalm 107:1*

The gathering included cooperation with neighboring natives and reflected a fragile peace that had allowed the colony to endure its most vulnerable period. Shared food and fellowship followed shared hardship—not triumph:

"Behold, how good and how pleasant it is for brethren to dwell together in unity!"

— *Psalm 133:1*

What made the First Thanksgiving significant was not its size or spectacle, but its timing. Gratitude preceded prosperity. Worship came before security. The settlers acknowledged God's mercy while their dependence was still fresh:

"In every thing give thanks: for this is the will of God in Christ Jesus concerning you."

— *1 Thessalonians 5:18*

The First Thanksgiving was not a national holiday.

It was a confession of dependence.

It was gratitude offered before growth marked the land.

And in that posture, providence was quietly honored—recognized not as entitlement, but as mercy.

---

5. Specific Providential Elements Recognized

Providential Example #1 — Survival Itself

When the remaining settlers gathered to give thanks, they did not do so from a position of comfort or abundance. Their gathering followed months of grief, loss, and uncertainty.

Many present had buried spouses, children, and close friends.

Some stood beside empty places where loved ones should have been.

Every person present had lived with the daily awareness that survival was not guaranteed.

The winter had stripped away illusions of strength and self-sufficiency. It had revealed how fragile their existence truly was. Life had continued—not because it was deserved, but because it had been **preserved**.

In this context, thanksgiving carried a different weight.

It was not an expression of triumph.

It was an acknowledgment of mercy.

Scripture speaks to this understanding:

"It is of the LORD's mercies that we are not consumed, because his compassions fail not. They are new every morning: great is thy faithfulness."
— *Lamentations 3:22–23*

The survivors recognized that the mere fact of their presence was evidence of God's kindness. Survival itself was not an entitlement. It was a gift—quietly given, undeserved, and deeply humbling.

This recognition shaped the tone of their gratitude.

They did not gather because hardship had ended.

They gathered because life had been spared.

Providence here was not measured by abundance, but by **continuance**. God had not removed sorrow, but He had sustained life. That distinction mattered deeply.

The thanksgiving they offered flowed from humility rather than pride. It acknowledged dependence rather than achievement. They gave thanks not for ease, but for endurance.

In recognizing survival as mercy, they set a pattern that Scripture consistently affirms: gratitude that arises from honest reflection, not inflated success.

Theological Reflection (Optional Transition Sentence)

True thanksgiving begins when survival is recognized as mercy rather than assumed as right.

Providential Example #2 — A Harvest That Was "Enough"

The harvest that followed the first year at Plymouth was not abundant by any generous standard. It did not erase the hardships of the past winter, nor did it guarantee security for the years ahead.

It was **modest**.

Every portion had been earned through labor by bodies still recovering from loss and illness. The fields yielded cautiously. Supplies were counted carefully. There was no sense that danger had passed or that prosperity had arrived.

And yet, it was **enough**.

There was food to eat. There was clothing to wear. There was provision sufficient to continue.

Scripture speaks directly to this kind of provision:

"And having food and raiment let us be therewith content."
— *1 Timothy 6:8*

God's provision here did not overwhelm with excess. It met the need of the moment without encouraging complacency or presumption. The harvest sustained life, but it did not create dependence on abundance.

This distinction mattered deeply.

An abundant harvest might have fostered false confidence. A meager harvest would have prolonged desperation. What they received was neither—it was **measured mercy**.
Providence provided what was necessary, not what was impressive.
The settlers recognized this. Their gratitude was not rooted in overflowing storehouses, but in the simple fact that what they had would carry them forward. Thanksgiving was offered not because everything was secure, but because God had once again shown Himself faithful.
This pattern echoes throughout Scripture. God often provides daily bread, not stored abundance. He supplies enough for obedience, not excess for comfort.
The harvest taught contentment.
It reinforced dependence.
It reminded the settlers that survival would continue to require humility, diligence, and trust.

Theological Reflection (Optional Transition Sentence)
God's providence often reveals itself not in excess, but in sufficiency.

Providential Example #3 — Peace With the Native Tribes
The gathering commonly remembered as the First Thanksgiving did not take place in isolation. It occurred within a fragile context shaped by vulnerability, uncertainty, and the ever-present possibility of conflict.
Peace with the surrounding Native tribes was not assumed.
It was **experienced**.
The gathering included cooperation with local native peoples—shared food, shared space, and shared time. This was not a casual arrangement. It represented trust built slowly, sustained through restraint, and preserved through mutual understanding.
This peace was neither accidental nor guaranteed.
The settlers remained few in number and physically weakened. The tribes surrounding them were capable of overwhelming the settlement if hostilities had arisen. The balance between survival and destruction was thin.
Yet peace endured.
Scripture speaks to the blessing of such unity:
"Behold, how good and how pleasant it is for brethren to dwell together in unity!"
— *Psalm 133:1*
Unity here did not imply sameness.
It did not erase differences.
It reflected restraint, respect, and cooperation.
Providence did not remove the potential for conflict.
It restrained it.

Peace created space for gratitude to be expressed without fear. It allowed the settlers to gather not in hiding, but openly. It affirmed that survival had been made possible not only through provision and endurance, but through relationships preserved during a time of weakness.

This peace mattered profoundly.

Without it, the harvest would not have sustained life. Without it, leadership and strength would have been irrelevant. Without it, the fragile settlement would not have lasted long enough to face another season.

Peace itself was a providential gift.

It was not earned through power.

It was not secured through dominance.

It was granted through restraint.

In Scripture, peace is often treated not as an absence of conflict, but as a **gift of God's governance**—a condition He allows when circumstances could easily produce chaos.

The settlers recognized this. Their thanksgiving was not limited to food on the table, but extended to peace beyond it.

Theological Reflection (Optional Transition Sentence)

When peace is granted where conflict is possible, it should be received as mercy, not assumed as right.

---

6. Thanksgiving as a Spiritual Discipline

For the Pilgrims, thanksgiving was not merely an emotional response to relief.

It was a **spiritual discipline**, deliberately practiced in the midst of uncertainty.

They understood thanksgiving as:

- **A way to honor God**
  Gratitude redirected attention away from human effort and toward divine mercy.
  Survival was acknowledged as God's provision, not personal achievement.
- **A safeguard against pride**
  Thanksgiving reminded them that endurance had not been earned.
  It restrained the temptation to interpret survival as success.
- **A reminder of dependence**
  Their future was still fragile.
  Gratitude kept them anchored in daily reliance rather than false security.

Thanksgiving was **not spontaneous—it was intentional**.

It required choosing acknowledgment before abundance and worship before certainty.

"Bless the LORD, O my soul, and forget not all his benefits."

— *Psalm 103:2*

Scripture consistently frames thanksgiving as an act of memory and humility.
"In every thing give thanks: for this is the will of God in Christ Jesus concerning you."
— *1 Thessalonians 5:18*
The Pilgrims gave thanks not because the land was secure, but because mercy had sustained them through loss.
Thanksgiving shaped their perspective before prosperity shaped their future.
It trained their hearts to recognize provision without presuming permanence.
Providence had preserved them.
Thanksgiving kept them mindful of **Who** had done so.
Their example teaches a lasting truth:
gratitude is not the result of security—it is the foundation of faithfulness.

---

7. Discussion Questions (Choose 2–3)

1. Why is gratitude often hardest after hardship?
2. How does thanksgiving protect the heart from pride?
3. What dangers arise when gratitude follows prosperity but not loss?
4. How does biblical thanksgiving differ from cultural celebration?

---

8. Personal & National Application

Personal

- Do I give thanks only when life is comfortable?
- Can I recognize God's mercy even after loss?

National

- Gratitude must precede prosperity
- Forgetting God often follows abundance
- Thanksgiving anchors memory and humility

"Beware that thou forget not the LORD thy God."
— *Deuteronomy 8:11*

---

9. Closing Reflection

The first Thanksgiving was not about success.
It was about acknowledgment.
The gathering did not follow prosperity, security, or ease. The future remained uncertain. Supplies were limited. Loss was still recent. Survival was fragile, not assured.
Yet gratitude was offered.
Scripture teaches that thanksgiving is not dependent on circumstance, but on recognition of God's mercy:

"O give thanks unto the LORD; for he is good: for his mercy endureth for ever."
— *Psalm 107:1*

They thanked God not because the future was secure, but because His mercy had sustained them through what should have ended them. Gratitude arose not from comfort, but from remembrance—remembrance of protection, provision, and restraint.

This reflects a consistent biblical principle.

God calls His people to give thanks not only after deliverance, but **in recognition of daily mercy**.

"In every thing give thanks: for this is the will of God in Christ Jesus concerning you."
— *1 Thessalonians 5:18*

The Thanksgiving gathering marked a conscious pause—a decision to acknowledge God before abundance could distract the heart. Gratitude preceded growth. Worship came before expansion.

Scripture warns that thanksgiving must come early, before prosperity hardens the soul:

"Beware lest thou forget the LORD… when thou hast eaten and art full."
— *Deuteronomy 8:11–12*

The Pilgrims did not wait for stability to give thanks. They recognized that survival itself was mercy, not entitlement.

"It is of the LORD's mercies that we are not consumed."
— *Lamentations 3:22*

Gratitude marked the colony before growth marked the land.

And in doing so, they acknowledged a truth that Scripture continually affirms: that thanksgiving is not the result of blessing—it is the proper response to mercy.

Providence had sustained them.

Gratitude rightly followed.

Optional Teaching Pause (Adult Class)

You might ask:

- *Why is gratitude most meaningful before circumstances improve?*
- *How does thanksgiving guard the heart against pride?*
- *What happens when gratitude is delayed until comfort arrives?*

10. Closing Scripture & Prayer Prompt

Read aloud:

"Let us come before his presence with thanksgiving."

— *Psalm 95:2*

Prayer Prompt:

"Lord, teach us to give thanks in all seasons, to remember Your mercy, and to walk humbly before You."

Lesson 8 — The Great Awakening

Series Title

God's Providence in American History: From the Pilgrims to the Present

Theme Verse

"Wilt thou not revive us again: that thy people may rejoice in thee?"
— *Psalm 85:6*

Lesson Aim (For the Teacher)

To show how God renewed spiritual life across the colonies through widespread repentance, conviction, and transformed hearts—creating moral unity before political unity ever existed. This lesson emphasizes **revival as an act of God**, not a human movement.

Time Flow (Minimum 40 Minutes)

- Opening Scripture & Prayer – 4 minutes
- Biblical Framework – 10 minutes
- Historical Narrative & Providential Examples – 18 minutes
- Discussion – 5 minutes
- Application & Closing Reflection – 3 minutes

---

1. Opening Scripture Reading

Read aloud together:

"If my people, which are called by my name, shall humble themselves, and pray, and seek my face, and turn from their wicked ways; then will I hear from heaven, and will forgive their sin, and will heal their land."
— *2 Chronicles 7:14*

---

2. Core Truth Statement

God often revives hearts before He reshapes history.

Spiritual renewal precedes lasting moral and cultural change.

---

3. Biblical Pattern: God Revives a People

Key Scriptures

"The sacrifices of God are a broken spirit: a broken and a contrite heart."
— *Psalm 51:17*

"Then shall we know, if we follow on to know the LORD."
— *Hosea 6:3*

"Times of refreshing shall come from the presence of the Lord."
— *Acts 3:19*

Teaching Point (Scripture-Anchored)

Revival in Scripture is marked by **repentance**, **humility**, and **renewed obedience**, not merely emotion or enthusiasm.

"12. Therefore also now, saith the LORD, turn ye even to me with all your heart, and with fasting, and with weeping, and with mourning:" "13. And rend your heart, and not your garments, and turn unto the LORD your God: for he is gracious and merciful, slow to anger, and of great kindness, and repenteth him of the evil."
— *Joel 2:12–13*

"8. Draw nigh to God, and he will draw nigh to you. Cleanse your hands, ye sinners; and purify your hearts, ye double minded." "9. Be afflicted, and mourn, and weep: let your laughter be turned to mourning, and your joy to heaviness." "10. Humble yourselves in the sight of the Lord, and he shall lift you up."
— *James 4:8–10*

True revival begins when God's people respond to His Word.

---

4. The Spiritual Condition of the Colonies

By the early 1700s, the colonies possessed an outward religious structure—but inward vitality had begun to fade.

Churches existed in nearly every community. Sermons were preached. Forms were maintained. Yet for many, faith had become inherited rather than embraced. Religious practice often settled into routine rather than conviction:

"This people draweth nigh unto me with their mouth, and honoureth me with their lips; but their heart is far from me."
— *Matthew 15:8*

Generational distance played a role. The first settlers had crossed oceans at great cost for conscience and obedience. Their children and grandchildren, however, had grown up amid relative stability. What had once been a hard-won faith increasingly became assumed rather than examined:

"And there arose another generation after them, which knew not the LORD."
— *Judges 2:10*

Moral compromise quietly increased. Prosperity softened urgency. Discipline waned. Attendance remained, but attentiveness diminished. The language of faith persisted while the fear of the Lord weakened:

"Having a form of godliness, but denying the power thereof."

— *2 Timothy 3:5*

Outward order remained.

Inward fire declined.

This pattern is not unique to colonial America. Scripture repeatedly shows that spiritual drift often follows seasons of blessing. When struggle recedes, dependence fades unless faith is intentionally renewed:

"Beware that thou forget not the LORD thy God… when thou hast eaten and art full."

— *Deuteronomy 8:11–12*

Yet decline itself was not the end of the story. Historically and biblically, this condition often precedes revival. God allows dryness to expose need, emptiness to awaken hunger, and routine to reveal the absence of power:

"Wilt thou not revive us again: that thy people may rejoice in thee?"

— *Psalm 85:6*

The spiritual condition of the colonies was fragile—but not forgotten. What appeared as decline was also preparation. God often permits spiritual barrenness so that renewal, when it comes, is unmistakably His work.

"I will pour water upon him that is thirsty, and floods upon the dry ground."

— *Isaiah 44:3*

This was the soil into which revival would soon fall.

---

5. The Great Awakening Begins

In the 1730s and 1740s, a spiritual stirring began to move through the American colonies—quietly at first, then with increasing clarity and power.

This movement did not arise from political ambition or institutional planning.

It emerged from **a renewed focus on the heart.**

- **Preaching emphasized personal repentance**
  Messages called individuals to examine their own standing before God.
  Faith was no longer assumed by heritage or church membership—it was tested by conscience.
- **Scripture was proclaimed plainly**
  The Word of God was preached with clarity and urgency.
  Listeners were encouraged to read, hear, and respond to Scripture personally.

- **Listeners were confronted with sin and grace**
  Conviction was paired with the offer of forgiveness.
  The gospel was presented not as moral improvement, but as spiritual rebirth.
- **Lives were visibly transformed**
  Testimonies of changed conduct followed changed hearts.
  Repentance bore fruit in humility, reconciliation, and renewed obedience.

"Now when they heard this, they were pricked in their heart."
— *Acts 2:37*

The movement spread rapidly:

- **Across colonies**
  Messages traveled beyond local communities, carried by itinerant preachers and shared testimony.
- **Across denominations**
  Though doctrinal differences remained, a shared emphasis on repentance and faith united many believers.
- **Without centralized leadership**
  No single authority controlled the movement.
  Its growth depended on response rather than organization.

This was not orchestrated—it was **ignited.**
"Not by might, nor by power, but by my spirit, saith the LORD of hosts."
— *Zechariah 4:6*
The Great Awakening revealed a consistent pattern of providence:
before God reshapes societies, He reshapes hearts.
The movement did not eliminate all problems.
It did not produce immediate political unity.
But it awakened conscience, renewed reverence for Scripture, and prepared the moral ground for responsibilities yet to come.
Providence did not thunder from above.
It stirred from within.

---

6. Specific Providential Marks of Revival — Widespread Conviction

The Great Awakening did not begin with organization, promotion, or emotional appeal. It began quietly—in the **hearts and consciences** of ordinary people.
Across towns and colonies, a similar pattern emerged.
People became deeply aware of personal sin. Not in abstract terms, but specifically and uncomfortably. Pride, dishonesty, bitterness, neglect of God, and hollow religion were named

openly. Confession was not coerced or staged; it arose naturally as individuals confronted Scripture and recognized their own condition before God.

This conviction led to visible change.

People sought reconciliation where relationships had been broken. Wrongs were acknowledged. Debts were addressed. Restitution was pursued where possible. Faith was no longer treated as inherited custom, but as personal responsibility.

Most notably, people **returned to Scripture**.

Bibles were read seriously rather than symbolically. Sermons were weighed against God's Word. Truth was examined rather than assumed. Conviction produced hunger—not merely for relief, but for righteousness.

Scripture describes this kind of awakening clearly:

"Now when they heard this, they were pricked in their heart."

— *Acts 2:37*

The language is significant. Conviction was not shallow. It pierced. It reached inward. It disrupted complacency and exposed false confidence.

Providence here did not rely on spectacle.

It relied on **truth applied by God**.

This conviction was widespread, but it was not uniform. It did not produce identical responses or expressions. What unified it was its source—not human persuasion, but the Spirit working through Scripture.

Importantly, this movement cannot be explained solely by personality or circumstance. The same response appeared across regions, among different congregations, and under varied leadership. The common element was not method, but message—God's Word brought to bear on conscience.

Conviction was deep, not manufactured.

It did not flatter the hearer.

It did not excuse sin.

It did not promise comfort without repentance.

It called people back to God.

Theological Reflection (Optional Transition Sentence)

True revival begins not with excitement, but with conviction that leads to repentance.

Providential Example #2 — Unity Across Colonies

One of the most remarkable features of the Great Awakening was not its intensity, but its **reach**.

The colonies were separated by distance, culture, and local identity. Communication was slow. Travel was difficult. There was no central authority coordinating belief or practice. And yet, across these divisions, a shared spiritual language began to emerge.

People who had never met one another began speaking in **common biblical terms**.

Scripture shaped sermons, conversations, and moral reflection. Words drawn from the Bible—repentance, grace, conviction, mercy, accountability—became familiar across regions.

Though styles of worship differed, the **substance** of belief increasingly aligned.

Shared convictions produced shared understanding.

This unity did not require uniformity. Colonies retained distinct customs and governance structures. Churches differed in form and emphasis. Yet beneath these differences grew a moral consensus shaped by Scripture rather than coercion.

Scripture describes this principle clearly:

"Can two walk together, except they be agreed?"

— *Amos 3:3*

Agreement here was not enforced by decree. It emerged through shared submission to God's Word. Unity was not created through political alignment, but through spiritual awakening.

Providence here worked internally before it worked externally.

Hearts were aligned before institutions were formed. Belief was clarified before governance was considered. Moral coherence developed before any attempt at collective action.

This mattered deeply for what would come later.

A people shaped by shared biblical understanding could cooperate without losing liberty. They could debate without fracturing entirely. They could resist tyranny morally rather than violently. Unity of conscience allowed diversity of expression.

God unified hearts **before** unifying governance.

This order is significant.

Unity imposed from above produces compliance.

Unity formed from conviction produces cooperation.

The Great Awakening created the latter.

It did not erase disagreement.

It did not eliminate tension.

But it established a shared moral framework within which disagreement could occur without dissolution.

Providence here was not loud.
It was **foundational.**

Theological Reflection (Optional Transition Sentence)
When God unites hearts through truth, cooperation follows without compulsion.

Providential Example #3 — Lasting Fruit
Specific Providential Marks of Revival — Lasting Fruit
The truest measure of the Great Awakening was not found in the intensity of its meetings, but in the **endurance of its effects**.
Emotional response alone does not define revival. Scripture consistently directs attention beyond the moment to what follows. The question is not whether people were moved, but whether lives were changed in ways that endured.
In the wake of the Awakening, several patterns became clear.
Church attendance increased—not briefly, but steadily. Worship was no longer treated as social custom alone, but as spiritual necessity. Congregations grew not through compulsion, but through conviction.
Education and literacy were emphasized with renewed urgency. The desire to read Scripture personally led families to value learning. Schools were established or strengthened. Knowledge was pursued not merely for advancement, but for understanding truth and responsibility before God.
Moral reform followed conviction.
Public conduct reflected inward change. Honesty, diligence, and accountability were increasingly valued. While society remained imperfect, there was a noticeable shift toward moral seriousness. God's authority was no longer assumed in name only; it was acknowledged as real and consequential.
Scripture provides a clear measure for such change:
"Ye shall know them by their fruits."
— *Matthew 7:16*
Fruit takes time.
It grows quietly.
It remains after emotion fades.
It reveals the nature of what produced it.
Providence here was not proven by crowds, but by continuity. The changes introduced during the Great Awakening did not disappear with the passing of prominent voices or dramatic gatherings. They shaped habits, institutions, and expectations across generations.
This endurance matters.

Lasting fruit indicates that the source was not merely human persuasion, but divine work rooted in truth. Where emotion subsides, conviction remains. Where excitement fades, discipline continues.

The Great Awakening did not perfect society.

It did not eliminate sin.

But it reoriented priorities.

God's authority was taken seriously.

Scripture was treated as foundational.

Life was viewed through the lens of accountability.

The change endured beyond emotion.

Theological Reflection (Optional Transition Sentence)

When God's work produces lasting fruit, it testifies that the source was deeper than feeling—it was truth.

---

7. Revival Without Perfection

Important clarification:

- Not every response was wise
- Some excesses occurred
- Discernment was necessary

Yet Scripture shows:

God often works through imperfect vessels.

"And the LORD said unto Gideon, The people that are with thee are too many for me to give the Midianites into their hands, lest Israel vaunt themselves against me, saying, Mine own hand hath saved me."
— Judges 7:2

"That no flesh should glory in his presence." — 1 Corinthians 1:29

Providence does not require flawlessness—only humility.

---

8. Discussion Questions (Choose 2–3)

1. Why does revival often follow spiritual complacency?
2. How can we distinguish true revival from emotional excitement?
3. Why is repentance central to lasting change?
4. What role does God's Word play in genuine revival?

---

9. Personal & National Application

Personal

- Do I respond humbly when God convicts my heart?
- Is my faith active or merely habitual?

National

- Moral unity often begins in the heart
- Revival cannot be legislated
- God changes nations by changing people

"Blessed are they which do hunger and thirst after righteousness."
— *Matthew 5:6*

---

10. Closing Reflection

Before America could act together,
it learned to repent together.

The Great Awakening did not begin with political resolve or national ambition. It began with conviction—quiet, personal, and deeply unsettling. Hearts were confronted before institutions were shaped. Conscience was awakened before responsibility could be carried.

Scripture reveals this order clearly:

"Wilt thou not revive us again: that thy people may rejoice in thee?"
— *Psalm 85:6*

Revival in Scripture is not enthusiasm alone. It is a return—back to truth, back to humility, back to the fear of the Lord.

The Great Awakening did not create a nation.
It shaped the **moral soil** from which one could grow.

God worked not by unifying laws first, but by aligning hearts. People across colonies, backgrounds, and distances were brought under a shared awareness of God's holiness and human accountability.

"Now when they heard this, they were pricked in their heart."
— *Acts 2:37*

Repentance preceded cooperation.
Conviction preceded consensus.
This reflects a consistent biblical pattern.
God prepares His people inwardly before entrusting them with outward responsibility.

"The fear of the LORD is the beginning of wisdom."
— *Proverbs 9:10*

Revival did not erase differences, but it created a shared moral language. Scripture became central. Sin was taken seriously. Obedience was understood as necessary, not optional.
This prepared hearts for responsibility—responsibility that would later require restraint, self-government, and mutual accountability.
"He that is faithful in that which is least is faithful also in much."
— *Luke 16:10*
The Great Awakening stands as a reminder that lasting unity is not forged by force, but by humility. God does not build nations on enthusiasm alone, but on repentance, truth, and reverence for His authority.
Revival did not guarantee righteousness.
But it created readiness.
And where hearts were prepared, God later entrusted responsibility.

Optional Teaching Pause (Adult Class)

You might ask:

- *Why does God often call for repentance before granting responsibility?*
- *How does shared conviction create unity without uniformity?*
- *What happens when responsibility outpaces spiritual readiness?*

---

11. Closing Scripture & Prayer Prompt

Read aloud:
"Create in me a clean heart, O God; and renew a right spirit within me."
— *Psalm 51:10*

Prayer Prompt:

"Lord, revive our hearts, humble us before You, and renew our love for Your truth."

Lesson 9 — Unity Through Revival

Series Title

God's Providence in American History: From the Pilgrims to the Present

Theme Verse

"Behold, how good and how pleasant it is for brethren to dwell together in unity!"
— *Psalm 133:1*

Lesson Aim (For the Teacher)

To show how spiritual revival produced a shared moral and biblical framework across the colonies, creating unity of purpose long before political independence existed.
This lesson emphasizes **unity born of truth**, not uniformity imposed by force.

Time Flow (Minimum 40 Minutes)

- Opening Scripture & Prayer – 4 minutes
- Biblical Framework – 10 minutes
- Historical Narrative & Providential Examples – 18 minutes
- Discussion – 5 minutes
- Application & Closing Reflection – 3 minutes

---

1. Opening Scripture Reading

Read aloud together:
"Endeavouring to keep the unity of the Spirit in the bond of peace."
— *Ephesians 4:3*

---

2. Core Truth Statement

True unity grows where people share a common submission to God's truth.
Unity is not created by agreement alone, but by shared allegiance.

---

3. Biblical Pattern: Unity Rooted in Truth

Key Scriptures

"Sanctify them through thy truth: thy word is truth."
— *John 17:17*

"Can two walk together, except they be agreed?"
— *Amos 3:3*
"That they all may be one… that the world may believe."
— *John 17:21*
Teaching Point (Scripture-Anchored)
Biblical unity flows from **shared truth**, **humility**, and **obedience**, not from forced conformity.
"I am a companion of all them that fear thee, and of them that keep thy precepts."
— Psalm 119:63
"1. If there be therefore any consolation in Christ, if any comfort of love, if any fellowship of the Spirit, if any bowels and mercies," "2. Fulfil ye my joy, that ye be likeminded, having the same love, being of one accord, of one mind." — Philippians 2:1–2
When truth is removed, unity becomes fragile or artificial.

---

4. The Colonies Before Unity
Prior to the Great Awakening, the colonies existed more as separate worlds than as a single people.
Geographic isolation shaped daily life. Travel between colonies was slow, difficult, and often dangerous. Communities were oriented inward, focused on local survival, trade, and governance rather than regional cooperation:
"Every man did that which was right in his own eyes."
— *Judges 21:25*
Denominational differences were pronounced. Puritans, Anglicans, Congregationalists, Baptists, Presbyterians, and others often viewed one another with suspicion. Theological distinctions, worship styles, and church governance varied widely. Shared faith in Scripture did not automatically produce shared fellowship:
"I am of Paul; and I of Apollos; and I of Cephas."
— *1 Corinthians 1:12*
Local identity outweighed any broader sense of unity. Colonists identified themselves by town, colony, or congregation—not by a common mission or shared responsibility. Loyalty was narrow. Cooperation was limited. There was little incentive to think beyond immediate borders:
"The way of a fool is right in his own eyes."
— *Proverbs 12:15*
Political structures did not bind the colonies together, and cultural differences reinforced separation. Economic interests competed. Leadership was local. There was no central authority, no shared vision, and no unifying cause.

There was no natural reason for unity.
What would later emerge as shared identity did not arise from convenience, strategy, or necessity. Unity was not forced. It was not negotiated. It was not planned:
"Except the LORD build the house, they labour in vain that build it."
— *Psalm 127:1*
The absence of unity is what makes the coming change so remarkable. What followed could not be explained by geography, politics, or ambition. Something deeper would have to move hearts before it could connect communities:
"Can two walk together, except they be agreed?"
— *Amos 3:3*
The colonies were separate in land, doctrine, and identity.
Only God could prepare them for unity—and He would do so not through government, but through revival.

---

5. Revival as the Unifying Agent
The Great Awakening did more than renew individual faith—it quietly **wove together a shared spiritual identity** across the colonies.
In a land marked by distance, denominational diversity, and local loyalties, revival accomplished ensuring unity not through authority, but through **common belief**.
The movement:

- **Spread common biblical language**
  Scripture became the shared vocabulary of faith.
  Sermons, letters, and conversations increasingly referenced the same passages and themes.
- **Reinforced shared moral values**
  Repentance, humility, and obedience were widely emphasized.
  These values transcended regional customs and economic differences.
- **Created mutual recognition among believers**
  Christians began to recognize one another as part of a larger spiritual community.
  Faith was no longer merely local—it was shared.
- **Encouraged cooperation across colonies**
  Churches supported one another through prayer, correspondence, and shared mission.
  Isolation gave way to awareness and partnership.

"And the multitude of them that believed were of one heart and of one soul."
— *Acts 4:32*
People began to see one another not merely as neighbors, but as **brothers and sisters in Christ**.

This unity did not erase all disagreement.
It did not remove cultural or theological distinctions.
But it established something deeper:
a shared submission to Scripture and a shared sense of accountability before God.
"Endeavouring to keep the unity of the Spirit in the bond of peace."
— *Ephesians 4:3*
God unified **hearts** before unifying **institutions**.
This sequence mattered.
When later challenges required cooperation beyond local boundaries, the spiritual groundwork had already been laid.
Revival had prepared people to think beyond themselves.
Providence did not force unity.
It **formed it**.
And in doing so, it demonstrated that lasting unity is born not of structure, but of shared conviction.

---

6. Specific Providential Effects of Unity
Providential Example #1 — Shared Worldview
As revival reshaped hearts, its effects extended beyond individual lives into the shared thinking of entire communities. One of the most significant outcomes was the emergence of a **common worldview** across the colonies.
Scripture moved from the margins of life to its center.
Families read the Bible regularly. Sermons were not only preached locally but circulated widely in printed form, read aloud in homes, and discussed across regions. Biblical phrases and references became familiar language, shaping how people understood duty, justice, authority, and responsibility.
This was not mere religious habit.
It was shared **orientation**.
People increasingly viewed life through Scripture's lens. Decisions were weighed in light of God's Word. Events were interpreted with reference to providence rather than chance. Right and wrong were discussed using biblical categories rather than personal preference alone.
Scripture describes this kind of relationship with God's Word:
"Thy testimonies also are my delight and my counsellors."
— *Psalm 119:24*
When Scripture functions as counselor, it shapes thought before it shapes action. It provides a framework for reasoning, not merely a source of comfort.
This shared worldview mattered profoundly.

The colonies remained diverse in customs, economies, and governance. Yet beneath those differences existed a common moral grammar. People could debate vigorously while still understanding one another's assumptions. Cooperation became possible because disagreement occurred within a shared framework of meaning.

Providence here did not eliminate difference.

It provided **common ground**.

Unity did not require sameness. It required shared reference points—Scripture serving as a trusted authority across regions. This allowed cooperation without coercion and accountability without centralized control.

A shared worldview made cooperation possible not because everyone agreed, but because they **reasoned from the same source**.

This was not imposed unity.

It was cultivated unity.

God's providence worked through revival to align hearts and minds before any attempt at formal union existed. What later emerged politically was built upon foundations already laid spiritually.

Theological Reflection (Optional Transition Sentence)

When God's Word shapes how people think, unity becomes possible without uniformity.

Providential Example #2 — Moral Consensus

As revival shaped individual conscience and a shared worldview emerged, another essential effect followed: the strengthening of **moral consensus** across communities.

This consensus did not eliminate disagreement or imperfection. It established shared expectations.

Personal responsibility was emphasized. Individuals were increasingly aware that actions carried consequences—not only socially, but before God. Integrity, diligence, and honesty were treated as moral obligations rather than optional virtues.

Community accountability followed naturally.

Families, churches, and local institutions reinforced shared standards of conduct. Wrongdoing was not ignored or excused lightly. Correction was expected, not resented. Moral failure was treated as serious because it affected both personal witness and communal trust.

Respect for law and order was strengthened, not weakened.

Revival did not produce contempt for authority. It clarified authority's purpose. Law was viewed as necessary for maintaining justice and protecting the vulnerable. Obedience was rendered not merely out of fear of punishment, but from conviction that order served God's purposes.

Scripture summarizes this principle clearly:
"Righteousness exalteth a nation: but sin is a reproach to any people."
— *Proverbs 14:34*
Righteousness here does not mean perfection. It refers to alignment with God's moral order—truth honored, wrong restrained, responsibility embraced.
Providence here worked through **internal discipline** rather than external enforcement.
When people govern themselves morally, less force is required to govern them socially. Trust increases because expectations are shared. Cooperation becomes possible because behavior is predictable. Liberty survives because restraint comes from within.
This moral alignment mattered profoundly.
Without it, unity would have been shallow and fragile. Liberty would have become license. Cooperation would have given way to chaos.
God's providence strengthened unity not by removing moral boundaries, but by **writing them on conscience**.

Theological Reflection (Optional Transition Sentence)
When righteousness is valued internally, order can be maintained externally without coercion.

Providential Example #3 — Preparedness for Responsibility
The unity formed through revival did not lead to unrest or rebellion. Instead, it produced **discipline**.
This discipline was not imposed suddenly or externally. It had been practiced for years in ordinary settings—homes, churches, and local communities. People learned to live under authority not as a burden, but as a responsibility.
Church life played a critical role.
Congregations were accustomed to self-governance under Scripture. Decisions were made collectively, guided by biblical principles. Disagreements were handled through counsel, correction, and reconciliation rather than force. Accountability was expected, not resented. Submission to Scripture shaped behavior.
Authority was not arbitrary; it was bounded. Leaders were respected, but measured against God's Word. Obedience was practiced thoughtfully, not blindly. This balance trained people to distinguish between rightful authority and overreach.
These patterns mattered deeply.
A people unfamiliar with self-restraint cannot suddenly bear greater responsibility. But those accustomed to governing themselves morally and spiritually are prepared to steward freedom wisely.
Scripture articulates this principle clearly:

"He that is faithful in that which is least is faithful also in much."
— *Luke 16:10*
Providence here worked patiently.
God did not thrust responsibility upon an unprepared people. He allowed discipline to develop gradually—through daily obedience, mutual accountability, and submission to truth. What appeared ordinary at the time proved foundational later.
Unity functioned as preparation.
It taught cooperation without compulsion.
It cultivated restraint without oppression.
It trained discernment without disorder.
By the time greater responsibilities emerged, the groundwork had already been laid. The habits required to steward liberty had been formed quietly, long before they were tested publicly.
Providence did not rush the process.
It matured it.

Theological Reflection (Optional Transition Sentence)
God often prepares His people for greater responsibility by first teaching them to be faithful in small, ordinary acts of obedience.

---

7. Unity Without Uniformity
An important clarification must be made.
The unity that emerged during the Great Awakening did **not** eliminate difference.

- **Differences remained**
  Colonies retained unique customs, leadership styles, and regional concerns.
- **Debates continued**
  Theological discussions, practical disagreements, and local disputes did not disappear.
- **Local traditions persisted**
  Worship styles, church governance, and cultural expressions varied widely.

Yet unity existed **above** those differences.
This unity was not enforced.
It was not institutional.
It was **spiritual**.
Biblical unity does not require sameness.
It does not flatten distinct callings or perspectives.
Instead, it **orders diversity under shared truth.**
"For as the body is one, and hath many members… so also is Christ."
— *1 Corinthians 12:12*

Scripture teaches that diversity of function strengthens the whole when it operates under a common head.

"But now hath God set the members every one of them in the body, as it hath pleased him."

— *1 Corinthians 12:18*

The Great Awakening demonstrated this principle in practice:

many voices, one message;

many communities, one Lord.

This kind of unity:

- Allows disagreement without division
- Permits distinction without hostility
- Sustains cooperation without coercion

"Let us therefore follow after the things which make for peace, and things wherewith one may edify another."

— *Romans 14:19*

Uniformity demands control.

Unity requires humility.

Providence did not remove difference.

It **disciplined it**—placing it in service to something greater.

And by doing so, God prepared a people capable of working together without surrendering conscience or conviction.

---

8. Discussion Questions (Choose 2–3)

1. Why does truth-based unity last longer than emotion-based unity?
2. What happens when unity is pursued without shared truth?
3. How did spiritual unity prepare the colonies for future challenges?
4. What threatens unity in the church today?

---

9. Personal & National Application

Personal

- Do I pursue unity through humility and truth?
- Am I willing to submit personal preferences for the sake of shared obedience?

National

- Unity rooted in moral truth strengthens society
- Forced unity eventually fractures
- Shared beliefs enable cooperation

"Let all things be done with charity."

— *1 Corinthians 16:14*

10. Closing Reflection

The unity formed through revival was not loud, political, or centralized.

It did not emerge through decrees, organizations, or shared strategy. Instead, it formed quietly—within hearts shaped by conviction and humility before God.

Scripture teaches that true unity begins inwardly, not structurally:

"Behold, how good and how pleasant it is for brethren to dwell together in unity!"

— *Psalm 133:1*

This unity was not uniformity.

It was shared submission.

People across regions, denominations, and communities were drawn together by a common recognition of God's authority and human accountability. Conviction softened pride. Humility restrained division. Scripture became the shared reference point.

"Can two walk together, except they be agreed?"

— *Amos 3:3*

Agreement did not come from coercion.

It came from conscience shaped by truth.

Revival fostered a shared humility—an understanding that no individual, no church, and no community stood above God's Word.

"God resisteth the proud, but giveth grace unto the humble."

— *James 4:6*

This humility made cooperation possible without erasing differences. It created moral alignment without political machinery. People learned to govern themselves spiritually before attempting to act together publicly.

Such unity is rarely dramatic—but it is powerful.

Scripture affirms that God entrusts responsibility to those who have first learned faithfulness:

"He that is faithful in that which is least is faithful also in much."

— *Luke 16:10*

The people shaped by revival did not yet realize the responsibility that lay ahead. They were not preparing for nationhood. They were learning submission, restraint, and obedience.

Yet in that quiet formation, God was preparing a people capable of bearing responsibility they did not yet see.

Unity was formed not by ambition—but by reverence.

Not by force—but by shared surrender to truth.

And when responsibility finally arrived, hearts had already been prepared.

-

Optional Teaching Pause (Adult Class)

You might ask:

- *Why does Scripture emphasize humility as the foundation of unity?*
- *How does shared submission to God's Word create stability without control?*
- *What dangers arise when unity is pursued without conviction?*

---

11. Closing Scripture & Prayer Prompt

Read aloud:

"Now the God of patience and consolation grant you to be likeminded one toward another."
— *Romans 15:5*

Prayer Prompt:

"Lord, unite our hearts in truth, humility, and obedience to Your Word."

SECTION III - THE AMERICAN REVOLUTION

Deliverance Against All Odds (1700–1783)

"Not by might, nor by power, but by my spirit, saith the LORD of hosts."
— **Zechariah 4:6**

Section Purpose

This section examines a conflict that—by every human measure—**should not have succeeded**.

The American Revolution was not won by superior strength, wealth, training, or unity. Again and again, events unfolded in ways that defied logic, strategy, and expectation.

This section does not celebrate war.

It examines **dependence**, **restraint**, and **deliverance**.

Here, we ask not:

"How did they win?"

But:

"Why were they preserved?"

Guiding Truth

God often delivers when success is humanly impossible—so that credit cannot be claimed by strength alone.

"When victory cannot be explained by power, attention must turn to providence."

Teaching Orientation (Leader Use)

As you enter this section, remind the class:

- God does not glorify violence
- God does not endorse pride
- God does not promise victory without humility

This section highlights:

- Prayer before strategy
- Preservation amid weakness
- Outcomes no one could fully control

Encourage the class to watch for **patterns of restraint, timing, and preservation**, not slogans or hero worship.

Lesson 10 — Impossibility of Victory

Series Title

God's Providence in American History: From the Pilgrims to the Present

Theme Verse

"For the battle is the LORD'S."

— *1 Samuel 17:47*

Lesson Aim (For the Teacher)

To show that, humanly speaking, the American colonies had **no reasonable path to victory**, and that repeated survival against overwhelming odds points to **preservation beyond human strength**.

This lesson emphasizes **dependence**, not daring.

Time Flow (Minimum 40 Minutes)

- Opening Scripture & Prayer – 4 minutes
- Biblical Framework – 10 minutes
- Historical Reality & Providential Examples – 18 minutes
- Discussion – 5 minutes
- Application & Closing Reflection – 3 minutes

---

1. Opening Scripture Reading

Read aloud together:

"Some trust in chariots, and some in horses: but we will remember the name of the LORD our God."

— *Psalm 20:7*

---

2. Core Truth Statement

God often allows circumstances to become humanly impossible so that deliverance cannot be mistaken for human achievement.

Impossibility strips away pride and forces reliance.

---

3. Biblical Pattern: God Delivers the Weak

Key Scriptures

"And he said unto me, My grace is sufficient for thee: for my strength is made perfect in weakness."

— *2 Corinthians 12:9*

"For when I am weak, then am I strong."

— *2 Corinthians 12:10*

"The LORD saveth not with sword and spear."

— *1 Samuel 17:47*

Teaching Point (Scripture-Anchored)

Throughout Scripture, God deliberately works through **weakness**, **imbalance**, and **dependence** so that outcomes testify to His power rather than human ability.

"And the LORD said unto Gideon, The people that are with thee are too many for me to give the Midianites into their hands, lest Israel vaunt themselves against me, saying, Mine own hand hath saved me."

— *Judges 7:2*

"Then he answered and spake unto me, saying, This is the word of the LORD unto Zerubbabel, saying, Not by might, nor by power, but by my spirit, saith the LORD of hosts." — Zechariah 4:6

---

4. The Reality the Colonies Faced

At the outbreak of war, the balance of power could not have been more uneven.

The British Empire was the strongest military force in the world. It had recently defeated France in a global conflict and stood at the height of its influence and confidence. Britain possessed:

- A professional standing army hardened by European warfare
- The world's most powerful navy, controlling major sea routes
- Vast financial resources drawn from a global empire
- Established supply lines spanning continents

From a purely military perspective, Britain was not merely superior—it was overwhelming:

"The horse is prepared against the day of battle: but safety is of the LORD."

— *Proverbs 21:31*

The American colonies, by contrast, were unprepared for sustained war. They had:

- No unified national army
- Militias with limited training and inconsistent discipline
- Minimal funding and unreliable currency
- Little manufacturing capacity for weapons, uniforms, or supplies
- Dependence on foreign trade that could be easily disrupted

Even more damaging than material weakness was internal division. The colonies were not united in purpose or conviction. Loyalists remained throughout the land. Regional rivalries persisted. Political disagreement was sharp and unresolved:

"Every kingdom divided against itself is brought to desolation."

— *Matthew 12:25*

There was no centralized command structure capable of coordinating large-scale resistance. Communication was slow. Decision-making was fragmented. Supplies were scarce. Morale fluctuated:

"Except the LORD keep the city, the watchman waketh but in vain."

— *Psalm 127:1*

Neutral observers did not expect victory. Many assumed the conflict would end quickly—either through suppression or collapse from within. The colonies were seen as fragile, divided, and outmatched:

"There is no wisdom nor understanding nor counsel against the LORD."

— *Proverbs 21:30*

Humanly speaking, the war should not have lasted—much less succeeded.

What followed cannot be explained by preparation, strength, or strategy alone. If the cause endured, it did so against every visible calculation. This is precisely where providence becomes visible—not by denying weakness, but by preserving life, leadership, and resolve when collapse seemed inevitable.

---

5. Specific Impossibilities That Should Have Ended the Cause

Impossibility #1 — Military Imbalance

From a purely military perspective, the colonial cause stood little chance of survival.

The opposing forces were not evenly matched. On one side stood the British Empire—the most powerful military force in the world at the time. It possessed a professional army, a dominant navy, established supply lines, and decades of combat experience across continents.

On the other side were the colonies.

Colonial forces were largely **untrained**. Many were farmers, tradesmen, and laborers who had little experience with formal warfare. Drilling was inconsistent. Discipline varied widely. Few had faced sustained combat.

They were also **poorly armed**.

Weapons were often outdated or mismatched. Ammunition was scarce. Uniforms were rare, making identification and coordination difficult. Supply chains were unreliable, leaving soldiers underfed, undersupplied, and exposed.

There was no standing army in the modern sense.

No centralized logistics system.

No reliable means of replacement or reinforcement.

In any conventional assessment, such a force should not have endured prolonged conflict—let alone challenged a global power.

Scripture captures this reality succinctly:

"The race is not to the swift, nor the battle to the strong."

— *Ecclesiastes 9:11*

This verse does not deny the value of strength or preparation. It reminds us that outcomes are not determined solely by human advantage.

Survival itself was improbable.

That the colonial forces did not collapse early—through desertion, defeat, or disorganization—requires explanation. Losses were heavy. Morale was fragile. Conditions were harsh. And yet, the effort continued.

Providence here was not seen in overwhelming strength.

It was seen in **persistence beyond expectation**.

The imbalance should have ended the cause quickly. It did not. The question is not whether the colonists were courageous—they were—but why courage alone did not fail under such odds.

This improbability sets the stage for every event that follows.

Before examining strategies, alliances, or victories, it must be acknowledged plainly: **the cause survived conditions that normally destroy movements before they mature**.

That survival demands careful reflection.

Theological Reflection (Optional Transition Sentence)

When human strength is insufficient, outcomes often reveal influences beyond human calculation.

Impossibility #2 — Financial Collapse

Beyond military weakness, the American cause faced a threat just as dangerous and far less visible: **financial collapse**.

At the outset of the conflict, the Continental Congress possessed **no authority to tax**. It could request funds from the colonies, but it could not compel payment. Contributions were inconsistent, delayed, or absent altogether. There was no reliable revenue stream to sustain a long war.

To meet immediate needs, Congress issued paper currency.

At first, it offered temporary relief. But without sufficient backing or control, the currency quickly **depreciated**. Inflation followed. Confidence eroded. Soldiers and suppliers alike grew wary of promises that could not be guaranteed.

The phrase "not worth a Continental" soon entered common use—not as mockery, but as painful reality.

Soldiers often went **unpaid for months**. When payment did arrive, it was frequently devalued. Supplies ran short. Clothing, food, and equipment were inconsistent. Families at home struggled while their men served under uncertain conditions.

Under such strain, mutiny and desertion were constant threats.

Armies do not remain intact indefinitely without provision. Loyalty weakens when promises cannot be kept. History shows that many causes have failed not on the battlefield, but in the ledger.

By all reasonable expectation, this one should have as well.

Scripture reminds us of the limits of human systems:

"Except the LORD keep the city, the watchman waketh but in vain."

— *Psalm 127:1*

This verse speaks not only to physical defense, but to **sustaining order itself**. Without God's governance, even the most vigilant effort collapses under its own weight.

Providence here did not erase financial hardship.

It restrained its consequences.

Despite unpaid wages and economic instability, the army did not dissolve entirely. Despite currency failure, the cause did not evaporate. Despite repeated moments when collapse seemed imminent, continuity remained.

This persistence is difficult to explain purely in economic terms.

Men continued to serve when logic suggested departure. Communities continued to support the effort when personal cost was high and return uncertain. Leadership held together despite constant pressure and limited resources.

Providence did not supply unlimited funds. It supplied **endurance**.

The financial weakness should have ended the cause before it matured. That it did not invites careful reflection—not on economic ingenuity alone, but on the sustaining hand that limited what failure could accomplish.

Theological Reflection (Optional Transition Sentence)

When systems fail and resources vanish, endurance itself becomes a testimony to providence.

Impossibility #3 — Internal Disunity

Even if military weakness and financial instability could somehow be endured, the American cause faced another threat capable of ending it entirely: **internal disunity**.

The colonies were not unified by default.

Loyalists remained throughout the conflict—some openly supportive of British authority, others quietly resistant to separation. Families were divided. Communities were fractured. Allegiances were not always clear, and trust was often strained.

Regional rivalries persisted.

Colonies differed in economic interests, religious traditions, and political priorities.

Cooperation was complicated by geography and local identity. What benefited one region often burdened another. Agreement required compromise, patience, and restraint—qualities not easily sustained under pressure.

Political disagreements were sharp.

Debates over authority, governance, military strategy, and sacrifice were constant. There was no single voice or centralized command capable of enforcing uniformity. Decisions required persuasion rather than compulsion, consensus rather than decree.

In most historical movements, such conditions prove fatal.

Internal division typically weakens resolve, erodes trust, and invites collapse from within.

Crisis amplifies differences rather than softening them. Unity under prolonged stress is rare.

And yet, the effort did not disintegrate.

Disagreements did not disappear—but they were **contained**. Debate did not give way to fragmentation. Despite tension and strain, cooperation endured long enough for the cause to continue.

Scripture speaks to the rarity and value of such unity:

"Behold, how good and how pleasant it is for brethren to dwell together in unity!"

— *Psalm 133:1*

This verse does not assume ease. It celebrates unity precisely because it is uncommon and fragile.

Providence here was not seen in perfect agreement.

It was seen in **sustained cooperation amid disagreement**.

God did not eliminate division.

He restrained its destructive power.

The colonies remained distinct, opinionated, and often contentious. But they did not collapse inward. Shared purpose outweighed unresolved differences. Commitment endured where fracture was expected.

This endurance is difficult to attribute solely to political skill or personal resolve. It reflects a deeper pattern already observed earlier: unity shaped by shared moral framework, mutual accountability, and discipline learned long before crisis arrived.
Providence governed not by erasing tension, but by preventing disintegration.

Theological Reflection (Optional Transition Sentence)
Unity that survives disagreement testifies to restraint greater than human resolve alone.

---

6. Providential Preservation, Not Immediate Victory
An important clarification must be made.
God's providence during the Revolutionary War did **not** appear as uninterrupted success.

- **The war was long**
  What many expected to last months stretched into years of exhaustion and uncertainty.
- **Losses were heavy**
  Soldiers died not only in battle, but from hunger, exposure, and disease.
- **Setbacks were frequent**
  Victories were often followed by retreats, discouragement, or renewed danger.

Providence did not guarantee triumph at every engagement.
It guaranteed **survival of the cause itself.**
Again and again, defeat seemed near:

- Armies were nearly destroyed
- Morale faltered
- Resources vanished

Yet collapse never fully came.
"We are troubled on every side, yet not distressed; we are perplexed, but not in despair; persecuted, but not forsaken; cast down, but not destroyed."
— 2 Corinthians 4:8–9
Scripture often distinguishes between **relief** and **preservation.**
God does not always remove the burden—but He sustains the bearer.
"My grace is sufficient for thee: for my strength is made perfect in weakness."
— 2 Corinthians 12:9
Providence preserved:

- Leadership when it could have fractured
- Unity when despair invited desertion
- Hope when circumstances denied it

The cause lived—often barely—long enough for the next step to unfold.

God's work was not loud.
It was **persistent**.

---

7. Why Impossibility Matters Spiritually

The impossibility of victory was not incidental.
It was instructive.
If victory had been easy:

- **Pride would have followed**
- **Dependence would have faded**
- **Gratitude would have been shallow**

Ease often produces forgetfulness.

"Lest when thou hast eaten and art full… then thine heart be lifted up, and thou forget the LORD thy God."
— *Deuteronomy 8:12–14*

God frequently allows difficulty to remain—not as punishment, but as protection.
He delays deliverance to:

- **Purify motives**
  Separating ambition from obedience.
- **Expose weakness**
  Revealing how little rests on human strength.
- **Invite prayer**
  Drawing hearts back to dependence.

"Before I was afflicted I went astray: but now have I kept thy word."
— *Psalm 119:67*

Impossibility strips away illusion.
It reminds people that survival itself is mercy.

"That no flesh should glory in his presence."
— *1 Corinthians 1:29*

Providence is clearest where boasting is impossible.
The lesson is not that hardship proves righteousness—
but that **dependence sustains obedience**.
And when victory finally came, it could not honestly be claimed as human achievement alone.

---

8. Discussion Questions (Choose 2–3)

1. Why does God sometimes allow His people to face overwhelming odds?
2. How does weakness prepare hearts for dependence?
3. What dangers come when success appears self-made?
4. How does this lesson shape how we interpret later victories?

---

9. Personal & National Application

Personal

- Where am I relying on my own strength instead of God?
- Do impossible circumstances drive me toward prayer or despair?

National

- Survival itself can be providential
- Strength can become a spiritual liability
- Dependence must not be forgotten after deliverance

"Cursed be the man that trusteth in man."

— *Jeremiah 17:5*

---

10. Closing Reflection

Before battles were won,

before independence was declared secure,

the cause itself was preserved—often against logic, probability, and human expectation.

Scripture repeatedly reminds us that God's work does not always appear as visible triumph.

Often, His hand is seen first in **restraint**—in what does *not* happen.

"Except the LORD had been on our side… then they had swallowed us up quick."

— *Psalm 124:1–3*

The cause should have collapsed.

Resources were insufficient. Unity was fragile. Leadership was tested. Circumstances pressed toward failure. Yet collapse did not come.

Providence often works quietly—

not by removing danger, but by **preventing disintegration**.

Scripture affirms this pattern:

"There is no wisdom nor understanding nor counsel against the LORD."

— *Proverbs 21:30*

God did not immediately grant victory.

He first preserved endurance.

The struggle continued not because conditions improved, but because destruction was restrained. Setbacks did not become surrender. Weakness did not become dissolution. The effort held together when fragmentation seemed inevitable.

This is a deeply biblical truth.

God often sustains His purposes by holding them together through pressure rather than eliminating pressure altogether.

"We are troubled on every side, yet not distressed; we are perplexed, but not in despair."
— *2 Corinthians 4:8*

Preservation preceded success.

Endurance came before achievement.

Only after the cause survived repeated tests could victory eventually follow. God ensured that what He intended to use was not lost before its purpose was fulfilled.

Providence did not shout.

It sustained.

And in that sustaining, the cause remained intact long enough for history to turn.

Optional Teaching Pause (Adult Class)

You might ask:

- *Why does God often preserve causes before granting success?*
- *How does restraint differ from rescue in Scripture?*
- *Where might God be preventing collapse in our own lives rather than removing difficulty?*

---

11. Closing Scripture & Prayer Prompt

Read aloud:

"The horse is prepared against the day of battle: but safety is of the LORD."
— *Proverbs 21:31*

Prayer Prompt:

"Lord, teach us to trust You when the path seems impossible, and to remember You when deliverance comes."

Lesson 11 — Washington at Valley Forge

Series Title

God's Providence in American History: From the Pilgrims to the Present

Theme Verse

"We went through fire and through water: but thou broughtest us out into a wealthy place."
— *Psalm 66:12*

Lesson Aim (For the Teacher)

To show how God preserved the Revolutionary cause during its most vulnerable season—when defeat seemed more likely than deliverance—by sustaining endurance, unity, and leadership under extreme hardship.

This lesson emphasizes **preservation through suffering**, not triumph through strength.

Time Flow (Minimum 40 Minutes)

- Opening Scripture & Prayer – 4 minutes
- Biblical Framework – 10 minutes
- Historical Narrative & Providential Examples – 18 minutes
- Discussion – 5 minutes
- Application & Closing Reflection – 3 minutes

---

1. Opening Scripture Reading

Read aloud together:

"It is good for me that I have been afflicted; that I might learn thy statutes."
— *Psalm 119:71*

---

2. Core Truth Statement

God often preserves His purposes by sustaining faith and leadership during seasons of extreme testing.

Victory is sometimes decided **before** the battlefield—during endurance.

3. Biblical Pattern: God Tests Before He Delivers

Key Scriptures

"Beloved, think it not strange concerning the fiery trial which is to try you."
— *1 Peter 4:12*

"The trying of your faith worketh patience."
— *James 1:3*

"Thou shalt remember all the way which the LORD thy God led thee… to humble thee, and to prove thee."
— *Deuteronomy 8:2*

Teaching Point (Scripture-Anchored)

Before God brings deliverance, He often allows **testing** that humbles pride, exposes weakness, and refines dependence.

"Now no chastening for the present seemeth to be joyous, but grievous: nevertheless afterward it yieldeth the peaceable fruit of righteousness unto them which are exercised thereby." — Hebrews 12:11
"For thou, O God, hast proved us: thou hast tried us, as silver is tried." — Psalm 66:10

---

4. The Reality of Valley Forge (Winter 1777–1778)

Valley Forge stands as one of the most severe tests of endurance in American history—not because of battle, but because of deprivation.

Approximately 12,000 Continental soldiers encamped there during the winter of 1777–1778. They arrived exhausted from months of campaigning, only to face conditions that stripped away any illusion of comfort or readiness. Supplies were not merely low—they were dangerously insufficient.

Many soldiers lacked basic necessities:

- Shoes, leaving bloody footprints in the snow
- Adequate clothing to withstand freezing temperatures
- Consistent food rations
- Proper shelter beyond crude huts hastily constructed from green timber

"The eyes of all wait upon thee; and thou givest them their meat in due season."
— *Psalm 145:15*

Hunger was constant. Rations were often reduced to flour mixed with water and baked into what soldiers called "firecakes." Meat was scarce. Hunger weakened bodies and spirits alike. Exposure and overcrowding allowed disease to spread rapidly through the camp. Typhus, dysentery, and pneumonia took hold among men already weakened by cold and malnutrition. Medical care was limited, sanitation was poor, and burial details became a grim routine:

"He knoweth our frame; he remembereth that we are dust."
— *Psalm 103:14*
By the time spring arrived, nearly one-quarter of the army—roughly 2,000 men—had died. Many perished without ever firing a shot. From a human perspective, this should have been the end of the Continental Army. No army so poorly supplied, so weakened by illness, and so neglected by its own government should have survived intact:
"Unless the LORD had been my help, my soul had almost dwelt in silence."
— *Psalm 94:17*
Yet the army did not dissolve. Discipline was maintained. Leadership remained. Soldiers reenlisted. Training continued under Baron von Steuben, quietly transforming a suffering force into a more unified and effective army:
"As thy days, so shall thy strength be."
— *Deuteronomy 33:25*
Valley Forge did not produce victory—it preserved the possibility of it. Providence was not seen in comfort or relief, but in endurance. The army survived the winter not because conditions improved, but because collapse was restrained.

---

5. Specific Providential Preservations

Providential Example #1 — The Army Did Not Mutiny

The winter conditions faced by the Continental Army created an environment where mutiny would have been expected—if not inevitable.
The soldiers endured **hunger**. Rations were inconsistent, inadequate, and often entirely absent. Men went days without sufficient food, relying on scant provisions while expending enormous physical energy simply to survive the cold.
They endured **exposure**. Clothing was inadequate. Shoes were worn through or nonexistent. Snow and ice cut into unprotected feet, leaving bloodied tracks behind. Shelter was crude, hastily constructed, and insufficient against the elements.
They endured **unpaid service**. Wages were delayed or worthless. Promises made by leadership could not always be kept—not from indifference, but from inability. Families at home suffered while soldiers remained uncertain whether their sacrifice would ever be honored.
They endured **frustration**. The war dragged on. Victory seemed distant. Supplies were unreliable. Leadership was burdened by limitations beyond its control.
Under such conditions, history records a familiar pattern: armies disintegrate.
Men desert. Discipline erodes. Mutiny erupts—not always from malice, but from desperation. Loyalty fractures when hope vanishes.
And yet, **the army largely remained intact**.

There were moments of unrest. There were complaints, grievances, and moments when collapse seemed imminent. But widespread mutiny did not occur. The force did not dissolve.

Unity—fragile and strained—held.

Scripture gives language to such preservation:

"When thou passest through the waters, I will be with thee; and through the rivers, they shall not overflow thee."

— *Isaiah 43:2*

This promise does not remove hardship. It limits its power to destroy.

Providence here did not provide comfort.

It provided **continuance.**

God did not shield the army from suffering.

He restrained suffering from breaking it apart.

Men continued to stand guard. Orders were followed. The chain of command remained functional. Commitment endured beyond what conditions alone would justify.

This preservation is not easily explained by morale, leadership, or discipline alone. Those factors mattered—but they were stretched beyond normal limits. Something else restrained collapse when it should have occurred.

Providence often works this way.

It does not eliminate pressure.

It prevents disintegration.

Unity held—not because circumstances improved, but because collapse was restrained.

Theological Reflection (Optional Transition Sentence)

God's providence is often revealed not in removing hardship, but in preventing hardship from destroying what He purposes to preserve.

Providential Example #2 — Leadership Was Preserved

The endurance of the Continental Army during its darkest winter cannot be separated from the preservation of its leadership—particularly that of George Washington.

Washington did not lead from a distance.

He **remained with the army**, refusing to abandon it even when circumstances made retreat or resignation understandable. He shared the same cold, uncertainty, and deprivation faced by his soldiers. His presence communicated commitment more powerfully than orders ever could.

Discipline was maintained—not through harshness, but through steadiness.

Washington resisted both despair and rash action. He balanced firmness with restraint, enforcing order while recognizing the limits of what suffering men could bear. Where others might have fractured under pressure, he persisted—day after day—holding together an army that should have dissolved.

He encouraged perseverance when hope was scarce.

Washington understood that morale mattered as much as strategy. He spoke honestly about hardship without surrendering resolve. He neither minimized suffering nor allowed it to define the future. His leadership provided **continuity** at a moment when continuity itself was fragile.

Scripture captures the importance of such leadership succinctly:

"Where there is no vision, the people perish."

— *Proverbs 29:18*

Vision here does not imply grand ambition. It refers to **direction**, purpose, and the ability to see beyond immediate misery. Washington's leadership provided that orientation—not by promising ease, but by sustaining resolve.

Providence here was not about brilliance or perfection.

Washington made mistakes.

He faced criticism.

He bore doubts—both his own and those of others.

Yet he endured.

Leadership was preserved when its loss would likely have ended the cause. Had Washington fallen—through resignation, removal, or despair—the fragile unity of the army may not have survived. His continued presence functioned as a stabilizing force during a season when every stabilizing element was under threat.

Providence often works this way.

God preserves leaders not because they are flawless, but because their preservation serves a purpose beyond themselves. The survival of the cause required the survival of leadership capable of bearing prolonged strain.

Washington did not remove hardship.

He remained faithful within it.

That endurance mattered.

Theological Reflection (Optional Transition Sentence)

God often preserves leaders not to spare them hardship, but to enable them to carry others through it.

Providential Example #3 — Prayer and Humility

Amid the hunger, cold, and uncertainty of the war, one pattern appears consistently in historical records: the deliberate turning of leaders and people toward **prayer**.

These were not casual gestures.

Days of prayer were proclaimed. Appeals for God's help were voiced openly. Dependence was acknowledged—not as weakness, but as necessity. In moments when human resources were exhausted and plans uncertain, leaders recognized that endurance required more than strategy. It required humility.

Prayer did not replace action. Soldiers still stood guard. Officers still planned. Supplies were still sought. But prayer framed these efforts within an honest recognition of limitation.

Scripture speaks directly to this posture:

"If my people, which are called by my name, shall humble themselves, and pray, and seek my face…"

— *2 Chronicles 7:14*

The emphasis begins with humility.

Prayer in this context was not a demand for ease or immediate deliverance. It was an acknowledgment that survival itself depended on God's sustaining hand. Leaders did not claim entitlement to success. They confessed need.

Providence here did not answer prayer by removing hardship.

Cold remained.

Hunger persisted.

Uncertainty continued.

But resolve was sustained.

Prayer provided perspective when circumstances threatened to overwhelm. It reminded leaders and soldiers alike that they were not carrying the burden alone. The recognition of dependence fostered patience, restrained despair, and steadied hearts under prolonged strain.

This humility mattered deeply.

Pride collapses quickly under hardship. Self-reliance fractures when plans fail. But humility endures because it does not rest on illusion. It accepts reality while trusting God's governance beyond what can be seen.

Providence often works through such humility.

God does not always change circumstances immediately.

He strengthens resolve within them.

Prayer did not shorten the winter.

It sustained the people through it.

Theological Reflection (Optional Transition Sentence)
When hardship remains and strength endures, humility before God often explains what resolve alone cannot.

---

6. Strength Formed in Weakness
Valley Forge was not merely a season the army survived.
It was a season that **reshaped what the army became**.
The winter of 1777–1778 stripped away illusions of strength.
What remained was either going to collapse—or be refined.
During this period:

- **Training improved**
  Under Baron von Steuben, soldiers learned discipline, order, and cohesion.
  The army began to function as a unified force rather than a collection of militias.
- **Discipline increased**
  Hardship exposed weaknesses in leadership and conduct—but correction followed.
  Order replaced chaos.
- **Unity strengthened**
  Shared suffering forged bonds that comfort never could.
  Soldiers endured together when desertion seemed reasonable.

God often uses deprivation to produce endurance.
"Behold, I have refined thee, but not with silver; I have chosen thee in the furnace of affliction." — *Isaiah 48:10*
What appeared to be wasted months became preparation months.
"And not only so, but we glory in tribulations also: knowing that tribulation worketh patience; and patience, experience; and experience, hope." — *Romans 5:3–4*
Valley Forge did not make the army comfortable.
It made the army **capable**.
Providence did not remove hardship—
it transformed hardship into readiness.

---

7. Why Valley Forge Matters
Valley Forge stands as a hinge point in the story of independence.
If the army had disbanded:

- **Independence would have ended**
- **The cause would have collapsed**
- **The war would be remembered as a failed rebellion**

There was no backup plan.
No reserve force.
No second army waiting.
The cause survived because the army did.
And the army survived not because conditions improved—
but because God restrained collapse.
"Except the LORD keep the city, the watchman waketh but in vain."
— *Psalm 127:1*
Providence did not preserve **comfort**.
It preserved **possibility**.
This distinction matters.
God often sustains the minimum necessary for obedience to continue:

- Enough strength to stand
- Enough resolve to remain
- Enough unity to endure

"The LORD is good unto them that wait for him, to the soul that seeketh him."
— *Lamentations 3:25*
Valley Forge teaches that survival itself can be victory—
when survival preserves God's unfolding purpose.
The army emerged weaker in body—
but stronger in resolve, discipline, and identity.
Providence did not rescue them *from* the winter.
It carried them *through* it.

---

8. Discussion Questions (Choose 2–3)

1. Why does God sometimes allow prolonged suffering instead of immediate relief?
2. How does hardship reveal true leadership?
3. What role does prayer play when circumstances do not improve?
4. Why is endurance often more difficult than action?

---

9. Personal & National Application

Personal

- Do trials drive me closer to God or toward discouragement?
- Am I faithful when progress feels stalled?

National

- Hardship can forge discipline
- Leadership matters most in crisis

- Preservation often comes quietly

"Let us not be weary in well doing."
— *Galatians 6:9*

---

10. Closing Reflection

Valley Forge was not glorious.
It was cold, hungry, and costly.
Suffering was constant. Morale was fragile. Survival itself was uncertain.
There were no decisive victories there.
No parades.
No celebration.
Yet Valley Forge became a place of preservation.
Scripture reminds us that God often works most deeply where hardship is prolonged rather than removed:
"Thou hast proved us, O God: thou hast tried us, as silver is tried."
— *Psalm 66:10*
The trial was not brief.
The hardship was not symbolic.
And yet, faith endured.
Men remained when desertion seemed logical. Commitment held when retreat would have been understandable. Unity survived where collapse was expected.
"Behold, how good and how pleasant it is for brethren to dwell together in unity!"
— *Psalm 133:1*
God did not rescue the army from suffering.
He strengthened them **within** it.
Scripture affirms that endurance itself is often God's chosen means of preservation:
"In the world ye shall have tribulation: but be of good cheer; I have overcome the world."
— *John 16:33*
Resolve was forged where comfort was absent. Leadership was tested where ease was removed. What could not be produced by victory was formed through endurance.
"Tribulation worketh patience; and patience, experience; and experience, hope."
— *Romans 5:3–4*
The cause was preserved not by sudden relief, but by sustained resolve. Valley Forge refined what battle alone could not.
Providence sometimes works not by rescue, but by **strengthening what must endure**.
God did not eliminate hardship.
He prevented surrender.

And in doing so, He preserved the cause long enough for history to turn.

Optional Teaching Pause (Adult Class)

You might ask:

- *Why does God sometimes allow prolonged hardship instead of immediate relief?*
- *What qualities are formed through endurance that victory cannot produce?*
- *Where might God be strengthening resolve rather than removing difficulty in our own lives?*

---

11. Closing Scripture & Prayer Prompt

Read aloud:

"But they that wait upon the LORD shall renew their strength."

— *Isaiah 40:31*

Prayer Prompt:

"Lord, strengthen us when relief is delayed, and teach us to trust You through endurance."

Lesson 12 — The Fog at Long Island

Series Title

God's Providence in American History: From the Pilgrims to the Present

Theme Verse

"Stand still, and see the salvation of the LORD."
— *Exodus 14:13*

Lesson Aim (For the Teacher)

To show how God preserved the Revolutionary cause at a moment when complete destruction was imminent—through restraint, timing, and circumstances no one could control. This lesson emphasizes **deliverance without combat.**

Time Flow (Minimum 40 Minutes)

- Opening Scripture & Prayer – 4 minutes
- Biblical Framework – 10 minutes
- Historical Narrative & Providential Examples – 18 minutes
- Discussion – 5 minutes
- Application & Closing Reflection – 3 minutes

---

1. Opening Scripture Reading

Read aloud together:

"He maketh the storm a calm, so that the waves thereof are still."
— *Psalm 107:29*

---

2. Core Truth Statement

God sometimes delivers His people not by victory, but by escape—and not by force, but by restraint.

When destruction is imminent, preservation itself becomes the miracle.

---

3. Biblical Pattern: Deliverance Through Timing and Restraint

Key Scriptures

"The LORD shall fight for you, and ye shall hold your peace."
— *Exodus 14:14*

"There failed not ought of any good thing which the LORD had spoken."
— *Joshua 21:45*

"Except the LORD had been my help, my soul had almost dwelt in silence."
— *Psalm 94:17*

Teaching Point (Scripture-Anchored)

In Scripture, God often delivers His people at the **last possible moment**, when no human option remains—so that His hand cannot be mistaken.
(Genesis 22:10–14; Psalm 124:1–8)

---

4. The Situation at Long Island (August 1776)

Only weeks after the Declaration of Independence, the Continental Army faced its first true test—not of ideals, but of survival.

British forces moved swiftly to crush the rebellion before it could solidify. In August 1776, the largest military expedition Britain had ever sent overseas arrived in New York. More than 30,000 seasoned troops—supported by naval power and experienced commanders—stood ready to strike. Opposing them was a fragile American force of roughly half that number, many of whom were untrained, poorly supplied, and newly enlisted.

"The horse is prepared against the day of battle: but safety is of the LORD."
— *Proverbs 21:31*

American positions on Long Island were badly chosen. Intelligence was incomplete. Defensive lines were extended and vulnerable. British troops executed a well-coordinated flanking maneuver through the Jamaica Pass—completely outmaneuvering the Americans and cutting off escape routes. Panic followed confusion. Units were overwhelmed or scattered.

The result was devastating:

- A crushing battlefield defeat
- Heavy American casualties and captures
- Thousands of Continental soldiers trapped on Brooklyn Heights
- British forces in perfect position to press a final, annihilating blow

From a military standpoint, nothing stood between the British army and total victory. The Continental Army was cornered against the East River with no clear path of retreat, limited supplies, and plummeting morale.

"Except the LORD had been on our side… then they had swallowed us up quick."
— *Psalm 124:1–3*

Humanly speaking, the rebellion should have ended there. A single decisive attack would have destroyed Washington's army, crushed colonial resistance, and ended any serious hope of independence. No reinforcements were coming. No strategic advantage remained. The cause rested on the edge of collapse.

Yet this moment—when defeat seemed inevitable—became the setting for one of the clearest displays of providence in the war. What followed did not involve superior strength, brilliant tactics, or sudden reinforcements.

It involved restraint, delay, darkness, and mercy.

"When my spirit was overwhelmed within me, then thou knewest my path."
— *Psalm 142:3*

Providence often reveals itself not at the height of confidence, but at the moment when survival itself seems unreasonable.

---

5. Why Destruction Was Certain

From a military standpoint, the situation at Long Island was beyond recovery.

The realities were stark and unforgiving.

Military Reality

By late August 1776:

- **British troops surrounded the American forces by land**
  Highly trained British regulars and Hessian troops had outmaneuvered colonial positions.
  Escape routes were cut off with precision.
- **The British navy controlled the water**
  The Royal Navy dominated the East River and surrounding waterways.
  Any attempt to flee by sea should have been detected and intercepted immediately.
- **Retreat appeared impossible**
  The American army was pinned against the river with no clear path of escape.
  Geography itself worked against survival.
- **Morale was collapsing**
  This was the army's first major test after declaring independence.
  Confidence gave way to shock, fear, and confusion.

Washington faced consequences that were unavoidable by human calculation:

- **Capture of the commanding general**
- **Destruction or imprisonment of the army**
- **The effective end of organized resistance**

There was no strategic maneuver left to execute.
No reinforcements to summon.
No advantage to exploit.
Humanly speaking, the war should have ended before it truly began.
"The race is not to the swift, nor the battle to the strong."
— *Ecclesiastes 9:11*
This moment exposes a critical truth about providence:
When every option disappears, **dependence becomes absolute**.
Washington could not outfight the enemy.
He could not outmaneuver superior forces.
He could only wait—exposed, vulnerable, and powerless.
Providence often waits until human solutions are exhausted
before revealing that **destruction is not inevitable**.
At Long Island, defeat was certain.
Deliverance would come—
not through strength,
not through strategy,
but through restraint and timing that no commander could control.

---

6. Specific Providential Interventions
Providential Example #1 — British Delay
At Long Island in August 1776, the American cause stood on the brink of collapse.
British forces held overwhelming advantages. Their army was larger, better trained, and better equipped. Their commanders had maneuvered effectively, placing American forces in a position of extreme vulnerability. The opportunity for a decisive victory lay directly before them.
From a military standpoint, the moment was clear.
A swift, aggressive advance could have crushed the Continental Army. Escape routes were limited. The Americans were exposed, outmatched, and disorganized. Many officers believed capture or destruction was imminent.
And yet, **the advance did not come**.
British commanders paused.
Despite possessing superior forces, clear advantage, and momentum, they chose restraint instead of immediate pursuit. Time passed. Hours slipped away. The pressure that should have closed tightened—but did not seal.

From a human perspective, the delay is difficult to explain fully. It cannot be reduced to a single reason or simple miscalculation. What matters most is not the explanation, but the **consequence**.

The pause created a window.

Scripture speaks to the governance of even opposing authorities:

"The king's heart is in the hand of the LORD, as the rivers of water: he turneth it whithersoever he will."

— *Proverbs 21:1*

"O Assyrian, the rod of mine anger… Howbeit he meaneth not so, neither doth his heart think so."

— *Isaiah 10:5–7*

These passages do not suggest that human leaders consciously serve God's purposes. They affirm that God can **restrain, redirect, or limit** actions—even when intent remains unchanged.

Providence here did not require British goodwill.

It required **restraint**.

The delay did not guarantee safety.

It allowed opportunity.

That opportunity would prove decisive.

Had the British pressed the attack immediately, the Continental Army would likely have been destroyed or captured. Leadership, morale, and momentum would have been lost in a single stroke. The cause itself may not have survived the year.

Instead, time—brief, fragile, and unexpected—was granted.

Providence here was not dramatic intervention.

It was **measured hesitation**.

God often preserves His purposes not by overpowering enemies, but by limiting how far their advantage is allowed to extend. Victory is sometimes delayed not by weakness, but by restraint beyond calculation.

This delay created the only window through which survival could pass.

Theological Reflection (Optional Transition Sentence)

When decisive moments pause without explanation, restraint itself may be the work of providence.

Providential Example #2 — Night Evacuation

As night fell following the British pause at Long Island, the American situation remained desperate.

The Continental Army was trapped. British forces held commanding positions. The East River lay behind the Americans, wide and dangerous. Any attempt at retreat risked discovery and destruction.

And yet, under cover of darkness and unusually heavy fog, a plan unfolded.

Small boats began ferrying troops across the East River. The operation required silence, precision, and endurance. Soldiers moved carefully, suppressing noise. Equipment was transported quietly. Supplies were removed as time allowed.

The work continued through the night.

Row by row, boatload by boatload, men crossed the water. Officers coordinated movement without modern communication. Orders were passed softly. Fear was present—but discipline held.

The risks were immense.

A single alarm.

A single premature discovery.

A single misstep.

Any one of these could have brought swift annihilation.

And yet, **the evacuation continued—undetected**.

Scripture gives voice to such deliverance:

"If it had not been the LORD who was on our side, now may Israel say;
If it had not been the LORD who was on our side, when men rose up against us:
Then they had swallowed us up quick."

— *Psalm 124:2–3*

This passage does not deny human effort. It acknowledges that effort alone is insufficient without God's restraint.

Providence here did not halt the enemy.

It concealed the escape.

British forces, positioned close enough to destroy the army by morning, remained unaware throughout the night. Patrols did not intercept the movement. The sounds of evacuation did not carry. The river crossing proceeded with remarkable order under extreme pressure.

This was not inevitability.

It was vulnerability protected.

The evacuation required courage, discipline, and coordination—but those alone cannot explain why discovery did not occur. Silence held when detection was likely. Darkness concealed when exposure was expected.

Providence here worked not through spectacle, but through **covering**.

God did not change the geography.

He governed the moment.

By morning, much of the Continental Army had crossed to safety. What should have ended the cause instead preserved it.

Theological Reflection (Optional Transition Sentence)

When escape requires silence and survival depends on concealment, restraint itself becomes deliverance.

Providential Example #3 — The Morning Fog

As the night evacuation neared completion, danger remained.

Not all troops had yet crossed. Dawn approached. With daylight would come exposure—movement visible from shore, boats silhouetted on the water, soldiers caught mid-retreat.

From a human perspective, the margin for survival had nearly vanished.

Then, as morning arrived, **a dense fog settled over the river and shoreline**.

Visibility dropped sharply. The water disappeared into gray stillness. The remaining troops were concealed from view. The shoreline—where discovery would have been immediate—was obscured.

British forces could not see the evacuation.

No signal was given.

No alarm was raised.

No attack followed.

The fog did not drift in gradually. It arrived **suddenly**, at precisely the moment concealment was most needed. It lingered long enough for the final boats to cross. And it lifted only after the evacuation was complete.

By the time visibility returned, **the American army was gone**.

What had been moments from destruction had passed into absence.

Scripture gives language to such moments:

"Clouds and darkness are round about him: righteousness and judgment are the habitation of his throne."

— *Psalm 97:2*

This verse does not describe chaos. It describes **authority concealed**—God governing without announcement, acting without display.

The fog was not commanded by men.
It was not predicted by plans.
It could not be controlled or summoned.
And yet, it arrived with precision.
Providence here was not dramatic rescue.
It was **perfect timing**.
God did not stop the enemy.
He prevented sight.
The fog did not guarantee victory.
It ensured survival.
Such moments resist explanation by strategy alone. Weather does not take sides. But it does have moments—and in this moment, restraint and concealment preserved what force could not.
The army escaped not because conditions improved, but because danger was **hidden** until escape was complete.

Theological Reflection (Optional Transition Sentence)
When concealment arrives at the moment of greatest exposure, timing itself bears the mark of providence.

---

7. Preservation Without Triumph
It is essential to clarify what happened—and what did not.
This moment was **not** a victory.

- **No ground was gained**
- **No enemy was defeated**
- **No tactical advantage was secured**
- **No celebration followed**

The American army did not prevail.
It did not reverse the battle.
It did not reclaim what was lost.
It simply **lived**.
From a human perspective, survival without success can feel meaningless.
But in God's economy, **preservation is often the greater mercy**.

"We are troubled on every side, yet not distressed;
we are perplexed, but not in despair;
persecuted, but not forsaken;
cast down, but not destroyed."
— *2 Corinthians 4:8–9*

Providence did not appear in triumph.

It appeared in restraint.

The cause of independence was kept alive—not advanced.

The future was protected—not secured.

This distinction matters deeply.

Had the army been destroyed at Long Island:

- Independence would have ended before it matured
- Leadership would have been lost
- Hope would have collapsed
- Later victories would never have been possible

God preserved **possibility**, not outcome.

He sustained **life**, not momentum.

Providence often works this way:

- Not by removing loss
- Not by erasing failure
- But by preventing **final collapse**

The absence of defeat is sometimes more important than the presence of success.

At Long Island, God did not grant victory.

He granted **time**.

And time, preserved by providence, would become the space in which future deliverance could unfold.

---

8. Why This Moment Matters

The significance of Long Island is not found in what was achieved—but in what was **averted.**

Had the Continental Army been destroyed at this moment:

- **The Revolution would have collapsed** before it truly began
- **Leadership would have been captured or killed**, including Washington himself
- **Organized resistance would have ceased**
- **Independence would have ended** as an idea rather than a reality

There was no reserve force waiting.

No second army prepared to rise.

No political mechanism capable of continuing the cause.

This was not a setback among many—it was a **point of extinction**.

Humanly speaking, the Revolution should have died on the shores of Long Island.

Yet it did not.

Not because strength prevailed.

Not because strategy succeeded.

Not because courage was sufficient.

But because **Providence intervened before the cause could die**.

"Our help is in the name of the LORD, who made heaven and earth."

— *Psalm 124:8*

This moment reveals a recurring biblical pattern:

God often acts **before collapse**, not after victory.

He preserves:

- When defeat is certain
- When options are exhausted
- When human wisdom has failed

Providence did not wait for triumph to justify itself.

It operated in weakness, confusion, and retreat.

What mattered most was not progress—but **continuation**.

The Revolution lived to fight another day because God preserved the people carrying it.

History often celebrates decisive victories.

Scripture teaches us to recognize **decisive survivals**.

At Long Island, God did not announce deliverance with power.

He whispered mercy through preservation.

And that preservation made everything else possible.

---

9. Discussion Questions (Choose 2–3)

1. Why does God sometimes deliver through escape rather than victory?
2. How does restraint play a role in providence?
3. What does this event teach us about timing?
4. Why is survival sometimes more important than success?

---

10. Personal & National Application

Personal

- Do I recognize God's hand when danger is avoided rather than conquered?
- Am I thankful for unseen protection?

National

- Preservation is not entitlement
- Escape can be as providential as victory
- Gratitude should follow deliverance

"If it had not been the LORD who was on our side…"
— *Psalm 124:1*

---

11. Closing Reflection

At Long Island, courage was insufficient.
Strategy failed.
Strength was outmatched.
From every human measure, defeat was certain.
The army faced destruction not because of cowardice or poor effort, but because the circumstances themselves were overwhelming. There was no superior tactic left to employ, no reserve of strength to draw upon, no path forward that promised success.
Yet the army lived.
Scripture often shows that when human means are exhausted, God's work becomes most visible:
"Stand still, and see the salvation of the LORD."
— *Exodus 14:13*
Providence did not appear in fire or force.
It came through delay, darkness, and fog.
Enemy decisions hesitated. Night concealed movement. A dense fog settled at precisely the moment it was needed, hiding the final withdrawal from view.
None of this was commanded by human authority.
None of it could be summoned by effort or skill.
"Clouds and darkness are round about him."
— *Psalm 97:2*
Scripture reminds us that God often delivers not by confrontation, but by concealment:
"Thou shalt hide them in the secret of thy presence from the pride of man."
— *Psalm 31:20*
At Long Island, God did not grant victory.
He granted escape.
And escape was mercy enough.
Providence restrained destruction when courage could not overcome force. It preserved life when strength could not secure success. What should have ended the cause instead preserved it.

"Our soul is escaped as a bird out of the snare of the fowlers."
— *Psalm 124:7*
The lesson is sobering.
God does not always deliver His people by making them stronger than their enemies.
Sometimes He delivers by limiting the enemy, restraining outcomes, and opening paths unseen.
Providence works not only in triumph, but in survival.
And at Long Island, survival itself testified that God's hand had not been withdrawn.

Optional Teaching Pause (Adult Class)
You might ask:

- *Why does God sometimes preserve life without granting immediate victory?*
- *How does concealment differ from confrontation in God's deliverance?*
- *Where might God be providing escape rather than triumph in our own lives?*

---

12. Closing Scripture & Prayer Prompt
Read aloud:
"The angel of the LORD encampeth round about them that fear him, and delivereth them."
— *Psalm 34:7*
Prayer Prompt:
"Lord, thank You for protection we often do not see. Teach us to trust You when escape is the only path forward."

Lesson 13 — Answered Prayer at Yorktown

Series Title

God's Providence in American History: From the Pilgrims to the Present

Theme Verse

"Through God we shall do valiantly: for he it is that shall tread down our enemies."
— *Psalm 60:12*

Lesson Aim (For the Teacher)

To show how God brought the Revolutionary conflict to a decisive close through the convergence of timing, restraint, cooperation, and circumstances beyond human control—illustrating that **answered prayer often comes through alignment rather than force alone**. This lesson emphasizes **God's orchestration**, not human certainty.

Time Flow (Minimum 40 Minutes)

- Opening Scripture & Prayer – 4 minutes
- Biblical Framework – 10 minutes
- Historical Narrative & Providential Examples – 18 minutes
- Discussion – 5 minutes
- Application & Closing Reflection – 3 minutes

---

1. Opening Scripture Reading

Read aloud together:

"The LORD hath made all things for himself: yea, even the wicked for the day of evil."
— *Proverbs 16:4*

---

2. Core Truth Statement

God often answers prayer by aligning circumstances beyond human planning, at precisely the needed moment.

Providence is frequently seen in convergence, not spectacle.

3. Biblical Pattern: God Brings Victory Through Alignment

Key Scriptures

"The preparations of the heart in man, and the answer of the tongue, is from the LORD."
— *Proverbs 16:1*

"For there are many devices in a man's heart; nevertheless the counsel of the LORD, that shall stand."
— *Proverbs 19:21*

"He shall bring forth thy righteousness as the light."
— *Psalm 37:6*

Teaching Point (Scripture-Anchored)

In Scripture, God often brings deliverance by **coordinating people, timing, and restraint** in ways no single group could control.

"11. He hath made every thing beautiful in his time: also he hath set the world in their heart, so that no man can find out the work that God maketh from the beginning to the end." — Ecclesiastes 3:11

"10. Declaring the end from the beginning, and from ancient times the things that are not yet done, saying, My counsel shall stand, and I will do all my pleasure:" — Isaiah 46:10

Answered prayer is sometimes recognized **after** alignment becomes visible.

---

4. The War's Uncertain State Before Yorktown

By 1781, the American Revolution had entered a long, grinding season of exhaustion rather than expectation.

What had once been fueled by conviction and urgency was now burdened by fatigue. The war had dragged on for more than six years, with no clear end in sight. Early confidence had faded. Victory no longer felt inevitable—if it ever had.

"Hope deferred maketh the heart sick."
— *Proverbs 13:12*

Public support wavered. Many colonists had endured years of hardship with little visible progress. Farms had been disrupted. Trade was damaged. Inflation had eroded savings. Soldiers went unpaid for long stretches. Families grew weary of sacrifice without resolution.

Resources were dangerously depleted:

- Supplies were scarce
- Clothing and equipment were inadequate
- Food shortages were common
- Foreign aid, though present, was uncertain and politically fragile

The Continental Army still existed—but barely. It survived more by endurance than by strength.

On the British side, confidence had also eroded. While Britain retained military superiority, the cost of sustaining a distant war across the Atlantic had grown heavy. Political pressure increased at home. Commanders faced conflicting objectives and incomplete information. Momentum had stalled.

Both sides were weary.

Both sides questioned how much longer the conflict could continue.

Few believed a decisive conclusion was near.

"The race is not to the swift, nor the battle to the strong."

— *Ecclesiastes 9:11*

From a human standpoint, the war appeared likely to end not with victory—but with collapse, compromise, or exhaustion. There was no single battle on the horizon that promised resolution. No overwhelming advantage had emerged. The conflict lingered in uncertainty.

Yet it was precisely in this moment—when expectation of resolution was lowest—that events began quietly aligning.

Providence does not always act when confidence is high.

Sometimes it waits until certainty has drained away.

"For my thoughts are not your thoughts, neither are your ways my ways, saith the LORD."

— *Isaiah 55:8*

What followed at Yorktown would not be the result of a single plan, a single leader, or a single nation's strength. It would come through timing, coordination, restraint, and convergence—elements no one fully controlled.

Providence was moving—but few could yet see it.

---

5. The Strategic Situation at Yorktown

By the summer of 1781, the Revolutionary War had entered a long, exhausting stalemate. British General **Lord Charles Cornwallis** positioned his forces at **Yorktown, Virginia**, believing the location offered safety rather than vulnerability. His assumptions were reasonable by every military standard of the time.

Cornwallis believed:

- **British naval dominance** would control the Chesapeake Bay
- **Reinforcements and supplies** could arrive by sea when needed
- **Evacuation was possible** if conditions deteriorated
- A defensive posture would allow Britain to **regain initiative**

From a human perspective, Yorktown appeared secure.

By contrast, the American situation remained fragile.

American and allied forces:

- **Were spread across vast territory** with limited communication

- **Struggled to coordinate operations**, even among allies
- **Faced shortages** of supplies, manpower, and reliable intelligence
- Had **few opportunities** to force a decisive engagement

Successful cooperation between American and French forces had been inconsistent at best. Timing, secrecy, and precise movement were required—yet these were the very areas where past efforts had often failed.

Humanly speaking, **too many variables had to align at once**:

- Naval movements
- Army positioning
- Secrecy and speed
- Enemy miscalculation
- Weather and geography

Any single failure would have preserved British control and prolonged the war indefinitely.

Victory at Yorktown did not rest on superior strength or certainty.

It rested on a convergence of events that no single leader controlled.

This was not a moment where human planning could guarantee success.

It was a moment where **answered prayer would have to bridge the gap between intention and outcome**.

"The steps of a good man are ordered by the LORD."

— *Psalm 37:23*

Yorktown set the stage for one of the clearest demonstrations of providential alignment in American history—not through one miracle, but through many precise convergences, arriving at exactly the right time.

---

6. Specific Providential Convergences

Providential Example #1 — Naval Timing

The final phase of the Revolutionary War hinged not on land alone, but on the **sea**.

For years, British naval dominance had shaped the conflict. Control of the waters allowed rapid movement of troops, steady resupply, and decisive reinforcement. Any American strategy that depended on isolating British forces required one condition that had proven elusive: **temporary loss of British naval control**.

At Yorktown, that condition emerged—briefly, unexpectedly, and decisively.

A French fleet arrived at the **Chesapeake Bay** at precisely the moment it was needed. Its timing was narrow. Its presence was critical. Had it arrived too early, it may have been forced to withdraw. Had it arrived too late, British forces would have escaped or been reinforced. Instead, it arrived **just in time**.

The fleet moved into position and **blocked British naval access**, preventing reinforcements from reaching General Cornwallis. Control of the bay shifted—not permanently, but long enough to alter the course of the war.

Equally significant was what followed.

The French fleet **maintained its position longer than expected**. Weather, logistics, and the constant risk of engagement made prolonged presence uncertain. Yet the fleet held, denying the British the opportunity to regain control of the waters during the critical window.

Meanwhile, British naval forces were **delayed**.

They did not arrive in time to challenge the blockade effectively. Efforts to regain naval superiority failed to materialize before the opportunity had passed. The delay was not dramatic, but it was decisive.

Scripture affirms God's authority over such realms:

"Thou rulest the raging of the sea: when the waves thereof arise, thou stillest them."

— *Psalm 89:9*

"They that go down to the sea in ships… these see the works of the LORD, and his wonders in the deep."

— *Psalm 107:23–24*

Providence here was not seen in constant control, but in **temporary governance**.

God did not permanently remove British naval strength.

He limited it **for a moment**.

That moment was enough.

The convergence of naval arrival, sustained presence, and enemy delay created conditions that had rarely existed during the war. What strategy alone could not secure, timing provided.

Providence here did not guarantee victory.

It made victory **possible**.

The sea—so often a source of British strength—became a boundary instead. Control shifted just long enough for land forces to act, encirclement to hold, and pressure to mount.

God governs seas as surely as land.

And sometimes, He governs them **just long enough**.

Theological Reflection (Optional Transition Sentence)
When independent forces converge at the precise moment needed, timing itself becomes a testimony to providence.

Providential Example #2 — Enemy Miscalculation
As events converged around Yorktown, British General Cornwallis made a series of decisions that, taken individually, appeared reasonable. Yet together, they placed his forces in a position from which escape became impossible.

Cornwallis chose a **defensive position** at Yorktown that was vulnerable to siege.

The location offered access to the sea and appeared suitable for resupply and evacuation if needed. From a conventional standpoint, it was defensible—provided naval support remained available. The assumption of continued British naval dominance shaped the decision.

But that assumption proved fragile.

Cornwallis **delayed retreat**.

Opportunities to reposition or withdraw existed earlier, when movement was still possible. Yet withdrawal was postponed. Confidence in expected support encouraged waiting rather than action. Time passed while conditions quietly shifted.

Most critically, Cornwallis **awaited reinforcements that never arrived**.

British naval forces did not appear when anticipated. Control of the Chesapeake remained contested. The window for escape narrowed and then closed entirely. What had seemed a temporary inconvenience became permanent isolation.

Scripture speaks directly to the limits of human calculation:

“There is no wisdom nor understanding nor counsel against the LORD.”

— *Proverbs 21:30*

This verse does not deny human intelligence or experience. It reminds us that even sound reasoning can be **bounded** by purposes beyond awareness.

Providence here did not require irrational choices.

It worked through **ordinary decisions**.

Cornwallis did not intend defeat.

He did not act with ignorance.

He made choices based on available information—yet that information proved incomplete.

Human decisions unknowingly aligned with God’s purposes.

What appeared to be strategic patience became entrapment. What seemed like a defensible position became confinement. What reliance on reinforcement became dependence without fulfillment.

Providence here was not coercive.
It was **directive through limitation**.
God did not override will.
He governed outcome.
The miscalculation was not dramatic. It was cumulative. Each delay, each assumption, each expectation quietly contributed to a narrowing set of options—until no viable alternative remained.
By the time Cornwallis recognized the reality of his position, the convergence was complete. Escape was no longer possible.

Theological Reflection (Optional Transition Sentence)
When human plans proceed without awareness of God's boundaries, even reasonable decisions may serve purposes never intended.

Providential Example #3 — Coordinated Movement
The success at Yorktown depended not only on timing and restraint, but on **coordination**—a factor that had often failed earlier in the war.
American and allied forces were required to move across significant distances, navigating difficult terrain, limited roads, and fragile supply systems. Communication was slow. Resources were scarce. Any premature disclosure could have alerted British forces and unraveled the plan.
And yet, movement proceeded with **remarkable precision**.
Forces moved swiftly and quietly. Marches were conducted with an unusual degree of discipline. Routes were adjusted without widespread confusion. The element of secrecy was maintained far longer than normally expected under such conditions.
Equally striking was the **synchronization**.
Separate contingents arrived within the same narrow window of time. Land forces aligned with naval positioning. Supply lines held just long enough. What typically fractured under pressure instead held together.
Scripture speaks to such ordering:
"The steps of a good man are ordered by the LORD: and he delighteth in his way."
— *Psalm 37:23*
This passage does not deny human planning or effort. It affirms that behind those efforts may stand a guiding hand that orders outcomes beyond human coordination alone.
Providence here was not miraculous in appearance.
It was **exceptional in effect**.
Coordination succeeded where it usually failed.

Earlier in the war, miscommunication, delay, and fragmentation had undermined operations repeatedly. At Yorktown, those familiar weaknesses were restrained. The very areas most prone to collapse became points of strength.

This convergence cannot be explained by competence alone.

Competence was present—but competence had been present before. What differed was the **alignment**. Independent movements, each vulnerable to disruption, unfolded in sequence rather than conflict.

Providence here was not about perfection.

It was about **completion**.

God did not remove obstacles.

He allowed them to be navigated.

Movement occurred without early exposure. Timing was maintained without precise control. Arrival occurred without collapse.

By the time all forces were in place, the convergence was complete.

What had required countless independent decisions unfolded as a single, unified outcome.

Theological Reflection (Optional Transition Sentence)

When coordination emerges where disorder has been the norm, alignment itself may testify to providence.

---

7. Prayer and Dependence

Historical records surrounding the Yorktown campaign reveal a consistent posture of humility rather than triumphalism. Leaders did not speak as though victory were guaranteed. Instead, there were:

- Appeals to God for guidance
- Acknowledgment of uncertainty
- Recognition that outcomes rested beyond human control

Correspondence from the period reflects restraint in language and awareness of dependence.

Victory was hoped for—but not presumed.

This posture aligns with Scripture:

"Call unto me, and I will answer thee, and shew thee great and mighty things, which thou knowest not."

— **Jeremiah 33:3**

Prayer did not replace strategy, labor, or sacrifice.

It framed them.

The leaders understood a vital truth:

Human effort functions best when it submits to divine sovereignty.

Providence was not treated as an excuse for inaction—but as the foundation for trust when action reached its limits.

---

8. Victory Without Excess

Important clarification:

- Yorktown did **not** immediately end all fighting
- The war officially continued after the surrender
- Loss, danger, and uncertainty still remained

Yet something decisive had changed.

The convergence at Yorktown—naval timing, coordinated movement, enemy miscalculation—created a turning point that could not be undone. Still, the response was not celebration without restraint.

There was no assumption that victory meant invincibility.

Scripture reminds us:

"For my thoughts are not your thoughts, neither are your ways my ways, saith the LORD."
— **Isaiah 55:8**

Providence often brings resolution **before people recognize finality**.

God closes doors quietly before history labels them closed.

Yorktown stands as a reminder that:

- God may answer prayer without removing all hardship
- Deliverance may arrive before peace is fully realized
- The end may be nearer than it appears—without being obvious

Victory came not as excess, but as sufficiency.

And sufficiency is often the clearest mark of providence.

---

9. Discussion Questions (Choose 2–3)

1. Why does God sometimes answer prayer through alignment rather than dramatic intervention?
2. What does Yorktown teach us about patience and timing?
3. How can we recognize God's hand in complex circumstances?
4. Why is humility important after success?

---

10. Personal & National Application

Personal

- Do I trust God to align circumstances beyond my control?
- Am I patient when answers take time?

National

- Success should lead to gratitude, not pride
- Alignment is not entitlement
- God's hand deserves recognition

"Not unto us, O LORD, not unto us, but unto thy name give glory."
— *Psalm 115:1*

---

11. Closing Reflection

At Yorktown, no single factor explains the outcome.
No one commander controlled every element.
No single decision guaranteed success.
No single strength ensured victory.
Instead, too many things aligned at once.
Naval movements, land forces, timing, weather, enemy decisions, and coordination across vast distances converged in a way that no individual mind could have planned or managed.
Scripture reminds us that God often works through convergence rather than command:
"The steps of a good man are ordered by the LORD."
— *Psalm 37:23*
At Yorktown, providence did not shout.
It **aligned**.
A fleet arrived when it should not have.
Reinforcements were delayed when they were needed.
Decisions were made that appeared reasonable—but proved decisive in ways unseen at the time.
"There are many devices in a man's heart; nevertheless the counsel of the LORD, that shall stand."
— *Proverbs 19:21*
No participant could see the whole picture. Each acted within limited knowledge, incomplete information, and human uncertainty. Yet the outcome unfolded with remarkable coherence.
This is a recurring biblical pattern.
God often governs history not by overriding human action, but by **ordering it**, allowing free decisions to intersect in ways that accomplish His purposes.

"He removeth kings, and setteth up kings."
— *Daniel 2:21*
Providence here was not dramatic intervention.
It was orchestration.
Events moved independently—yet arrived together.
Yorktown stands as a reminder that God's hand is often most evident where control is absent and outcomes exceed explanation.
Victory did not hinge on brilliance alone.
It rested on convergence.
Providence does not always announce itself with thunder.
Sometimes it is recognized only afterward—when all that aligned could not reasonably have aligned on its own.
And in that convergence, God's sovereign ordering becomes unmistakable.

Optional Teaching Pause (Adult Class)
You might ask:

- *Why does God often work through convergence rather than visible intervention?*
- *How does limited human perspective magnify God's sovereignty?*
- *Where might God be aligning unseen factors in our own lives?*

---

12. Closing Scripture & Prayer Prompt
Read aloud:
"The LORD shall fight for you, and ye shall hold your peace."
— *Exodus 14:14*
Prayer Prompt:
"Lord, help us recognize Your hand when circumstances align, and keep us humble when deliverance comes."

Lesson 14 — Declaration of Dependence

Series Title

God's Providence in American History: From the Pilgrims to the Present

Theme Verse

"Some trust in chariots, and some in horses: but we will remember the name of the LORD our God."

— *Psalm 20:7*

Lesson Aim (For the Teacher)

To show that even at the moment of political resolve, the leaders of the American cause publicly acknowledged their dependence on God—appealing not to power, wealth, or certainty, but to **Divine Providence**.

This lesson emphasizes **humble appeal**, not self-confidence.

Time Flow (Minimum 40 Minutes)

- Opening Scripture & Prayer – 4 minutes
- Biblical Framework – 10 minutes
- Historical Narrative & Providential Examples – 18 minutes
- Discussion – 5 minutes
- Application & Closing Reflection – 3 minutes

---

1. Opening Scripture Reading

Read aloud together:

"The LORD bringeth the counsel of the heathen to nought: he maketh the devices of the people of none effect."

— *Psalm 33:10*

---

2. Core Truth Statement

True courage is not confidence in oneself, but willingness to act while acknowledging dependence on God.

Faith does not deny risk—it entrusts outcomes.

---

3. Biblical Pattern: Appeals Made in Dependence

Key Scriptures

"Commit thy works unto the LORD, and thy thoughts shall be established."
— *Proverbs 16:3*
"Except the LORD build the house, they labour in vain that build it."
— *Psalm 127:1*
"Trust in the LORD with all thine heart; and lean not unto thine own understanding."
— *Proverbs 3:5*

Teaching Point (Scripture-Anchored)

In Scripture, decisive action is often paired with **explicit dependence on God**, not claims of self-sufficiency.
(Psalm 37:5; James 4:13–15)
Faith moves forward while surrendering control.

---

4. The Historical Moment of the Declaration

When the Declaration of Independence was signed in 1776, the outcome of the conflict was anything but certain.
The colonies were still militarily weak. The Continental Army was poorly trained, unevenly supplied, and far from unified. British forces remained the most powerful military presence in the world, supported by professional troops, naval dominance, and global resources. Defeat was not merely possible—it was expected by many observers.
"Put not your trust in princes, nor in the son of man, in whom there is no help."
— *Psalm 146:3*
The decision to declare independence was not made from a position of strength.
It was made in the face of risk.
Signing the Declaration was not a symbolic gesture or a distant political statement. Under British law, it constituted open rebellion. Those who placed their names on the document were knowingly exposing themselves to the full consequences of treason.
The cost was understood.
Those involved risked:

- **Property** — Confiscation of homes, land, and businesses
- **Freedom** — Imprisonment or exile
- **Reputation** — Social ruin and historical condemnation if the cause failed
- **Life itself** — Execution by hanging if captured

"For which of you, intending to build a tower, sitteth not down first, and counteth the cost?"
— *Luke 14:28*

Many signers were already established men with families, livelihoods, and standing in their communities. They were not reckless idealists. They were aware that failure would not simply mean defeat—it would mean devastation.

Yet they signed.

Not because victory was guaranteed.

Not because protection was assured.

But because conscience compelled action.

"We ought to obey God rather than men."

— *Acts 5:29*

At that moment, the Declaration became more than a political document.

It became a confession of dependence.

Appealing not to military strength or human certainty, the signers placed their trust in "the Supreme Judge of the world" and committed themselves to one another "with a firm reliance on the protection of Divine Providence."

Providence was not promised.

It was appealed to.

True faith often moves forward not when outcomes are clear,

but when obedience demands action despite uncertainty.

"Commit thy way unto the LORD; trust also in him; and he shall bring it to pass."

— *Psalm 37:5*

What followed would test that reliance severely.

But at this moment, history turned—not on assurance,

but on conviction.

---

5. Specific Providential Recognitions in the Declaration

Providential Example #1 — Unified Language of Dependence

Despite deep disagreements among the colonies—political, regional, and economic—the Declaration speaks with **remarkable theological unity**.

The document openly acknowledges:

- A **Creator** who endows rights
- A **Supreme Judge of the world**
- **Divine Providence** governing outcomes

This was not required language. It was chosen.

The signers did not merely assert independence from Britain; they expressed **dependence upon God** as the moral authority above all human governments.

"Appealing to the Supreme Judge of the world for the rectitude of our intentions…"

— *Declaration of Independence*

Scripture affirms the significance of such agreement:
"Can two walk together, except they be agreed?"
— *Amos 3:3*
Providence here is seen not in victory, but in **consensus**.
Men who disagreed on many matters agreed on this:
Human authority is accountable to God.
Unity at this level—under threat of death—was neither automatic nor guaranteed.

Providential Example #2 — Public Appeal to God Under Oath
The Declaration was not a private document. It was a **public, binding appeal**, signed with full awareness of consequences.
By signing, the representatives knowingly risked:
• Property confiscation
• Imprisonment
• Execution
And yet they closed the document with these words:
"With a firm reliance on the protection of Divine Providence…"
This was not rhetoric meant to inspire the public alone.
It was a **statement of personal trust**.
Scripture speaks directly to such reliance:
"The LORD is my light and my salvation; whom shall I fear?"
— *Psalm 27:1*
Providence here is not inferred—it is **explicitly confessed**.
They did not claim certainty of success.
They claimed reliance on God's protection.
That distinction matters deeply.

Providential Example #3 — Timing Before Outcome
The Declaration was issued **before victory was visible**.
At the time of signing:
• The war was far from won
• British military power remained overwhelming
• Defeat was entirely possible
This was not a celebration of success—it was an act of faith amid uncertainty.
Scripture captures this posture:
"Commit thy way unto the LORD; trust also in him; and he shall bring it to pass."
— *Psalm 37:5*

Providence here is seen in **timing**, not triumph.
They acted before outcomes were known, acknowledging that the future rested beyond their control. The Declaration did not claim that God would bless rebellion—it entrusted the cause to His judgment.
That restraint is significant.

Teaching Insight (Summary Statement)
The Declaration of Independence is better understood as a **Declaration of Dependence**.
It does not glorify human strength.
It does not predict guaranteed success.
It openly submits intentions and outcomes to God.
Providence is recognized not as entitlement, but as **appeal**.

Optional Transition Sentence for the Lesson
Before independence was secured, dependence was confessed.

---

6. The Language of the Declaration
The Declaration of Independence is often remembered for its bold assertions, but its **language reveals restraint as much as resolve**.
Notably, the document does **not** claim certainty of success.
It does **not** assert guaranteed victory.
It does **not** portray independence as inevitable.
Instead, its language consistently reflects:

- Appeals to a **higher moral authority**
- Recognition of **accountability before God**
- An explicit closing appeal to
  "the protection of Divine Providence"

This wording was not politically required.
It was not demanded by law.
It was deliberately chosen.
The signers framed their cause not as self-justifying rebellion, but as a moral appeal made under divine oversight. They acknowledged that history—and judgment—ultimately belong to God.
Scripture affirms this posture:
"The fear of the LORD is the beginning of wisdom."
— **Proverbs 9:10**

Wisdom does not begin with confidence in outcome.
It begins with reverence toward God.
By invoking Providence, the Declaration placed the cause under God's authority rather than above it. The appeal was not to destiny, but to responsibility.
Providence was not used as a slogan.
It was invoked as a submission.

---

7. Dependence Without Presumption

Important clarification:

- The Declaration does **not** claim divine approval for every action
- It does **not** guarantee blessing
- It does **not** promise ease or success

Instead, it expresses:

- Moral conviction rooted in conscience
- Submission to God's ultimate judgment
- Willingness to accept consequences, whatever they might be

The signers did not presume God's favor.
They entrusted themselves to God's oversight.
This posture mirrors a clear biblical pattern:
"If it be so, our God whom we serve is able to deliver us…
But if not, be it known unto thee… we will not serve thy gods."
— **Daniel 3:17–18**
Biblical dependence does not demand deliverance.
It remains faithful even if deliverance does not come.
The Declaration reflects this same spirit. Its signers pledged their lives, fortunes, and sacred honor—not because success was assured, but because obedience to conscience required action.
Providence was acknowledged, not manipulated.
Dependence was expressed, not assumed.
This is the difference between faith and presumption.
Faith obeys and entrusts outcomes to God.
Presumption acts and demands God justify the action.
The Declaration stands as an example of dependence that **moves forward without certainty**, trusting that God judges righteously—even when outcomes remain unknown.

8. Why This Matters Spiritually

How a cause is framed often shapes how it is remembered—and how it is lived.
If the Declaration had presented the cause as:

- Inevitable
- Self-powered
- Guaranteed

then pride would have followed naturally. Success would have been attributed to intellect, resolve, or destiny rather than to God's restraint and mercy.
Scripture consistently warns that **confidence divorced from humility leads to downfall:**
"Pride goeth before destruction, and an haughty spirit before a fall."
— **Proverbs 16:18**
Instead, the Declaration framed the cause as:

- **Humble** — acknowledging moral accountability
- **Risk-aware** — recognizing real consequences
- **God-conscious** — appealing to divine oversight rather than human certainty

This posture mattered spiritually because it placed the nation's future **outside human control** and **under God's judgment.**
The appeal was not, *"We cannot fail."*
It was, *"We will act, and we entrust the outcome to God."*
Scripture affirms this posture:
"God resisteth the proud, but giveth grace unto the humble."
— **James 4:6**
Grace does not accompany presumption.
It accompanies humility.
By acknowledging Providence rather than claiming inevitability, the Declaration left room for correction, repentance, and dependence. It did not sanctify every future decision—it established a posture of accountability.
This matters because **nations, like individuals, are shaped not only by what they believe—but by how they believe it.**
Confidence rooted in pride demands success.
Faith rooted in humility submits to God's will.
Providence responds not to certainty, but to submission.

9. Discussion Questions (Choose 2–3)

1. Why is dependence important at moments of decision?
2. How does acknowledging God change how we view risk?
3. What dangers come with presuming God's blessing?
4. How does biblical faith differ from confidence in outcomes?

---

10. Personal & National Application

Personal

- Do I commit plans to God or assume success?
- Am I willing to obey even when outcomes are uncertain?

National

- Dependence must accompany responsibility
- Appeals to God require humility
- Blessing is not entitlement

"Boast not thyself of tomorrow; for thou knowest not what a day may bring forth."
— *Proverbs 27:1*

---

11. Closing Reflection

The Declaration was not a claim of strength.
It was a confession of risk.
Those who signed did not act from a position of certainty or safety. They did not declare independence because victory was assured, nor because the future was clear. They acted knowing that failure could mean loss of property, freedom, or life itself.
Scripture reminds us that faith is not rooted in visible assurance:
"Now faith is the substance of things hoped for, the evidence of things not seen."
— *Hebrews 11:1*
At the moment of resolve, the appeal was not to military power, political calculation, or human wisdom—but to Providence.
This appeal reflected a biblical posture long established in Scripture:
"Commit thy way unto the LORD; trust also in him; and he shall bring it to pass."
— *Psalm 37:5*
The Declaration acknowledged human limitation. It recognized uncertainty. It placed responsibility not on confidence in outcome, but on trust in God's governance.
True faith does not wait for guarantees.
"Trust in the LORD with all thine heart; and lean not unto thine own understanding."
— *Proverbs 3:5*

To act in faith is not to claim control—it is to surrender it. The signers stepped forward with open hands, knowing that obedience sometimes requires movement before security arrives.
This pattern echoes throughout Scripture.
God repeatedly calls His people to act not when success is visible, but when obedience is required.
"By faith Moses… chose rather to suffer affliction with the people of God."
— *Hebrews 11:24–25*
The Declaration stands, therefore, not merely as a political document, but as a moment of moral resolve—where uncertainty was met with trust, and responsibility was embraced without assurance.
Providence was not invoked as decoration.
It was acknowledged as necessity.
True faith does not demand certainty.
It steps forward in trust.

Optional Teaching Pause (Adult Class)

You might ask:

- *Why does Scripture often connect faith with risk rather than safety?*
- *How does appealing to Providence differ from claiming divine endorsement?*
- *Where might God be calling us to act in trust without visible guarantees?*

---

12. Closing Scripture & Prayer Prompt

Read aloud:
"Commit thy way unto the LORD; trust also in him; and he shall bring it to pass."
— *Psalm 37:5*

Prayer Prompt:

"Lord, teach us to act with conviction while remaining fully dependent on You."

Lesson 15 — British Strategic Blunders

Series Title

God's Providence in American History: From the Pilgrims to the Present

Theme Verse

"There is no wisdom nor understanding nor counsel against the LORD."
— *Proverbs 21:30*

Lesson Aim (For the Teacher)

To show how repeated misjudgments, delays, and miscalculations by a vastly superior power contributed to the preservation of the Revolutionary cause—illustrating that **God often works through human limitation and error without endorsing pride or violence**.

This lesson emphasizes **divine overruling**, not ridicule.

Time Flow (Minimum 40 Minutes)

- Opening Scripture & Prayer – 4 minutes
- Biblical Framework – 10 minutes
- Historical Narrative & Providential Examples – 18 minutes
- Discussion – 5 minutes
- Application & Closing Reflection – 3 minutes

---

1. Opening Scripture Reading

Read aloud together:

"The LORD bringeth the counsel of the heathen to nought: he maketh the devices of the people of none effect."
— *Psalm 33:10*

---

2. Core Truth Statement

When human plans oppose God's purposes, even the strongest powers are hindered by their own limitations.

God does not need to overpower—He often **overrules**.

---

3. Biblical Pattern: God Overrules Human Counsel

Key Scriptures

"A man's heart deviseth his way: but the LORD directeth his steps."
— *Proverbs 16:9*

"Surely the wrath of man shall praise thee: the remainder of wrath shalt thou restrain."
— *Psalm 76:10*

"He taketh the wise in their own craftiness."
— *Job 5:13*

Teaching Point (Scripture-Anchored)

Throughout Scripture, God restrains, redirects, or frustrates human counsel when it conflicts with His purposes—often without dramatic intervention.
(Isaiah 19:11–14; Acts 5:38–39)

---

4. The British Advantage

At the outset of the war, the balance of power was overwhelmingly in Britain's favor.

Britain possessed:

- **The world's strongest navy**, capable of controlling major ports, blockading coastlines, and transporting troops and supplies across the Atlantic
- **A professional, disciplined standing army**, trained through years of European warfare and accustomed to coordinated command
- **Global resources and supply lines**, drawing wealth, weapons, and manpower from an extensive empire
- **Experienced commanders**, many of whom had fought and won conventional wars against established European powers

The British military was not improvised.

It was refined.

It was feared.

It was proven.

By contrast, the American colonies faced the conflict with severe disadvantages. Most colonial soldiers were volunteers or short-term enlistees. Training was inconsistent. Supplies were unreliable. Uniforms, weapons, and ammunition were often scarce. Coordination between colonies was fragile at best.

"There is no king saved by the multitude of an host: a mighty man is not delivered by much strength."
— *Psalm 33:16*

From a human standpoint, victory should have been **decisive and swift.**

Military logic favored Britain.
Financial logic favored Britain.
International opinion largely favored Britain.
Many assumed the rebellion would collapse once confronted by sustained force. The expectation was not whether Britain would win—but how quickly resistance would be crushed.
"The horse is prepared against the day of battle: but safety is of the LORD."
— *Proverbs 21:31*
Yet history unfolded differently.
Despite overwhelming advantage, Britain failed to deliver a decisive blow early in the war. Opportunities to end the conflict passed. Campaigns stalled. Momentum shifted unexpectedly. What should have been a short suppression became a prolonged struggle.
This imbalance highlights a recurring biblical pattern:
Power does not guarantee outcome.
Strength does not ensure success.
"Not by might, nor by power, but by my spirit, saith the LORD of hosts."
— *Zechariah 4:6*
The British advantage was real.
The colonial weakness was undeniable.
Yet the outcome would ultimately reveal that providence does not align itself automatically with visible strength. History would show that what appeared inevitable was quietly restrained—and that overwhelming power was repeatedly checked by forces beyond human calculation.

---

5. Repeated Strategic Miscalculations
Providential Example #1 — Underestimating Colonial Resolve
At the outset of the conflict, British leadership widely assumed that resistance in the colonies would be **brief and fragmented**.
The prevailing expectation was that colonial opposition would collapse under pressure. Economic dependence, regional divisions, and lingering loyalty to the Crown were believed to outweigh the will to sustain prolonged resistance. Many assumed that a show of force would restore order quickly.
That assumption proved deeply flawed.
Colonial resolve did not evaporate. It **hardened**.
Despite early losses, shortages, and uncertainty, resistance continued year after year. Communities endured hardship. Militias regrouped. Leaders persisted. The willingness to endure suffering outlasted expectations shaped by imperial experience.

Scripture speaks to such misjudgment:
"Pride goeth before destruction, and an haughty spirit before a fall."
— *Proverbs 16:18*
This does not suggest that British leaders were uniquely arrogant. It reveals a broader truth: **human authority often misjudges moral resolve**, especially when conviction is rooted in conscience rather than convenience.
Providence here was not about superior strength.
It was about **endurance beyond calculation**.
British planners believed time was on their side. Instead, time became an ally of resistance. What was expected to be a short suppression turned into a prolonged conflict that drained resources, morale, and political support at home.
The conflict lasted far longer than anticipated—not because resistance was easy, but because it was sustained.
Providence here worked quietly.
God did not instantly reverse power.
He allowed resolve to **outlast expectation**.
Human plans underestimated the depth of conviction formed by years of religious teaching, communal accountability, and moral reasoning. What imperial logic dismissed as weakness proved to be resilience.
This underestimation was not dramatic.
It was cumulative.
Each passing year eroded confidence that submission would come quickly. Each failure to end resistance reinforced the reality that resolve had been misread.
Providence often advances not by sudden reversal, but by **patient exposure of faulty assumptions**.

Theological Reflection (Optional Transition Sentence)
When human authority misjudges conscience-driven resolve, time itself may become an instrument of providence.

Providential Example #2 — Failure to Adapt Strategy
Throughout much of the conflict, British leadership approached the war as though it were **a temporary rebellion**, not a prolonged struggle requiring adaptation.
Initial strategy assumed that overwhelming force, decisive engagements, and conventional European tactics would quickly restore control. The war was treated as a problem to be suppressed rather than a conflict that would demand sustained flexibility.
That assumption shaped decisions.

British forces relied heavily on traditional formations, established supply lines, and set-piece engagements—methods well suited to European battlefields, but less effective in the varied terrain and decentralized conditions of the colonies.

Opportunities for decisive action did arise.

At several points, British commanders held advantages in manpower, equipment, and positioning. Yet these opportunities were not always pursued with urgency. Caution, overconfidence, or adherence to established doctrine often delayed action when swift engagement might have altered outcomes.

Scripture speaks to the danger of inflexibility:

"Be not righteous over much; neither make thyself over wise: why shouldest thou destroy thyself?"

— *Ecclesiastes 7:16*

And to the limits of human power when governed by God:

"He bringeth the princes to nothing; he maketh the judges of the earth as vanity."

— *Isaiah 40:23*

These passages do not condemn order or discipline. They caution against **rigidity that resists necessary adjustment**.

Providence here did not strip Britain of strength.

It allowed strength to be **misapplied**.

The empire possessed immense resources, experienced officers, and global reach. Yet its strategy remained tethered to assumptions that no longer matched reality. While colonial forces adapted—often out of necessity—imperial strategy adjusted slowly, constrained by tradition and expectation.

This imbalance mattered.

Wars are not won by strength alone, but by the ability to apply strength appropriately.

Providence often works not by removing power, but by limiting how effectively it can be used.

God often allows rigidity to undermine strength.

British strategy did not fail in a single moment. It faltered gradually, as repeated assumptions went uncorrected and opportunities passed without decisive action. What could have ended the conflict sooner instead prolonged it—contributing to exhaustion, expense, and eventual withdrawal.

Providence here was quiet.

No single mistake determined the outcome.

No dramatic collapse occurred.

Instead, **inflexibility accumulated**, narrowing options over time until strength could no longer secure the intended result.

Theological Reflection (Optional Transition Sentence)

When power refuses to adapt, God may allow its own rigidity to become its limitation.

Providential Example #3 — Distance and Delay

Throughout the conflict, British command was constrained by **distance**—a factor that repeatedly shaped outcomes in ways no battlefield strength could overcome.

Orders issued from London required **weeks or even months** to reach commanders in the field. By the time instructions arrived, conditions on the ground had often changed. Situations that demanded immediate response were addressed after opportunity had already passed.

This delay created hesitation.

Field commanders, uncertain whether to act independently or await further instruction, sometimes paused rather than pressed advantage. Decisions were deferred. Momentum slowed. What appeared to be prudence often resulted in lost opportunity.

The effect was cumulative.

Delays introduced inconsistency. Strategy shifted unevenly. Commanders operated with partial guidance, while colonial forces—operating closer to decision-makers—responded more quickly to changing conditions.

Scripture speaks to God's authority even within human decision-making structures:

"The king's heart is in the hand of the LORD, as the rivers of water: he turneth it whithersoever he will."

— *Proverbs 21:1*

This verse does not suggest confusion or incompetence. It affirms that God may govern outcomes by **limiting coordination**, even among powerful authorities.

Providence here did not require error.

It worked through **delay**.

Each postponed order gave American forces time—time to withdraw, regroup, resupply, or simply survive another season. Each hesitation allowed the weaker force to avoid decisive engagement when destruction seemed imminent.

Distance did not weaken British power.

It limited its **application**.

The empire's global reach became a constraint rather than an advantage. Control extended across oceans—but speed did not. Decisions made far from the conflict could not always match the urgency required on the ground.

Delays consistently favored the survival of the weaker force.

This pattern appeared again and again. Not because American forces were always stronger or wiser—but because time itself became a shield. Providence worked through geography, communication, and the unavoidable reality of distance.
God did not alter the map.
He governed its consequences.

Theological Reflection (Optional Transition Sentence)
When distance delays power, time itself may become an instrument of providence.

---

6. Restraint Without Cruelty
Important clarification:

- Britain did not lack military power
- Total destruction of colonial resistance was possible
- Brutal suppression could have been pursued more aggressively

From a purely military standpoint, the British Empire possessed the means to devastate population centers, impose harsher controls, and crush resistance through overwhelming force. History shows that empires often choose such paths when rebellion arises.
Yet in this conflict, **restraint repeatedly limited the reach of British power**.
This restraint was influenced by:

- Political considerations at home
- Concern for public opinion
- Hesitation to treat fellow English subjects as irredeemable enemies

The result was not kindness—but it was **measured force rather than annihilation**.
This restraint mattered because it:

- Reduced widespread civilian devastation
- Preserved social structures within the colonies
- Prevented immediate collapse of organized resistance

Scripture affirms that God often restrains human power even when it intends destruction:
"Surely the wrath of man shall praise thee: the remainder of wrath shalt thou restrain."
— **Psalm 76:10**
Providence does not always stop conflict.
Sometimes it **limits how far conflict is allowed to go**.
The British did not abandon their objectives—but their full capacity for cruelty was never fully unleashed. In that restraint, space remained for endurance, recovery, and continued resistance.
Providence was present not in the absence of power—but in its containment.

---

7. Providence Without Humiliation

This lesson is not written to mock British missteps or glorify colonial cleverness.
Scripture warns against pride rooted in hindsight:
"Let not him that girdeth on his harness boast himself as he that putteth it off."
— **1 Kings 20:11**
Rather, this lesson highlights a deeper truth:

- Intelligence does not guarantee wisdom
- Power does not guarantee success
- Careful plans do not override God's purposes

British commanders were experienced.
Resources were abundant.
Strategies were thoughtful by human standards.
Yet outcomes repeatedly failed to match expectations.
Scripture explains why:
"He frustrateth the tokens of the liars, and maketh diviners mad; that turneth wise men backward, and maketh their knowledge foolish."
— **Isaiah 44:25**
Providence does not humiliate nations for sport.
It humbles confidence that excludes God.
This restraint preserved dignity even in failure. Britain withdrew defeated—but not destroyed. The conflict ended with negotiation rather than annihilation, allowing history to move forward rather than collapse into vengeance.
Providence was not revealed through mockery—but through **limits placed on human certainty**.
God's purposes advanced not through humiliation, but through restraint, miscalculation, and mercy.

---

8. Discussion Questions (Choose 2–3)

1. Why does God sometimes allow powerful nations to misjudge situations?
2. How does pride affect decision-making?
3. Why is restraint sometimes more providential than force?
4. What dangers arise when strength is assumed to guarantee success?

---

9. Personal & National Application

Personal

- Do I rely on planning without prayer?
- Am I open to God redirecting my assumptions?

National

- Power must be exercised humbly
- Wisdom requires submission to God
- Restraint can be providential

"Trust in the LORD with all thine heart."

— *Proverbs 3:5*

---

10. Closing Reflection

The Revolution was not preserved by brilliance alone.

Skill mattered. Courage mattered. Sacrifice mattered.

But again and again, survival depended on something less visible—and less controllable.

Power hesitated.

Decisions faltered.

Opportunities passed.

What should have been decisive moments dissolved instead into delay, restraint, or inaction.

Scripture repeatedly reminds us that God governs not only action, but outcome:

"The LORD bringeth the counsel of the heathen to nought: he maketh the devices of the people of none effect."

— *Psalm 33:10*

Providence here was seen not in dramatic reversals, but in **withheld conclusions**. Plans that appeared sound did not proceed. Strength that could have crushed resistance did not press its advantage. Moments that should have ended the cause instead passed without final consequence.

This, too, is a biblical pattern.

God often works through restraint as much as intervention.

"There are many devices in a man's heart; nevertheless the counsel of the LORD, that shall stand."

— *Proverbs 19:21*

What did not happen proved as important as what did.

Battles not pursued.

Attacks delayed.

Decisions reconsidered.

Scripture teaches that such restraint is not weakness—it is governance.
"The king's heart is in the hand of the LORD… he turneth it whithersoever he will."
— *Proverbs 21:1*
Providence did not remove danger.
It limited outcome.
Again and again, collapse seemed reasonable—yet it did not come. The effort survived not because it was unstoppable, but because it was **preserved**.
This challenges a common misunderstanding of God's work.
Providence is not always visible as victory.
Sometimes it appears as **non-finality**.
God sustains His purposes not only by advancing them—but by preventing their premature end.
The Revolution endured because providence restrained destruction long enough for history to turn.

Optional Teaching Pause (Adult Class)
You might ask:

- *Why does Scripture emphasize God's control over human counsel?*
- *How does restraint reveal sovereignty as clearly as intervention?*
- *Where might God be preserving something today by limiting outcomes rather than producing success?*

---

11. Closing Scripture & Prayer Prompt
Read aloud:
"He disappointeth the devices of the crafty, so that their hands cannot perform their enterprise."
— *Job 5:12*
Prayer Prompt:
"Lord, grant us wisdom, humility, and submission to Your will in all our plans."

Lesson 16 — Independence Secured

Series Title

God's Providence in American History: From the Pilgrims to the Present

Theme Verse

"If the LORD delight in us, then he will bring us into this land."
— *Numbers 14:8*

Lesson Aim (For the Teacher)

To show that independence was not secured through strength or certainty, but through **preservation over time**, culminating in an outcome that demanded humility, gratitude, and responsibility before God.

This lesson emphasizes **deliverance completed**, not entitlement earned.

Time Flow (Minimum 40 Minutes)

- Opening Scripture & Prayer – 4 minutes
- Biblical Framework – 10 minutes
- Historical Narrative & Providential Examples – 18 minutes
- Discussion – 5 minutes
- Application & Closing Reflection – 3 minutes

---

1. Opening Scripture Reading

Read aloud together:

"Except the LORD had been on our side… then they had swallowed us up quick."
— *Psalm 124:2–3*

---

2. Core Truth Statement

Deliverance becomes dangerous when it is mistaken for self-achievement rather than God's mercy.

What God preserves must be stewarded with humility.

---

3. Biblical Pattern: Deliverance Followed by Responsibility

Key Scriptures

"And thou shalt remember the LORD thy God: for it is he that giveth thee power to get wealth."
— *Deuteronomy 8:18*

"To whomsoever much is given, of him shall be much required."
— *Luke 12:48*

"Righteousness exalteth a nation."
— *Proverbs 14:34*

Teaching Point (Scripture-Anchored)

In Scripture, deliverance is always followed by **accountability**. God rescues not to remove responsibility, but to **transfer it.**
(Deuteronomy 6:10–12; Joshua 24:14–15)
Freedom increases obligation.

---

4. The End of the War (1783)

With the signing of the Treaty of Paris in 1783, the Revolutionary War formally came to an end.

By its terms:

- **Britain formally recognized American independence**, acknowledging the failure of its efforts to reclaim the colonies
- **Hostilities officially ceased**, ending years of bloodshed, uncertainty, and exhaustion
- **The colonies emerged intact**, not fragmented into competing regions or reclaimed territories

The war was over—but peace did not bring immediate stability.

The condition of the nation was sobering.

America was:

- **Financially strained**
  - Massive war debt burdened both the Continental Congress and individual states
  - Currency had depreciated severely
  - Soldiers returned home unpaid or underpaid
- **Politically fragile**
  - The Articles of Confederation offered limited authority
  - States guarded their independence fiercely
  - National unity remained fragile and untested

- **Socially divided**
    - Loyalists and patriots lived side by side, often in tension
    - Families and communities bore unresolved wounds
    - Questions of justice, restitution, and reconciliation remained unanswered
- **Spiritually vulnerable to pride**
    - Victory tempted the nation toward self-congratulation
    - Survival could easily be misinterpreted as self-achievement
    - Gratitude could quietly give way to presumption

"When thou hast eaten and art full… then thine heart be lifted up, and thou forget the LORD thy God."

— *Deuteronomy 8:12–14*

The war had ended, but the greater test was just beginning.

Freedom secured through sacrifice now demanded stewardship.

Liberty preserved by providence now required humility.

Survival achieved through restraint now called for wisdom.

"Except the LORD build the house, they labour in vain that build it."

— *Psalm 127:1*

The question before the nation was no longer whether it could endure oppression—but whether it could govern itself without losing the virtues that had sustained it through crisis.

History shows that victory can be as dangerous as defeat.

Peace can test character more severely than war.

The hardest work still lay ahead:

- Learning restraint after conflict
- Choosing unity over rivalry
- Preserving humility after deliverance

Providence had carried the nation through war.

Whether the nation would walk wisely in peace remained to be seen.

---

5. Providential Preservation Recognized

Providential Example #1 — Survival to the End

By any ordinary measure, the cause should not have endured.

From its earliest days, the effort faced near collapse. Military defeats accumulated. Supplies ran short. Confidence wavered. Support fluctuated. At multiple points, the continuation of resistance depended on margins so narrow they were nearly invisible.

The struggle was marked by **years of uncertainty**.

There were no guarantees of success. Victory was not assured. Many involved did not expect to see a favorable outcome within their lifetimes. The passage of time did not steadily improve conditions—it often intensified strain.

And yet, the cause endured.

Despite repeated setbacks, it was not extinguished. Despite moments when collapse appeared inevitable, survival continued. The effort remained intact long enough for circumstances to shift, alliances to form, and outcomes to unfold.

Scripture gives language to this kind of endurance:

"It is of the LORD's mercies that we are not consumed, because his compassions fail not."

— *Lamentations 3:22*

This verse does not speak of triumph.

It speaks of **restraint**.

Providence here was not seen in uninterrupted progress. It was seen in **continued existence**.

The cause survived not because it was always strong, but because it was **not allowed to be destroyed**.

That distinction matters.

Survival itself testified to mercy.

God did not remove hardship.

He limited its reach.

God did not prevent loss.

He prevented annihilation.

Each season that ended without collapse was itself a providential moment. Each year that passed without total defeat represented restraint applied where destruction seemed reasonable.

Providence often works this way.

It does not always announce itself with victory.

It reveals itself through **preservation**.

The survival of the cause was not inevitable. It was sustained—moment by moment, decision by decision, restraint by restraint—until survival became history.

Theological Reflection (Optional Closing Sentence)

When destruction does not occur despite every reason it should, mercy itself becomes evidence of providence.

Providential Example #2 — Peaceful Recognition

When the conflict reached its conclusion, the opportunity for continued destruction remained. Britain possessed the ability to prolong hostilities. Retaliation, continued resistance, or renewed campaigns were possible. Pride, vengeance, or refusal to concede could have extended bloodshed for years.

Instead, a different course was taken.

British leadership chose **negotiation over renewed war**. The loss was acknowledged rather than contested through continued violence. Terms were pursued through diplomacy rather than force.

This restraint mattered.

The decision prevented further devastation. Communities already exhausted by years of conflict were spared additional suffering. Resources were preserved. Lives were not expended in a final struggle to reclaim what had been lost.

Providence here was not seen in victory.

It was seen in **limitation**.

Scripture speaks to this principle:

"When a man's ways please the LORD, he maketh even his enemies to be at peace with him."
— *Proverbs 16:7*

This verse does not suggest that peace arises from moral perfection or mutual agreement. It affirms that God may restrain hostility when continued conflict would only multiply loss.

The choice of peaceful recognition allowed **stability to begin**.

A fragile transition followed. Structures had to be built. Trust had to be formed. A nation did not emerge fully formed—it began in uncertainty. But peace provided the necessary space for order to take root.

Providence here did not erase consequences.

It limited escalation.

The end of war did not resolve every division.

It prevented new ones from being forged in blood.

God often preserves the future not by granting triumph, but by **ending destruction at the right moment**.

Peaceful recognition was not guaranteed. It was chosen—within boundaries God governs.

Theological Reflection (Optional Closing Sentence)

When restraint follows victory, preservation may matter more than triumph.

Providential Example #3 — Leadership Transition Without Collapse

As the war concluded, the greatest danger did not lie in external threat—but in **internal transition**.

History shows that revolutions often unravel after victory. Military authority lingers. Power consolidates. Order fractures. New nations frequently exchange one form of domination for another.

That outcome was possible here.

The Continental Army had gained influence. Military leaders held loyalty and force. Civil structures were young and untested. The temptation to retain power—or to rule by force "for stability's sake"—was real.

Yet that collapse did not occur.

Military authority **yielded to civil governance**.

Power was restrained rather than extended. Leadership transitioned without violence, purges, or consolidation of control. The army did not seize authority. The sword returned to its sheath.

Order was preserved—not imposed.

Scripture captures the weight of such restraint:

"He that ruleth his spirit is better than he that taketh a city."

— *Proverbs 16:32*

This verse elevates **self-governance over conquest**. It reminds us that restraint requires greater strength than domination.

Providence here extended beyond battlefield success.

God did not merely preserve the cause through war.

He preserved the people through peace.

Leadership transition without collapse is not automatic. It requires humility, discipline, and submission to limits. That such a transition occurred—without civil war, military takeover, or fragmentation—speaks to restraint applied at a critical moment.

Providence here was quiet but decisive.

Power was not seized.

Authority was not abused.

Stability was allowed to form.

This preservation mattered deeply.

A nation cannot be sustained by victory alone. It must be sustained by **order under restraint**.

The willingness to step back from power ensured that what had been preserved through hardship was not lost through pride.

Providence often completes its work not at the moment of triumph, but in what follows it.

Theological Reflection (Optional Closing Sentence)
When power is relinquished rather than retained, restraint itself bears witness to providence.

---

6. Independence Was Not the End
Important clarification:

- Independence did not guarantee righteousness
- Freedom did not ensure unity
- Victory did not secure virtue

The conclusion of the war marked the end of British rule—but it did not mark the end of spiritual danger.
History often tempts nations to believe that **deliverance equals arrival**. Scripture repeatedly corrects that assumption. The Bible shows that moments of rescue are often followed by seasons of spiritual vulnerability.
Israel's history offers a sober warning:
"And there arose another generation after them, which knew not the LORD, nor yet the works which he had done for Israel."
— **Judges 2:10**
The danger was not external oppression—it was internal forgetfulness.
Deliverance can be forgotten faster than bondage because pain imprints memory, while relief invites distraction. Once hardship lifts, vigilance often fades. What was once sought through prayer is soon assumed through prosperity.
Scripture records the tragic progression that follows forgotten deliverance:
"And they forsook the LORD God of their fathers… and followed other gods."
— **Judges 2:12**
Independence removed an external master—but it did not remove the need for submission to God. Liberty created opportunity, not maturity.
Providence preserved freedom—but what would be done with that freedom remained an unanswered question.

---

7. The Spiritual Danger After Deliverance
The Bible consistently reveals a pattern after great deliverance:

- Gratitude fades
- Pride grows
- Dependence weakens

This danger is not theoretical—it is repeated throughout Scripture.
Moses warned Israel while they were still preparing to enter the land:

"Beware lest thou forget the LORD, which brought thee forth out of the land of Egypt."
— **Deuteronomy 8:11**
The warning was not against open rebellion—but against quiet neglect.
As blessing increases, the heart is tempted to shift trust:

- From God to systems
- From prayer to policy
- From dependence to confidence

Scripture explains why remembrance is essential:
"Lest when thou hast eaten and art full… then thine heart be lifted up, and thou forget the LORD."
— **Deuteronomy 8:12–14**
Freedom must be guarded—not merely by laws, but by memory.
Without deliberate remembrance:

- Liberty becomes license
- Confidence replaces humility
- Prosperity dulls conscience

Providence delivers—but it does not force gratitude. That responsibility belongs to those who benefit from what God has preserved.
Freedom survives only where remembrance remains.

---

8. Discussion Questions (Choose 2–3)

1. Why is the period after deliverance spiritually dangerous?
2. How can a nation remember God after success?
3. What responsibilities come with freedom?
4. How does gratitude protect against pride?

---

9. Personal & National Application
Personal

- Do I give God credit after deliverance?
- Am I faithful once pressure lifts?

National

- Freedom requires moral restraint
- Blessing demands stewardship
- Gratitude guards liberty

"Happy is that people, whose God is the LORD."
— *Psalm 144:15*

---

10. Closing Reflection

Independence was not claimed.

It was granted.

It did not arrive as the result of uninterrupted strength or flawless execution. It endured through weakness, restraint, and preservation far beyond human capacity to secure.

Scripture reminds us that what survives beyond expectation does so by God's allowance, not human entitlement:

"Except the LORD build the house, they labour in vain that build it."

— *Psalm 127:1*

The cause was preserved not because it was invincible, but because God restrained destruction long enough for it to stand. Weakness did not destroy it. Delay did not undo it. Failure did not finish it.

Providence sustained what human strength could not secure.

"Not by might, nor by power, but by my spirit, saith the LORD of hosts."

— *Zechariah 4:6*

Independence endured through:

- **Weakness**, which exposed human limits
- **Restraint**, which prevented collapse
- **Providence**, which governed outcomes unseen

God preserved the opportunity—but preservation was not the same as approval.

Scripture is clear that what God grants must be stewarded with fear and humility:

"For unto whomsoever much is given, of him shall be much required."

— *Luke 12:48*

The greater question did not end with survival.

It began there.

What would be done with what God had preserved?

Would liberty be governed by truth—or consumed by self-will?

Would independence lead to humility—or pride?

"Righteousness exalteth a nation: but sin is a reproach to any people."

— *Proverbs 14:34*

Providence had granted opportunity, not permanence. Preservation created responsibility, not exemption.

God had restrained destruction.

Now faithfulness would be tested.

Independence was not the end of God's dealings—but the beginning of accountability under His hand.

Optional Teaching Pause (Adult Class)

You might ask:

- *Why does Scripture link blessing with responsibility rather than security?*
- *How does preservation differ from endorsement?*
- *What dangers follow when what God preserves is treated as entitlement?*

---

11. Closing Scripture & Prayer Prompt

Read aloud:

"Now therefore fear the LORD, and serve him in sincerity and in truth."

— *Joshua 24:14*

Prayer Prompt:

"Lord, keep us humble after deliverance, grateful for Your mercy, and faithful with the freedom You provide."

SECTION IV - CONSTITUTION & EARLY REPUBLIC

Preserving Liberty Through Wisdom and Restraint

"Every purpose is established by counsel: and with good advice make war."
— **Proverbs 20:18**

Section Purpose

Winning independence did not guarantee stability.
Deliverance had been granted—but **preservation required wisdom.**
This section examines the fragile years that followed the Revolution, when unity was tested not by war, but by governance. The challenge was no longer survival under oppression, but **self-government under freedom.** Here, we see God's providence not through rescue from enemies, but through **restraint, counsel, and cooperation** among imperfect men.

Lessons in This Section

- **Lesson 17:** The Constitutional Convention Prayers
- **Lesson 18:** Ratification Against All Odds
- **Lesson 19:** Washington's Inauguration
- **Lesson 20:** Early National Revivals
- **Lesson 21:** Preservation of Unity

Guiding Truth

Freedom is preserved not by power alone, but by humility, counsel, and submission to God.

(Optional Closing Line for Print or Teaching)

"Liberty survives only where restraint is willingly embraced."

Teaching Orientation (Leader Use)

As you enter this section, remind the class:

- Victory can unite temporarily; wisdom must unite permanently
- Self-government requires moral self-control
- Institutions reflect the character of the people who build them

Encourage the class to watch for:

- Appeals to God for wisdom
- Recognition of human limitation
- The dangers of pride after success

Lesson 17 — The Constitutional Convention Prayers

Series Title

God's Providence in American History: From the Pilgrims to the Present

Theme Verse

"If any of you lack wisdom, let him ask of God."

— *James 1:5*

Lesson Aim (For the Teacher)

To show how the framers of the Constitution, facing division and uncertainty, acknowledged their limitations and appealed to God for wisdom—demonstrating that **self-government requires humility before God**.

This lesson emphasizes **dependence after deliverance**, not confidence in intellect alone.

Time Flow (Minimum 40 Minutes)

- Opening Scripture & Prayer – 4 minutes
- Biblical Framework – 10 minutes
- Historical Narrative & Providential Examples – 18 minutes
- Discussion – 5 minutes
- Application & Closing Reflection – 3 minutes

---

1. Opening Scripture Reading

Read aloud together:

"Trust in the LORD with all thine heart; and lean not unto thine own understanding."

— *Proverbs 3:5*

---

2. Core Truth Statement

When human wisdom reaches its limits, God invites His people to ask for divine guidance.

Self-government begins with self-distrust and reliance on God.

---

3. Biblical Pattern: Seeking God's Wisdom

Key Scriptures

"Except the LORD build the house, they labour in vain that build it."
— *Psalm 127:1*

"O LORD, I know that the way of man is not in himself."
— *Jeremiah 10:23*

"In the multitude of counsellors there is safety."
— *Proverbs 11:14*

Teaching Point (Scripture-Anchored)

In Scripture, God's people are repeatedly warned that **human understanding alone is insufficient** for righteous governance; wisdom must be sought from God.
(1 Kings 3:9; Psalm 25:4–5)

Asking for wisdom is an act of humility, not weakness.

---

4. The Crisis at the Constitutional Convention (1787)

By the summer of 1787, the weaknesses of the young nation could no longer be ignored.
The **Articles of Confederation**, written during wartime urgency, were proving inadequate for peace.
By nearly every measure, the system was failing.
The nation faced:

- **Economic instability**
  - Interstate trade disputes disrupted commerce
  - Debts from the Revolutionary War went unpaid
  - Inflation and unreliable currency undermined trust
- **Political paralysis**
  - Congress lacked authority to enforce laws
  - National decisions depended on unanimous or near-unanimous consent
  - States acted increasingly as independent rivals rather than a unified people
- **Social unrest**
  - Events such as **Shays' Rebellion** revealed growing desperation
  - Armed resistance to taxation signaled deep instability
  - Leaders feared that liberty might collapse into disorder

"Where there is no vision, the people perish."
— *Proverbs 29:18*

When delegates gathered in Philadelphia, unity was assumed—but quickly shattered.
Inside the convention:

- **States clashed over representation**
    - Large states demanded proportional representation
    - Small states feared domination and loss of voice
- **Regional interests collided**
    - Commercial states and agrarian states disagreed sharply
    - Slavery and economic policy created moral and political fault lines
- **Trust eroded**
    - Motives were questioned
    - Compromise felt increasingly impossible
    - Delegates openly discussed abandoning the effort

Debate grew intense.

Progress stalled.

Frustration mounted.

At several points, adjournment without agreement seemed inevitable.

"Only by pride cometh contention."

— *Proverbs 13:10*

Humanly speaking, failure was likely.

There was:

- No guarantee of consensus
- No assurance that states would accept any final document
- No certainty that continued unity was even desirable

Yet the delegates remained.

They debated.

They argued.

They reconsidered.

They returned again to the table.

This persistence itself reflected restraint—a refusal to abandon the work simply because agreement was difficult.

"The discretion of a man deferreth his anger; and it is his glory to pass over a transgression."

— *Proverbs 19:11*

Providence does not always appear in sudden clarity.

Sometimes it works through prolonged tension—holding people in the room long enough for humility to replace certainty.

The Constitutional Convention did not move forward because division vanished.

It moved forward because collapse was restrained.

The question was no longer whether the Articles would survive.

The question was whether humility, patience, and restraint would.

Providence often reveals itself not by eliminating disagreement—but by preventing it from destroying what must still be built.

---

5. The Call for Prayer

At a moment of impasse:

- The respected elder statesman, Benjamin Franklin rose
- He reminded the assembly of past dependence on God
- He urged daily prayer for divine guidance

This appeal acknowledged:

- Human limitation
- Need for humility
- Dependence on providence

"God governs in the affairs of men."

21 And he changeth the times and the seasons: he removeth kings, and setteth up kings: he giveth wisdom unto the wise, and knowledge to them that know understanding: (Daniel 2:21)

The appeal was not ceremonial—it was corrective.

---

6. Providence Through Humility and Counsel

Providential Example #1 — Recognition of Dependence

As independence was secured, the danger did not disappear—it **changed form**.

Victory removed an external authority, but it did not create wisdom. Independence granted freedom, but it did not guarantee unity. The absence of a ruling power did not ensure the presence of restraint.

Leaders recognized this reality.

Rather than assuming that success implied competence or moral clarity, there was a conscious acknowledgment of **continued dependence upon God**. Calls to prayer reflected an understanding that the nation now faced challenges as great as those it had overcome.

Victory did not guarantee wisdom.

Independence did not ensure unity.

Freedom required restraint.

This recognition was not symbolic.

It acknowledged that the greatest threats often emerge **after success**, when pride tempts leaders to trust outcomes rather than principles. The willingness to seek counsel beyond human authority revealed an awareness of limitation rather than entitlement.

Scripture speaks directly to this posture:

"The fear of the LORD is the beginning of wisdom."
— *Proverbs 9:10*

Wisdom, in biblical terms, does not begin with power.

It begins with **reverence and humility**.

Providence here did not consist in granting new victories.

It consisted in **restraining pride**.

Calls to prayer served as a safeguard. They reminded leaders and citizens alike that liberty could be squandered as easily as it could be lost. The acknowledgment of dependence placed boundaries on ambition and reminded the nation that authority—newly held—remained accountable.

Providence often works this way.

God does not always add strength.

Sometimes He preserves by cultivating **humility**.

The recognition of dependence created space for counsel, deliberation, and patience. It slowed rash decisions and encouraged reflection at a moment when unchecked confidence could have led to fragmentation or authoritarian control.

Providence here was preventative.

It guarded the future not by granting certainty, but by reinforcing **reverent caution**.

Theological Reflection (Optional Closing Sentence)

When humility follows victory, wisdom may yet guide freedom.

Providential Example #2 — Continued Cooperation

Following the recognition of dependence and the call to prayer, a crucial outcome emerged: **cooperation did not dissolve**.

The period after independence was fragile. Delegates represented diverse regions, interests, and convictions. Disagreements were real and often sharp. Fatigue from years of conflict compounded frustration. The temptation to withdraw, dominate, or abandon the process altogether was strong.

Yet the work continued.

Delegates **remained engaged** rather than retreating into isolation. Conversations resumed even after disagreement. Dialogue continued where division could have hardened.

Compromise, though difficult, was pursued again.

This did not mean uniformity.

It did not eliminate tension.

It did not guarantee immediate agreement.

But it preserved **participation**.

Scripture identifies pride as the chief threat to such cooperation:

"Only by pride cometh contention: but with the well advised is wisdom."

— *Proverbs 13:10*

This verse does not condemn conviction. It warns against pride that refuses counsel and insists on victory rather than understanding.

Providence here was not about agreement on every point.

It was about **continued willingness to engage**.

Humility made disagreement survivable. It allowed conversation to outlast frustration. It restrained the impulse to abandon the process when outcomes were uncertain or unsatisfying.

This mattered deeply.

Many revolutions fracture not because enemies remain, but because cooperation fails after victory. When dialogue collapses, power fills the vacuum. When compromise is abandoned, coercion follows.

That collapse did not occur here.

Providence worked through restraint.

God did not eliminate disagreement.

He preserved **engagement.**

The willingness to continue talking, listening, and revising was itself a providential safeguard. It kept authority from hardening prematurely and allowed solutions to emerge through deliberation rather than force.

Humility made agreement possible—not inevitable, but attainable.

Theological Reflection (Optional Closing Sentence)

When dialogue endures despite disagreement, humility may be the quiet work of providence.

Providential Example #3 — Enduring Framework

As deliberation continued and compromise endured, what finally emerged was not a celebration of human confidence—but a framework shaped by **sobering realism**.

The Constitution that resulted reflected a clear understanding of human nature.

Rather than assuming virtue, it **anticipated weakness**. Rather than concentrating authority, it **distributed power**. Rather than trusting individuals implicitly, it placed restraints upon offices, institutions, and ambition itself.

This was not accidental.

Checks and balances were intentionally woven into the structure. Authority was divided rather than centralized. Power was limited not because leaders lacked confidence, but because they possessed **wisdom born of humility**.

Scripture affirms this understanding:

"He that ruleth his spirit is better than he that taketh a city."
— *Proverbs 16:32*
"The heart is deceitful above all things, and desperately wicked: who can know it?"
— *Jeremiah 17:9*
These verses do not deny leadership.
They warn against **unchecked authority**.
Providence here was not expressed through expansion.
It was expressed through **restraint**.
The framework assumed that even well-intentioned leaders could err. It recognized that concentration of power invites abuse. It acknowledged that liberty survives only when authority is limited by principle rather than personality.
This sober view of human nature shaped the structure itself.
Rather than trusting that future leaders would always act wisely, the framework constrained what leaders could do—even when intentions were good. In doing so, it protected against both corruption and zeal unchecked by accountability.
Providence here worked through foresight.
God did not grant perfect leaders.
He allowed a system that **anticipated imperfection**.
That endurance matters.
Structures built on optimism alone collapse under strain. Structures grounded in humility endure because they assume the need for correction. The longevity of the framework testifies not to human brilliance, but to wisdom that recognized limits.
God's wisdom often appears not as expansion, but as restraint.

Theological Reflection (Optional Closing Sentence)
When authority is limited by design, humility may be the lasting work of providence.

---

7. Prayer Did Not Remove Difficulty
Important clarification:

- Prayer did not eliminate disagreement
- It did not produce instant harmony
- It did not guarantee perfection

The Constitutional Convention did not become peaceful or effortless after prayer was introduced. Deep divisions remained. Debates continued. Frustration did not vanish.
Prayer did not change the **complexity of the task**—it changed the **posture of the participants**.

Scripture consistently shows that prayer is not a mechanism for bypassing struggle. It is a means of **enduring it rightly**.

The Apostle Paul testified:

"And he said unto me, My grace is sufficient for thee: for my strength is made perfect in weakness."

— **2 Corinthians 12:9**

God often answers prayer not by removing the burden, but by supplying the strength to carry it.

At the Convention:

- Disagreements were still sharp
- Compromise remained difficult
- Progress was slow and uncertain

Yet something essential changed. Appeals shifted from personal certainty to collective humility. Pride softened. Listening increased. Endurance replaced withdrawal.

Prayer reminded the delegates that:

- Wisdom was not automatic
- Human reason had limits
- Accountability existed beyond the room

Scripture affirms this kind of reorientation:

"Commit thy works unto the LORD, and thy thoughts shall be established."

— **Proverbs 16:3**

Prayer did not guarantee the best possible document. It guarded against the worst possible outcome—abandonment.

Providence often sustains perseverance when collapse seems likely.

Prayer did not remove struggle.

It restrained pride.

It renewed patience.

It preserved the process.

8. Discussion Questions (Choose 2–3)

1. Why is humility essential for self-government?
2. What dangers arise when leaders rely solely on intellect?
3. How does prayer change decision-making?
4. Why does Scripture emphasize counsel and restraint?

---

9. Personal & National Application

Personal

- Do I seek God's wisdom before major decisions?
- Am I willing to admit when I lack understanding?

National

- Freedom requires moral wisdom
- Institutions reflect the character of their builders
- Dependence on God must continue after deliverance

"Happy is the man that findeth wisdom."
— *Proverbs 3:13*

---

10. Closing Reflection

The Constitution was not born of confidence alone.

It emerged from a sober recognition of human weakness—an understanding shaped not by cynicism, but by experience. Those who gathered did not assume virtue would prevail automatically. They assumed, instead, that unchecked power would eventually corrupt.

Scripture speaks plainly to this reality:

"The heart is deceitful above all things, and desperately wicked: who can know it?"
— *Jeremiah 17:9*

Wisdom was sought not because failure was inevitable,
but because pride would have guaranteed it.

The framers did not deny human capability—but they distrusted human nature. They understood that good intentions alone could not sustain liberty. Restraint was necessary. Accountability was essential. Power had to be limited because human judgment is fallible.

This aligns with Scripture's insistence that wisdom begins with humility:

"The fear of the LORD is the beginning of wisdom."
— *Proverbs 9:10*

Providence often works through humble counsel rather than decisive assertion. It moves not through domination, but through deliberation—through men willing to admit limits, listen carefully, and restrain themselves for the sake of order.

"Where no counsel is, the people fall: but in the multitude of counsellors there is safety."
— *Proverbs 11:14*
The Constitution reflects this wisdom. It assumes disagreement. It anticipates misuse of power. It builds friction into authority—not because unity is unimportant, but because restraint is necessary.
Scripture affirms that such restraint is strength, not weakness:
"He that ruleth his spirit is better than he that taketh a city."
— *Proverbs 16:32*
Providence was not seen in a perfect system, but in a guarded one—one that recognized the need for balance, accountability, and humility under God.
The Constitution did not eliminate human weakness.
It acknowledged it.
And in that acknowledgment, God's providence worked—not by exalting confidence, but by honoring humility.

Optional Teaching Pause (Adult Class)
You might ask:

- *Why does Scripture treat humility as foundational to wisdom?*
- *How does acknowledging human weakness protect liberty?*
- *What happens when systems are built on optimism rather than restraint?*

---

11. Closing Scripture & Prayer Prompt
Read aloud:
"Give therefore thy servant an understanding heart."
— *1 Kings 3:9*
Prayer Prompt:
"Lord, grant us wisdom beyond our understanding and humility to seek You continually."

Lesson 18 — Ratification Against All Odds

Series Title

God's Providence in American History: From the Pilgrims to the Present

Theme Verse

"For the LORD giveth wisdom: out of his mouth cometh knowledge and understanding."
— *Proverbs 2:6*

Lesson Aim (For the Teacher)

To show how the Constitution—despite deep opposition, fear, and division—was ratified through patience, persuasion, and restraint, illustrating that **God's providence often works through orderly process rather than force**.

This lesson emphasizes **preservation through consensus**, not coercion.

Time Flow (Minimum 40 Minutes)

- Opening Scripture & Prayer – 4 minutes
- Biblical Framework – 10 minutes
- Historical Narrative & Providential Examples – 18 minutes
- Discussion – 5 minutes
- Application & Closing Reflection – 3 minutes

---

1. Opening Scripture Reading

Read aloud together:

"He that is slow to wrath is of great understanding: but he that is hasty of spirit exalteth folly."
— *Proverbs 14:29*

---

2. Core Truth Statement

God often preserves unity not by silencing disagreement, but by guiding patient dialogue toward shared responsibility.

Lasting agreement requires time, humility, and restraint.

---

3. Biblical Pattern: Unity Through Counsel and Patience

Key Scriptures

"Where no counsel is, the people fall: but in the multitude of counsellors there is safety."
— *Proverbs 11:14*

"Let every man be swift to hear, slow to speak, slow to wrath."
— *James 1:19*

"The wisdom that is from above is first pure, then peaceable, gentle."
— *James 3:17*

Teaching Point (Scripture-Anchored)

Scripture teaches that durable unity is forged through **patient counsel, measured speech, and willingness to listen**, rather than haste or force.
(Ecclesiastes 7:8; Proverbs 15:22)

---

4. The Fragility of Ratification

When the Constitutional Convention concluded its work, the crisis was not resolved—it had only entered a new and uncertain phase.

The Constitution existed on paper, but its survival depended entirely on acceptance.

Across the states, **fear was widespread and sincere**.

Many Americans believed they had only recently escaped tyranny—and were wary of creating another form of it.

Concerns included:

- **Centralized power**
  - A stronger federal government raised alarms
  - Memories of distant authority under Britain were still fresh
  - Many feared that liberty could again be eroded gradually
- **Loss of local control**
  - States worried about surrendering sovereignty
  - Smaller states feared domination by larger ones
  - Citizens questioned whether their voices would still matter
- **Limited trust**
  - The colonies had long histories of rivalry
  - Economic and regional interests differed sharply
  - Unity had been tested but not yet secured

"Put not your trust in princes, nor in the son of man, in whom there is no help."
— *Psalm 146:3*

Unlike ordinary legislation, ratification was not handled by Congress alone.

The Constitution required approval through **separate state conventions**, each representing the people directly.

This process ensured legitimacy—but it also multiplied risk.

- Each state debated independently
- Rejection by key states could unravel the entire effort
- There was no mechanism to compel agreement

Opposition was vocal and organized.

Pamphlets warned of:

- Future tyranny
- Loss of rights
- Concentration of power in distant hands

Supporters defended the framework, but persuasion—not force—was the only tool available.

"A soft answer turneth away wrath."

— *Proverbs 15:1*

Ratification did not move forward with confidence.

It moved forward cautiously, slowly, and unevenly.

Margins were narrow.

Votes were delayed.

Decisions were revisited.

At several moments, a single reversal could have undone years of sacrifice and debate.

"Except the LORD keep the city, the watchman waketh but in vain."

— *Psalm 127:1*

Humanly speaking, fragmentation was entirely possible.

The nation stood at a crossroads:

- Unity without certainty
- Liberty without guarantee
- A future that depended on restraint rather than force

Providence did not remove fear.

It restrained collapse.

The Constitution was not preserved by overwhelming enthusiasm—but by patience, humility, and the willingness of divided people to remain engaged rather than withdraw.

Providence often works not by silencing doubt, but by preventing doubt from becoming destruction.

5. Specific Providential Preservations

Providential Example #1 — Debate Without Collapse

As the work of national formation unfolded, disagreement was unavoidable—and often intense.

States differed sharply over representation, authority, commerce, and governance. Interests conflicted. Regional priorities clashed. Convictions were deeply held, and compromise was difficult. At multiple points, the process appeared fragile.

History offers many examples of such moments ending in violence.

Revolutions frequently fracture when debate hardens into coercion. When disagreement is no longer contained by principle, force replaces persuasion. Authority is seized rather than reasoned, and collapse follows.

That outcome was possible here.

Yet it did not occur.

Despite strong disagreement, the states **did not resort to violence**. Debate remained within lawful and deliberative channels. Arguments were made, withdrawn, revised, and reconsidered. Dialogue replaced coercion when passions ran high.

This preservation of process mattered deeply.

Scripture speaks to the blessing attached to such restraint:

"Blessed are the peacemakers: for they shall be called the children of God."

— *Matthew 5:9*

Peace in this context was not the absence of disagreement.

It was the **presence of restraint**.

Providence here was not seen in unanimous agreement.

It was seen in **continued engagement without rupture**.

The ability to argue strongly without destroying the process itself is rare. It requires humility, patience, and submission to something higher than immediate victory. That such restraint endured through prolonged debate speaks to preservation beyond human temperament alone.

God did not remove disagreement.

He restrained its consequences.

Debate sharpened ideas without shattering unity. Conflict exposed weaknesses without ending cooperation. The process survived long enough for solutions to emerge—not because agreement was easy, but because violence was refused.

Providence preserved **the means** by which outcomes could be reached.

And that preservation ensured that what emerged was not imposed by force, but formed through deliberation.

Theological Reflection (Optional Closing Sentence)

When disagreement does not destroy dialogue, restraint itself may be the work of providence.

Providential Example #2 — Willingness to Amend

As debate continued and concerns intensified, agreement did not come through insistence alone—but through **humility expressed as willingness to adjust**.

Significant fears were raised.

Some states worried about centralized authority. Others feared the loss of local governance, individual liberties, or long-term imbalance of power. These concerns were not dismissed as obstruction. They were recognized as legitimate expressions of caution born from hard experience.

Rather than forcing acceptance, leaders chose a different path.

Concerns were addressed through:

- **Promises of future amendments**
- **Recognition of legitimate fears**
- **Commitment to ongoing correction**

This approach acknowledged an important truth: no framework created by fallible people would be complete or perfect at its inception.

Scripture speaks to the wisdom of such restraint:

"He that covereth a transgression seeketh love; but he that repeateth a matter separateth very friends."

— *Proverbs 17:9*

This verse does not encourage ignoring truth. It commends **restraint that preserves relationship**, allowing space for reconciliation and growth rather than division.

Providence here was not expressed through immediate resolution.

It was expressed through **patience with imperfection**.

The willingness to amend acknowledged limits without surrendering conviction. It allowed trust to grow where fear could have hardened resistance. Agreement was secured not by denying concerns, but by committing to address them over time.

This humility mattered deeply.

Many political systems fracture because leaders insist on finality too quickly. When correction is denied, resistance becomes entrenched. When adjustment is permitted, cooperation survives.

Providence here preserved unity by allowing **room for correction**.

God did not grant flawless agreement.

He preserved a posture that allowed improvement without collapse.

The commitment to amend reflected a sober understanding of human nature: that wisdom unfolds over time, and that enduring structures must allow for refinement.

Theological Reflection (Optional Closing Sentence)
When correction is welcomed rather than feared, humility may be preserving unity by God's design.

Providential Example #3 — Narrow Margins, Timely Decisions
As the ratification process moved forward, success did not come through overwhelming agreement.
It came through **narrow margins**.
Several states ratified the Constitution by **slim votes**, only after prolonged debate marked by real uncertainty and deep concern. Arguments were revisited repeatedly. Positions shifted slowly. Decisions were delayed until the last possible moment.
The outcome was fragile.
A single reversal in any key state could have unraveled the entire effort. Momentum was never guaranteed. Each vote carried disproportionate weight, and failure remained a realistic possibility until the process was complete.
This was not inevitability.
It was vulnerability.
Scripture speaks to the significance of what appears small or limited:
"A little that a righteous man hath is better than the riches of many wicked."
— *Psalm 37:16*
Providence often works **not through abundance**, but through sufficiency.
The narrowness of these decisions reveals restraint at work. No coercion forced agreement. No overwhelming majority silenced opposition. Instead, persuasion, patience, and timing carried the process forward just far enough to hold unity together.
These were **timely decisions**.
Votes occurred when debate had done its work—when concerns had been heard, when concessions had been made, and when delay would have risked collapse rather than improvement. Agreement arrived not early, but **before fracture became irreversible**.
Providence here was not dramatic intervention.
It was **precision at the margins**.
God did not guarantee ease.
He preserved **just enough agreement** at the moment it was needed.

Throughout Scripture, God's purposes often advance under similar conditions—where outcomes rest on narrow ground and human control is minimal. Such margins reveal dependence rather than dominance.
Providence often works at the margins.

Theological Reflection (Optional Closing Sentence)
When preservation depends on narrow outcomes rather than force, restraint itself bears the mark of providence.

---

6. Restraint Over Force
Important clarification:

- Ratification was not inevitable
- It was not imposed
- It was not rushed

The Constitution did not become law through coercion, intimidation, or military authority. It was submitted to the people of the states, debated publicly, and approved only after extended deliberation.
This was a remarkable restraint of power.
Those who supported the Constitution possessed influence, momentum, and urgency—but they did not force agreement. Instead, persuasion was chosen over domination, patience over pressure.
Scripture consistently honors this pattern:
"He that is slow to anger is better than the mighty; and he that ruleth his spirit than he that taketh a city."
— **Proverbs 16:32**
Power that restrains itself reflects wisdom, not weakness.
Ratification unfolded through:

- Open debate
- Public explanation
- Willingness to delay
- Acceptance of uncertainty

Even when approval seemed close, force was withheld. Threats were avoided. Compulsion was rejected.
The apostle Paul instructs:
"If it be possible, as much as lieth in you, live peaceably with all men."
— **Romans 12:18**

Providence was visible not in speed, but in restraint.
Not in pressure, but in patience.
Not in domination, but in disciplined self-control.
God often preserves His purposes through what leaders refuse to do.

---

7. Why Ratification Matters Spiritually

If ratification had failed:

- Unity would have collapsed
- Regional conflict was likely
- The experiment in self-government might have ended

The fragile alliance formed through war could have dissolved into rivalry, distrust, or open conflict. Victory over a common enemy did not guarantee peace among former allies.
Ratification mattered because it preserved **possibility**, not perfection.
Scripture reminds us that God's guidance does not eliminate risk—it calls for trust:
"Commit thy way unto the LORD; trust also in him; and he shall bring it to pass."
— **Psalm 37:5**
Ratification was an act of commitment under uncertainty.
It required:

- Trust without guarantees
- Agreement without uniformity
- Hope without certainty

Spiritually, this moment teaches an enduring truth:
God often preserves opportunity rather than outcome.
Structure rather than success.
Responsibility rather than ease.
The Constitution did not promise righteousness.
It assumed fallibility.
It depended on virtue it could not enforce.
Providence did not guarantee what the nation would become.
It preserved the space in which obedience—or disobedience—could unfold.
That preservation was itself an act of mercy.

8. Discussion Questions (Choose 2–3)

1. Why is patience essential for lasting agreement?
2. How does humility make compromise possible?
3. What dangers arise when disagreement is silenced instead of addressed?
4. How does this lesson apply to the church today?

9. Personal & National Application

Personal

- Do I listen carefully before forming conclusions?
- Am I willing to engage disagreement patiently?

National

- Unity requires restraint
- Process matters as much as outcome
- Wisdom grows through counsel

"Better is the end of a thing than the beginning thereof."
— *Ecclesiastes 7:8*

10. Closing Reflection

Ratification was not a moment of triumph.
It was a season of patient endurance.
Debate was prolonged. Disagreement was sharp. Outcomes were uncertain. The process tested resolve not through external threat, but through internal tension. Unity was not assumed—it was fragile.
Scripture reminds us that endurance is often the soil in which wisdom grows:
"Better is the end of a thing than the beginning thereof: and the patient in spirit is better than the proud in spirit."
— *Ecclesiastes 7:8*
Providence did not preserve unity by removing disagreement.
It preserved unity by **guiding disagreement toward responsibility**.
Voices differed. Fears were expressed. Concerns were not silenced. Yet the process held. Dialogue continued. Compromise emerged not through coercion, but through restraint.
This reflects a consistent biblical principle.
God does not require immediate agreement to accomplish His purposes. He governs outcomes through patience, counsel, and measured response.
"Where no counsel is, the people fall: but in the multitude of counsellors there is safety."
— *Proverbs 11:14*

Disagreement, when submitted to truth and governed by humility, does not destroy unity—it refines it.

Scripture warns against haste in matters of weight:

"He that believeth shall not make haste."

— *Isaiah 28:16*

Ratification demanded time. It required listening. It forced leaders to acknowledge limits and address legitimate concerns rather than overpower them.

Providence honored restraint.

"Only by pride cometh contention: but with the well advised is wisdom."

— *Proverbs 13:10*

Unity endured not because differences vanished, but because responsibility prevailed over reaction. The process was preserved long enough for agreement to mature.

Ratification stands as a reminder that God often sustains unity not through unanimity, but through patience.

Providence did not rush the outcome.

It steadied the process.

And in that endurance, unity was preserved—not as triumph, but as trust exercised under God's hand.

Optional Teaching Pause (Adult Class)

You might ask:

- *Why does Scripture associate patience with wisdom?*
- *How can disagreement strengthen unity when governed rightly?*
- *Where might God be calling us to endurance rather than immediacy?*

---

11. Closing Scripture & Prayer Prompt

Read aloud:

"Teach me thy way, O LORD; I will walk in thy truth."

— *Psalm 86:11*

Prayer Prompt:

"Lord, grant us patience, wisdom, and humility as we seek unity under Your guidance."

Lesson 19 — Washington's Inauguration

Series Title

God's Providence in American History: From the Pilgrims to the Present

Theme Verse

"He that ruleth his spirit is better than he that taketh a city."
— *Proverbs 16:32*

Lesson Aim (For the Teacher)

To show how God preserved the young nation through a peaceful transfer of authority marked by humility, restraint, and public acknowledgment of dependence on God.
This lesson emphasizes **submission to responsibility**, not celebration of power.

Time Flow (Minimum 40 Minutes)

- Opening Scripture & Prayer – 4 minutes
- Biblical Framework – 10 minutes
- Historical Narrative & Providential Examples – 18 minutes
- Discussion – 5 minutes
- Application & Closing Reflection – 3 minutes

---

1. Opening Scripture Reading

Read aloud together:
"By me kings reign, and princes decree justice."
— *Proverbs 8:15*

---

2. Core Truth Statement

God preserves liberty when leaders willingly restrain themselves and acknowledge His authority.

The true test of leadership is not gaining power, but **how it is held and transferred**.

---

3. Biblical Pattern: Authority Under God

Key Scriptures

"Let every soul be subject unto the higher powers."
— *Romans 13:1*

"For rulers are not a terror to good works, but to the evil."
— *Romans 13:3*

"Except the LORD keep the city, the watchman waketh but in vain."
— *Psalm 127:1*

Teaching Point (Scripture-Anchored)

In Scripture, legitimate authority is always **delegated**, **limited**, and **accountable to God**.
(Deuteronomy 17:18–20; 1 Peter 5:2–3)
Power restrained is power preserved.

---

4. The Moment of Inauguration (1789)

When George Washington took the oath of office in 1789, the ceremony did not mark the end of uncertainty—it marked the beginning of responsibility.

The Constitution had been ratified, but it remained **untested**.

No one knew whether its balance of power would hold, whether its limits would be honored, or whether ambition would eventually overwhelm restraint.

The nation itself was still **fragile**.

- The wounds of war were recent
- Financial stability was uncertain
- Regional loyalties remained strong
- Trust in centralized authority was cautious at best

Many Americans feared that the presidency—however carefully defined—could become a new form of monarchy in time.

"Put not your trust in princes, nor in the son of man, in whom there is no help."
— *Psalm 146:3*

Nothing about this moment was automatic.

There was **no historical precedent** for a peaceful transfer of executive authority under a written constitution.

No one could point to a model and say, *"This is how it works."*

Every action would establish expectation.

Every decision would set direction.

Every restraint—or lack of it—would echo forward.

Fear of tyranny had not faded with independence.
It lingered in memory and conscience.

- Power had corrupted before
- Authority had overreached before
- Liberty had been lost gradually before

"It is better to trust in the LORD than to put confidence in man."
— *Psalm 118:8*

Washington himself recognized the weight of the moment.
He did not enter office with triumph, but with **reluctance and sobriety**.
He acknowledged personal inadequacy and publicly appealed to divine guidance.
This posture mattered.
Providence often works not merely through events—but through the spirit with which responsibility is accepted.
"God resisteth the proud, but giveth grace unto the humble."
— *James 4:6*

The survival of the republic now depended not on revolution, but on restraint.

- Would power be exercised within limits?
- Would law remain above personality?
- Would authority serve rather than dominate?

There was no guarantee the republic would endure.
There was only the opportunity to walk carefully, humbly, and deliberately.
Providence did not promise permanence.
It provided a moment.
What followed would depend on whether that moment was stewarded with wisdom.
"Commit thy way unto the LORD; trust also in him; and he shall bring it to pass."
— *Psalm 37:5*

---

5. Specific Providential Preservations

Providential Example #1 — Reluctant Acceptance of Office

As the new nation moved from framework to function, leadership once again presented both opportunity and risk.
The office of the presidency carried immense authority. Its shape would influence expectations, precedent, and public trust for generations. The first person to hold it would not merely occupy the role—he would **define it**.
In this moment, ambition would have been dangerous.

George Washington **did not seek the presidency**. He did not campaign for it. He did not present himself as indispensable. Instead, he expressed reluctance and hesitation, acknowledging his limitations and the weight of responsibility involved.

This reluctance mattered.

Washington **accepted the office unwillingly**, not because he doubted the necessity of leadership, but because he understood the burden of authority. He spoke openly of personal inadequacy and concern about meeting the expectations placed upon him.

Scripture speaks directly to this posture:

"God resisteth the proud, but giveth grace unto the humble."

— *James 4:6*

Humility here was not a performance.

It was a disposition.

Providence in this moment did not place power in the hands of someone eager to possess it. Instead, authority was entrusted to one who approached it with caution, restraint, and self-awareness.

This preserved **trust**.

Reluctant acceptance reassured a wary public that the office existed to serve the nation—not the ambition of the individual. It set a precedent that leadership was a duty rather than a prize.

Providence here worked preventatively.

God did not remove power from human hands.

He placed it where humility could restrain it.

The acceptance of office without appetite for domination reduced fear, stabilized expectations, and encouraged unity at a critical moment. Authority was exercised not to expand influence, but to preserve order.

Humility preserved trust—and trust allowed the young nation to move forward.

Theological Reflection (Optional Closing Sentence)

When leadership is accepted with reluctance rather than ambition, humility may be God's means of preservation.

Providential Example #2 — Public Acknowledgment of God

At the moment when authority was formally assumed, the new nation did not present leadership as self-derived or self-sustaining.

An **oath was taken**.

This was not merely a procedural requirement. An oath acknowledged accountability beyond human oversight. It recognized that authority, once granted, remained answerable to a higher standard.

Scripture was present.

The inclusion of Scripture underscored that governance was not to be guided by impulse or power alone, but by principles believed to be enduring and binding. The Word of God served not as ornament, but as reference—an acknowledgment that wisdom does not originate solely in office.

God's guidance was **publicly acknowledged.**

This acknowledgment was deliberate and visible. Dependence was not confined to private devotion or personal belief. It was expressed openly, before the people, at the outset of authority.

Scripture speaks clearly to this posture:

"In all thy ways acknowledge him, and he shall direct thy paths."

— *Proverbs 3:6*

This verse does not promise ease.

It promises **direction.**

Providence here was not expressed through guarantee of success.

It was expressed through **orientation of authority.**

By acknowledging God publicly, leadership established a precedent: power would be exercised under accountability, not autonomy. Authority would proceed with reference to something greater than human judgment alone.

This mattered deeply.

Public acknowledgment of God restrained expectations of absolute authority. It reminded both leaders and citizens that governance required humility, wisdom, and moral grounding.

Providence here worked through **example.**

God did not remove the burdens of leadership.

He framed them within acknowledged dependence.

The declaration of reliance at the very beginning helped preserve trust, temper ambition, and set a tone of responsibility that extended beyond ceremony.

Dependence was not hidden—it was declared.

Theological Reflection (Optional Closing Sentence)

When authority begins with acknowledgment of God, restraint may guide power from its first step.

Providential Example #3 — Civilian Authority Established

As the presidency began, another critical preservation took place—one that would shape the nation far beyond a single term.

Authority was exercised **within limits.**

Washington **submitted to the Constitution**, acknowledging that his power derived from law rather than personal authority. He did not present himself as the source of order, but as a servant of an established framework. Decisions were made within defined boundaries, not personal discretion.

Civilian authority was **affirmed**.

Military leadership did not dominate governance. The habits of command forged during war did not carry over unchecked into civil life. Authority flowed through constitutional processes rather than force or personality.

This mattered profoundly.

New nations often struggle at this juncture. Military success can overshadow civil order. Leaders accustomed to command may resist limitation. Power, once gained, is rarely relinquished easily.

That danger was present—but it was restrained.

Washington **set precedent for restraint**.

By respecting civilian governance and constitutional limits, he established expectations that authority would be temporary, accountable, and bounded. The office was defined not by what it could seize, but by what it would **refuse** to claim.

Scripture affirms the source and nature of such authority:

"For there is no power but of God: the powers that be are ordained of God."

— *Romans 13:1*

This verse does not sanctify every use of power.

It affirms that legitimate authority operates **under God's ordering**, not above it.

Providence here was not dramatic.

No spectacle marked the moment.

No force was displayed.

No declaration of dominance was made.

Instead, order was preserved quietly.

Providence was seen not in expansion, but in **submission**—submission of authority to law, of leadership to structure, and of power to restraint.

This preservation mattered deeply.

Civilian authority established at the beginning prevented future confusion between force and governance. It safeguarded liberty by anchoring power to accountability rather than personality.

Providence often works this way.

God does not always display His hand through dramatic acts. Sometimes He preserves by ensuring that power remains **properly ordered**.

Providence was seen in order, not spectacle.

Theological Reflection (Optional Closing Sentence)

When authority submits to law rather than exceeding it, order itself may testify to providence.

---

6. Why This Moment Matters

If leadership at this moment had:

- Seized excessive power
- Ignored constitutional restraint
- Dismissed accountability

the fragile republic could have collapsed into a different form of tyranny—one born not of monarchy, but of fear, admiration, or unchecked authority.

The inauguration of George Washington was not merely ceremonial. It was formative.

For the first time, a national executive authority was exercised under:

- A written constitution
- Defined limits
- Public accountability
- Temporary tenure

Nothing forced restraint except character.

Washington stood at a crossroads where precedent would matter more than personality. Every action would quietly answer an unspoken question:

Would power be accumulated—or restrained?

Providence was evident not in dramatic declarations, but in deliberate moderation.

Washington did not rule by impulse. He proceeded cautiously, aware that how authority was exercised mattered as much as who exercised it.

Scripture reminds us:

"Better is the end of a thing than the beginning thereof: and the patient in spirit is better than the proud in spirit."

— **Ecclesiastes 7:8**

Beginnings are dangerous moments. Ambition often hides behind necessity. Pride often justifies itself as urgency.

Providence preserved liberty in this moment not through strength, but through self-control—setting a pattern that power would be **limited**, **accountable**, and **temporary**.

---

7. Authority Without Idolatry

Important clarification:

- Leaders are servants, not saviors
- Respect is not worship

- Gratitude is not blind allegiance

The reverence shown to Washington was understandable—but it was not unlimited. The danger of hero-dependence has always threatened free societies. When admiration becomes reliance, liberty erodes quietly.

Scripture repeatedly warns against confusing instruments with sources:

"Put not your trust in princes, nor in the son of man, in whom there is no help."

— **Psalm 146:3**

Washington himself reinforced this truth by:

- Submitting to constitutional limits
- Deferring to law rather than personality
- Acknowledging dependence on God rather than his own wisdom

Authority was exercised without self-exaltation.

Leadership was displayed without idolatry.

This distinction matters spiritually.

Biblical leadership does not draw strength from admiration, but from humility. It recognizes that all authority is borrowed, temporary, and accountable to God.

"For there is no power but of God: the powers that be are ordained of God."

— **Romans 13:1**

Providence was visible in this moment not because a great man rose—but because a great man **refused to place himself above the office**, the law, or the Lord.

Liberty was preserved not by charisma, but by submission.

---

8. Discussion Questions (Choose 2–3)

1. Why is restraint essential in leadership?
2. How does humility build public trust?
3. What dangers arise when leaders seek power?
4. How does biblical authority differ from domination?

---

9. Personal & National Application

Personal

- Do I handle responsibility with humility?
- Am I willing to submit to limits?

National

- Peaceful transfer of power matters
- Authority must remain accountable
- Liberty depends on restraint

"Serve the LORD with fear, and rejoice with trembling."
— *Psalm 2:11*

---

10. Closing Reflection

Washington's inauguration was not triumphant—it was sobering.

Power was not seized.

It was accepted with reluctance, carried with prayer, and restrained by conscience.

From the beginning, leadership was framed not as entitlement, but as burden.

Scripture consistently presents authority as a trust received from God, not a possession claimed by man:

"For there is no power but of God: the powers that be are ordained of God."
— *Romans 13:1*

Washington did not present himself as sufficient for the task. He openly expressed inadequacy and dependence, reflecting a posture Scripture honors:

"God resisteth the proud, but giveth grace unto the humble."
— *James 4:6*

This humility was not weakness—it was restraint guided by reverence.

The public acknowledgment of God at the inauguration signaled something essential: liberty was not secured by strength alone, but by submission to higher authority.

"In all thy ways acknowledge him, and he shall direct thy paths."
— *Proverbs 3:6*

Providence preserved liberty not through spectacle or force, but through precedent.

Washington's willingness to submit himself to constitutional limits established a pattern that power must serve law, not dominate it. This aligns with Scripture's warning that unrestrained authority corrupts:

"He that ruleth his spirit is better than he that taketh a city."
— *Proverbs 16:32*

Leadership framed by humility created stability where ambition might have undone it. The moment mattered not because of ceremony, but because restraint was chosen when opportunity for dominance existed.

Providence was seen not in dramatic assertion, but in disciplined submission.

Liberty endured because power bowed.

And in that humility, God's preserving hand was quietly at work.

11. Closing Scripture & Prayer Prompt

Read aloud:

"Not unto us, O LORD, not unto us, but unto thy name give glory."

— *Psalm 115:1*

Prayer Prompt:

"Lord, grant our leaders humility, wisdom, and restraint, and help us honor You above all authority."

Lesson 20 — Early National Revivals

Series Title

God's Providence in American History: From the Pilgrims to the Present

Theme Verse

"Wilt thou not revive us again: that thy people may rejoice in thee?"
— *Psalm 85:6*

Lesson Aim (For the Teacher)

To show how God renewed spiritual life in the early Republic through seasons of revival—reminding a newly formed nation that **liberty requires ongoing dependence on God**, not past deliverance alone.

This lesson emphasizes **renewal after establishment**, not complacency.

Time Flow (Minimum 40 Minutes)

- Opening Scripture & Prayer – 4 minutes
- Biblical Framework – 10 minutes
- Historical Narrative & Providential Examples – 18 minutes
- Discussion – 5 minutes
- Application & Closing Reflection – 3 minutes

---

1. Opening Scripture Reading

Read aloud together:

"Blessed are they which do hunger and thirst after righteousness: for they shall be filled."
— *Matthew 5:6*

---

2. Core Truth Statement

God's providence does not end with political freedom; it continues through spiritual renewal.

A nation may be free—and still spiritually weak.

---

3. Biblical Pattern: Renewal After Deliverance

Key Scriptures

"Nevertheless he left not himself without witness."
— *Acts 14:17*

"If my people… shall humble themselves, and pray."
— *2 Chronicles 7:14*

"Times of refreshing shall come from the presence of the Lord."
— *Acts 3:19*

Teaching Point (Scripture-Anchored)

In Scripture, seasons of deliverance are often followed by seasons of **spiritual drift**, requiring renewed repentance and dependence on God.
(Judges 2:10–12; Psalm 80:18–19)

Revival restores what success can erode.

---

4. The Spiritual Condition of the Early Republic

Following independence, the new nation entered a season of rapid transition.

Externally, progress was visible.

- **Political structures were established**
  The Constitution was implemented, governance stabilized, and authority was exercised through lawful process rather than force.
- **Economic opportunity expanded**
  Trade increased, land was settled, and many experienced the hope of prosperity after years of deprivation.
- **National confidence increased**
  Survival against overwhelming odds fostered optimism and a growing belief in the nation's future.

Yet beneath these encouraging developments, **spiritual warning signs emerged**.

In many regions:

- **Church attendance waned**, particularly in urban centers and frontier communities
- **Religious practice became less urgent**, as survival gave way to success
- **Moral complacency grew**, with gratitude quietly replaced by presumption

Confidence increasingly rested in:

- Institutions rather than humility
- Prosperity rather than dependence
- Stability rather than vigilance

"Beware that thou forget not the LORD thy God… when thy silver and thy gold is multiplied, and all that thou hast is multiplied."
— *Deuteronomy 8:11–13*
This pattern was not new.
Scripture repeatedly records seasons where deliverance was followed by drift.

- After peace came neglect
- After blessing came forgetfulness
- After provision came pride

"Then the children of Israel did evil in the sight of the LORD, and forgat the LORD their God."
— *Judges 3:7*
The early Republic faced the same spiritual tension found throughout biblical history:
Would freedom deepen faith—or diminish it?
Liberty can strengthen obedience when paired with gratitude.
It can also weaken reverence when paired with self-reliance.
"The fear of the LORD is the beginning of wisdom."
— *Proverbs 9:10*
The nation's greatest vulnerability was not external threat—but internal drift.
Providence had preserved the nation through crisis.
Whether the nation would remain attentive to God in comfort remained an open question.
History shows that prosperity tests faith more subtly—and sometimes more severely—than persecution.
This was the soil into which revival would later come:
Not because God had abandoned the nation,
but because the nation had begun to forget its dependence on Him.

---

5. The Rise of Early National Revivals

In the years following independence, signs of spiritual drift became increasingly evident. Political freedom had been secured, but spiritual vitality had weakened in many places. Confidence in institutions began to replace dependence on God. Moral seriousness softened. Faith, in some regions, became inherited rather than lived.
In response, God stirred renewal—not through legislation or coercion, but through conscience.
Across the young nation, there arose:

- Renewed preaching of Scripture
- Clear calls to repentance
- Emphasis on personal faith, holiness, and obedience
- Renewed concern for moral responsibility before God

These movements were not uniform, but they shared common features:

- Scripture was central, not peripheral
- Sin was confronted honestly
- Grace was proclaimed clearly
- Personal transformation was emphasized over external conformity

The revivals:

- Crossed regional lines
- Affected entire communities, not just individuals
- Influenced education, missions, and social conscience
- Reinforced the connection between liberty and responsibility

Significantly, these awakenings did not originate from government authority. They arose from pulpits, homes, camp meetings, and local churches.

Scripture reminds us:

"Not by might, nor by power, but by my spirit, saith the LORD of hosts."

— **Zechariah 4:6**

Providence worked not through law, but through hearts.

Before laws could restrain behavior, consciences had to be awakened.

Before liberty could endure, character had to be renewed.

God again demonstrated a consistent pattern: **spiritual renewal precedes moral stability**.

---

6. Specific Providential Effects of Revival

Providential Example #1 — Moral Reawakening

One of the clearest effects of revival was not political action, but **moral reawakening**.

As revival spread, attention shifted inward. Individuals examined their own lives rather than focusing solely on external conditions. There was renewed concern for righteousness—not merely as an abstract ideal, but as a personal responsibility before God.

Conviction over personal sin became common.

People responded to Scripture with seriousness. Confession was not coerced. Change was not imposed. Instead, hearts were stirred by an awareness of God's holiness and their own need for alignment with it.

This conviction produced **desire for godly living**.

Behavior followed belief. Families adjusted habits. Communities emphasized integrity, honesty, and responsibility. Moral restraint was strengthened not by law alone, but by conscience informed by Scripture.

Scripture affirms the societal impact of such renewal:

"Righteousness exalteth a nation: but sin is a reproach to any people."

— *Proverbs 14:34*

This verse does not promise prosperity or immunity from hardship.
It identifies **moral alignment** as stabilizing.
Providence here did not operate through force.
It worked through **transformation of the heart**.
Moral renewal strengthened social stability because it addressed the roots of disorder. When individuals accept responsibility before God, communities gain coherence. Trust increases. Accountability becomes mutual rather than imposed.
Revival did not eliminate conflict.
It **reordered priorities**.
People were reminded that freedom without virtue collapses inward. Liberty requires restraint. Rights require responsibility. Revival reinforced these truths not by argument alone, but by lived conviction.
Providence here was preventative.
God did not wait for collapse to correct course.
He stirred conscience before fracture.
This moral reawakening did not produce perfection—but it produced **orientation**. It reminded individuals and communities alike that righteousness is not merely personal—it has collective consequence.
Moral renewal strengthened social stability because it aligned conduct with conviction.

Theological Reflection (Optional Closing Sentence)
When conscience is awakened before disorder spreads, revival may be God's means of preserving stability.

Providential Example #2 — Expansion of Education and Missions
One of the enduring effects of revival was not limited to immediate moral response—it extended into **long-term investment in knowledge and truth**.
As revival renewed concern for righteousness, it also awakened concern for **understanding**. Faith was not treated as sentiment alone. It was something to be taught, explained, preserved, and passed on.
This revival energy fueled **education**.
Schools and colleges were founded or strengthened with the conviction that an informed conscience mattered. Literacy was emphasized so that individuals could read Scripture for themselves rather than rely solely on secondhand instruction. Education was viewed not as a threat to faith, but as a servant of it.
Mission efforts expanded alongside learning.

Revival stirred concern not only for personal faith, but for the spiritual condition of others—both nearby and distant. Scripture distribution increased. Teaching accompanied proclamation. Faith was shared with the understanding that truth must be communicated clearly to endure.
Scripture speaks directly to the danger of neglected instruction:
"My people are destroyed for lack of knowledge."
— *Hosea 4:6*
This verse does not condemn ignorance alone.
It warns of **loss through neglect**.
Providence here worked through **preparation**, not urgency alone.
God did not allow revival to burn out quickly. He channeled its energy into structures that could preserve truth beyond a single generation. Education and missions became vessels through which revival's influence could continue even after the initial fervor subsided.
This mattered deeply.
Emotional response fades.
Conviction requires reinforcement.
Truth must be taught to endure.
By strengthening literacy, education, and Scripture access, revival safeguarded future conscience. It ensured that moral reawakening would not depend solely on memory, but on **instruction anchored in God's Word**.
Providence here was generational.
God used revival not only to awaken hearts, but to **preserve truth across time**. What began as renewed devotion matured into sustained teaching, enabling faith to be examined, understood, and transmitted faithfully.
Revival preserved more than passion.
It preserved **knowledge**.

Theological Reflection (Optional Closing Sentence)
When revival strengthens instruction as well as devotion, God may be preserving truth for generations yet unseen.

Providential Example #3 — Social Restraint and Compassion
One of the most visible effects of revival was not confined to worship gatherings—it appeared in **how people treated one another**.
Spiritual renewal encouraged **restraint**.
As conscience was awakened, individuals became more aware of personal responsibility. Ethical conduct was emphasized not merely as social expectation, but as obedience before

God. Dishonesty, cruelty, and neglect were increasingly recognized as sins, not merely personal failings.

This restraint fostered **compassion**.

Care for the poor, the vulnerable, and the overlooked increased. Communities took greater responsibility for their own members. Assistance was offered not as entitlement, but as stewardship—an expression of faith lived outwardly.

Scripture defines such faith clearly:

"Pure religion and undefiled before God and the Father is this, To visit the fatherless and widows in their affliction, and to keep himself unspotted from the world."

—*James 1:27*

This verse unites two truths:

- **Compassion toward others**
- **Moral restraint within oneself**

Revival did not remove hardship from society.

It reshaped how hardship was addressed.

Ethical responsibility increased because people recognized that freedom without compassion leads to exploitation. Community accountability strengthened because individuals understood that personal conduct affected collective stability.

Providence here did not operate through legislation alone.

It worked through **transformed lives**.

When hearts changed, behavior followed. Care was offered voluntarily rather than imposed. Responsibility was assumed rather than enforced. Revival produced a moral climate where compassion and restraint reinforced one another.

This mattered deeply.

Societies fracture when compassion disappears or restraint collapses. Revival countered both tendencies by renewing conscience and reinforcing accountability.

Providence here was practical.

God expressed His preserving work not through spectacle, but through ordinary acts of faithfulness—neighbors caring for neighbors, communities guarding moral standards, individuals choosing righteousness in daily life.

Providence expressed itself through **transformed lives**.

Theological Reflection (Optional Closing Sentence)
When compassion grows alongside restraint, revival may be God's means of preserving both conscience and community.

---

7. Revival Without Perfection
Important clarification:

- Revivals did not eliminate sin
- Not every emotional response was wise
- Excesses and imbalances occurred
- Discernment remained necessary

The Bible never portrays revival as flawless. Even in seasons of genuine spiritual awakening, human weakness remains present. Emotion can outpace understanding. Zeal can exceed wisdom. Not every claim reflects true transformation.
Yet Scripture affirms that God does not wait for perfect conditions before working.
"The sacrifices of God are a broken spirit: a broken and a contrite heart, O God, thou wilt not despise."
— **Psalm 51:17**
"For thus saith the high and lofty One that inhabiteth eternity… I dwell… with him also that is of a contrite and humble spirit."
— **Isaiah 57:15**
God revives **imperfect people**, not perfected ones.
Revival does not mean:

- Sin disappears
- Judgment is suspended
- Discipline is unnecessary

It means hearts are softened, consciences awakened, and direction corrected.
Providence works patiently—allowing growth, correction, and refinement over time.
The spiritual fruit of these revivals was not measured by emotional intensity alone, but by:

- Lasting moral reform
- Increased commitment to Scripture
- Renewed emphasis on education and discipleship
- A deeper awareness of accountability before God

Revival did not make the nation righteous.
It preserved the possibility of righteousness.
Providence once again restrained decline—not by removing weakness, but by renewing humility.

---

8. Discussion Questions (Choose 2–3)

1. Why does spiritual renewal remain necessary after success?
2. How can prosperity dull spiritual hunger?
3. What distinguishes true revival from emotional enthusiasm?
4. How does revival benefit both church and society?

---

9. Personal & National Application

Personal

- Am I pursuing renewal or relying on past faith?
- Do I hunger for righteousness?

National

- Spiritual vitality cannot be legislated
- Renewal sustains liberty
- Dependence must be continual

"Renew our days as of old."

— *Lamentations 5:21*

---

10. Closing Reflection

The early Republic learned a vital truth:

freedom achieved does not mean faith preserved.

Political independence removed external rule, but it did not remove internal need. Liberty could establish opportunity, yet it could not sustain virtue on its own. Scripture warns that freedom, when detached from truth, quickly turns inward:

"For, brethren, ye have been called unto liberty; only use not liberty for an occasion to the flesh."

— *Galatians 5:13*

Providence did not cease with independence. Instead, it continued quietly—working not through new institutions, but through renewed hearts.

Revival addressed what laws could not: conscience.

As Scripture spread and conviction deepened, God renewed spiritual awareness among a people learning how to live responsibly with freedom:

"Wilt thou not revive us again: that thy people may rejoice in thee?"

— *Psalm 85:6*

This renewal was not dramatic power, but inward correction. It reminded the nation that liberty requires restraint, and blessing requires remembrance:

"Beware that thou forget not the LORD thy God."
— *Deuteronomy 8:11*
Providence often preserves by restoring what fades quietly. Revival did not replace liberty—it guarded it by recalling hearts to accountability before God.
Without such renewal, freedom becomes fragile. With it, liberty gains moral footing strong enough to endure.
Providence was still at work—not by granting something new, but by renewing what had already been given.

---

11. Closing Scripture & Prayer Prompt
Read aloud:
"Create in me a clean heart, O God; and renew a right spirit within me."
— *Psalm 51:10*
Prayer Prompt:
"Lord, renew our hearts, restore our hunger for righteousness, and keep us dependent on You."

Lesson 21 — Preservation of Unity

Series Title

God's Providence in American History: From the Pilgrims to the Present

Theme Verse

"Behold, how good and how pleasant it is for brethren to dwell together in unity!"
— *Psalm 133:1*

Lesson Aim (For the Teacher)

To show how God preserved unity in the early Republic not by removing disagreement, but by restraining division, encouraging compromise, and cultivating shared responsibility—demonstrating that **unity must be maintained intentionally after freedom is secured**. This lesson emphasizes **preservation through restraint**, not forced agreement.

Time Flow (Minimum 40 Minutes)

- Opening Scripture & Prayer – 4 minutes
- Biblical Framework – 10 minutes
- Historical Narrative & Providential Examples – 18 minutes
- Discussion – 5 minutes
- Application & Closing Reflection – 3 minutes

---

1. Opening Scripture Reading

Read aloud together:

"Endeavouring to keep the unity of the Spirit in the bond of peace."
— *Ephesians 4:3*

---

2. Core Truth Statement

Unity is not self-sustaining; it must be guarded through humility, restraint, and shared commitment to truth.

Freedom multiplies choices—unity requires discipline.

---

3. Biblical Pattern: Unity Requires Guarding

Key Scriptures

"Only by pride cometh contention."
— *Proverbs 13:10*

"If it be possible, as much as lieth in you, live peaceably with all men."
— *Romans 12:18*

"Let nothing be done through strife or vainglory; but in lowliness of mind."
— *Philippians 2:3*

Teaching Point (Scripture-Anchored)

Scripture teaches that unity is preserved not by eliminating differences, but by cultivating **humility**, **self-restraint**, and **commitment to shared truth**.
(Psalm 133:1; Colossians 3:12–14)
Unity fractures when pride replaces humility.

---

4. The Fragile State of the Early Republic

After independence and the formation of a constitutional government, the young nation entered a period of uneasy balance.
Victory in war had secured freedom—but it had not erased division.
Beneath the surface of shared achievement, **significant fractures remained.**

- **Regional differences were strong**
  The priorities of New England, the Mid-Atlantic, and the Southern states often conflicted.
  Economic systems, cultural traditions, and local loyalties shaped how citizens understood government and liberty.
- **Economic interests diverged**
  Debates emerged over debt, taxation, trade, and monetary policy.
  Farmers, merchants, creditors, and laborers viewed national policy through very different lenses.
- **Political disagreements intensified**
  Competing visions for the future of the republic took shape.
  Questions about federal authority, state sovereignty, and individual liberty produced sharp and sometimes personal disputes.
- **Distrust between factions existed**
  Suspicion grew that opposing views threatened the survival of the nation itself.
  Motives were questioned, and loyalty was not always assumed.

"Only by pride cometh contention."
— *Proverbs 13:10*
Unity, it became clear, was **not guaranteed by shared victory**.
The bonds forged under external threat now faced the test of internal disagreement.
The discipline required for war did not automatically translate into the patience required for peace.
"A kingdom divided against itself is brought to desolation."
— *Matthew 12:25*
The survival of the republic now depended on something different than courage or sacrifice.
It required:

- Restraint instead of reaction
- Dialogue instead of dominance
- Shared moral reference instead of raw power

Providence had preserved unity in crisis.
Whether unity could be preserved in freedom would depend on humility, wisdom, and continued moral alignment.
History would soon reveal that internal division often poses a greater threat to a nation than any external enemy.
Providence had carried the nation this far.
Its continued preservation would test whether liberty could be stewarded as faithfully as it had been won.

---

5. Specific Providential Preservations

Providential Example #1 — Peaceful Disagreement

As disagreements intensified, the risk was not merely division—it was **escalation**.
Debates were sharp. Positions were strongly held. Emotions ran high. Issues under discussion touched power, authority, regional interest, and long-term consequence. History shows that such moments often turn volatile.
That outcome was possible here.
Yet conflict remained **largely verbal**.
Arguments were made openly, forcefully, and repeatedly—but they were argued through words rather than weapons. Institutions were used rather than bypassed. Procedures were followed even when outcomes were uncertain or frustrating.
This restraint mattered.
Processes absorbed pressure that might otherwise have erupted into violence. Debate was channeled through councils, conventions, and lawful assemblies. Disagreement did not disappear—but it was **contained**.

Scripture speaks to this kind of restraint:
"The discretion of a man deferreth his anger; and it is his glory to pass over a transgression."
— *Proverbs 19:11*
This verse does not praise indifference.
It praises **delayed reaction**.
Providence here was not seen in immediate harmony.
It was seen in **controlled response**.
God preserved unity not by silencing disagreement, but by restraining how disagreement was expressed. Reaction was slowed. Anger was deferred. Decisions were delayed long enough for reason to reassert itself.
This pattern appears repeatedly in Scripture.
God often preserves His people by governing **pace**—slowing impulse, tempering reaction, and allowing space for reflection. When anger is deferred, destruction is often prevented.
Providence here worked quietly.
No dramatic intervention stopped violence.
Violence simply did not take hold.
Discretion became a safeguard. Process became a buffer. Time became an ally. Together, these restrained escalation when passion could have overtaken judgment.
Unity was preserved not by agreement, but by restraint.

Theological Reflection (Optional Closing Sentence)
When anger is deferred and process is honored, restraint itself may be the work of providence.

Providential Example #2 — Willingness to Compromise
As disagreement continued, unity was not preserved through one side prevailing over another.
It was preserved through **compromise**.
Participants on all sides recognized limits—limits of persuasion, limits of certainty, and limits of what any single group could justly demand. Rather than pressing every advantage, leaders accepted that enduring unity would require **mutual concession**.
This choice was costly.
Compromise meant relinquishing preferred outcomes. It meant accepting solutions that were **imperfect**, provisional, and sometimes personally unsatisfying. Yet those involved understood that insisting on total agreement risked something far worse than dissatisfaction—**collapse**.
Scripture speaks to the wisdom of such restraint:
"Better is a dry morsel, and quietness therewith, than an house full of sacrifices with strife."
— *Proverbs 17:1*

This proverb does not glorify scarcity.
It elevates **peace over excess.**
Providence here was not expressed through ideal solutions.
It was expressed through **shared restraint.**
Mutual concessions allowed dialogue to continue. Recognition of limits kept debate from hardening into hostility. Acceptance of imperfect outcomes preserved cooperation long enough for stability to form.
This mattered deeply.
Many conflicts fail not because solutions are unavailable, but because parties refuse to accept anything short of total victory. When compromise is rejected, unity fractures and force fills the void.
That did not occur here.
Providence worked through humility.
God did not grant flawless agreement.
He preserved **sufficient agreement.**
The willingness to compromise acknowledged a biblical truth: human wisdom is partial, and peace often requires accepting less than ideal outcomes for the sake of greater good. Mutual restraint guarded the future more effectively than insistence ever could.
Providence often works this way.
It restrains ambition on every side, preserving unity not by eliminating disagreement, but by tempering it with humility.

Theological Reflection (Optional Closing Sentence)
When peace is chosen over perfection, restraint itself may be the instrument of providence.

Providential Example #3 — Shared Moral Framework
Despite significant differences in region, interest, and opinion, unity did not dissolve because a **shared moral framework** remained intact.
Disagreements were real.
Perspectives varied.
Solutions were contested.
Yet beneath these differences, a common moral language persisted.
Scripture continued to inform conscience.
Biblical concepts—right and wrong, justice and restraint, accountability and responsibility—remained part of the shared vocabulary. Even when conclusions differed, arguments were often framed within a common understanding of moral obligation rather than raw self-interest.

This mattered deeply.

When societies lose shared moral reference points, disagreement quickly becomes irreconcilable. Without common standards, debate turns into power struggle, and unity fractures under competing claims.

That did not happen here.

Accountability was still valued.

Leaders expected to answer not only to constituents, but to higher principles. Appeals were made to conscience, not merely advantage. Decisions were weighed in moral terms, not solely practical ones.

Scripture captures the stabilizing role of such grounding:

"Righteousness exalteth a nation: but sin is a reproach to any people."

— *Proverbs 14:34*

This verse does not claim that righteousness eliminates disagreement.

It affirms that righteousness **stabilizes** a people.

Providence here was not expressed through uniformity.

It was expressed through **continuity of moral reference**.

Because Scripture-informed conscience remained influential, disagreement could occur without dissolving into hostility. Compromise did not feel like surrender of principle, but negotiation within shared ethical boundaries.

This shared framework acted as a **moral guardrail**.

It limited how far disagreement could go. It restrained extremes. It preserved mutual recognition of responsibility—even among those who strongly opposed one another's positions.

Providence often works this way.

God preserves unity not by forcing agreement, but by sustaining the values that make agreement possible. When conscience remains informed and accountability respected, division does not have the final word.

Shared values supported continued unity—not because differences disappeared, but because restraint endured.

Theological Reflection (Optional Closing Sentence)
When conscience remains anchored in shared truth, unity may endure even amid disagreement.

---

6. Unity Without Uniformity
Important clarification:

- Unity did not mean sameness
- Disagreement was permitted
- Debate was expected

The unity preserved in the early republic was not based on identical opinions, backgrounds, or interests. Differences remained—regional, economic, theological, and political. What mattered was not the absence of disagreement, but the manner in which disagreement was handled.
Biblical unity has never required uniformity. Scripture consistently affirms that God works through diversity ordered by love and humility.
"Forbearing one another in love."
— **Ephesians 4:2**
This kind of unity:

- Honors conscience rather than suppressing it
- Allows disagreement without dissolving relationship
- Requires patience, restraint, and charity

The early nation learned—sometimes imperfectly—that:

- Debate could occur without violence
- Strong convictions did not require coercion
- Order could be preserved without forced agreement

Scripture describes this balance clearly:
"Endeavouring to keep the unity of the Spirit in the bond of peace."
— **Ephesians 4:3**
Unity was not achieved by erasing difference, but by placing shared commitments—law, process, and moral responsibility—above personal victory.
Providence preserved unity not by eliminating diversity, but by restraining pride and encouraging mutual endurance.

7. Why Preservation Matters

Unity is easiest during:

- Crisis
- War
- Shared external threat

In such moments, differences are temporarily overshadowed by survival.

Unity is hardest during:

- Peace
- Prosperity
- Expansion

When danger passes, restraint weakens. Gratitude fades. Personal interest rises. Without vigilance, division grows quietly.

Scripture repeatedly warns of this pattern:

"And the people served the LORD all the days of Joshua… And there arose another generation after them, which knew not the LORD."

— **Judges 2:7, 10**

Preservation matters because unity does not sustain itself automatically. It must be guarded intentionally—especially after deliverance.

The early republic faced a dangerous transition:

- From dependence to confidence
- From survival to growth
- From shared sacrifice to competing interests

Providence preserved unity during this fragile season—not by removing disagreement, but by restraining collapse.

Scripture reminds us:

"Behold, how good and how pleasant it is for brethren to dwell together in unity!"

— **Psalm 133:1**

Unity is not a permanent achievement. It is a maintained discipline.

God's providence in this era did not guarantee harmony—but it preserved the opportunity for continued cooperation. The survival of unity after victory was itself a quiet mercy.

---

8. Discussion Questions (Choose 2–3)

1. Why is unity harder to preserve than to form?
2. How does humility protect unity?
3. What role does restraint play in peace?
4. How can unity be maintained amid disagreement?

---

9. Personal & National Application

Personal

- Am I quick to listen and slow to react?
- Do I value unity enough to practice restraint?

National

- Unity requires ongoing effort
- Freedom magnifies responsibility
- Shared truth sustains peace

"Let all things be done with charity."
— *1 Corinthians 16:14*

---

10. Closing Reflection

The early Republic survived not because disagreement disappeared,
but because division was restrained.

Differences were real. Convictions were strong. Passions often ran high. Yet collapse did not follow conflict, because restraint governed response. Scripture reminds us that preservation often depends not on agreement, but on self-control:

"He that is slow to anger is better than the mighty; and he that ruleth his spirit than he that taketh a city."
— *Proverbs 16:32*

Unity endured because pride was checked. Leaders recognized that force would destroy what persuasion could preserve. Rather than silencing opposition, they allowed debate to run its course—trusting process over pressure:

"Only by pride cometh contention: but with the well advised is wisdom."
— *Proverbs 13:10*

Processes were honored even when outcomes were uncertain. Law restrained impulse. Patience replaced coercion. This restraint reflected a sober understanding of human nature:

"The discretion of a man deferreth his anger; and it is his glory to pass over a transgression."
— *Proverbs 19:11*

Most importantly, shared values remained central. Though opinions differed, a common moral language—shaped by Scripture—still informed conscience and accountability:

"Righteousness exalteth a nation."
— *Proverbs 14:34*

Providence did not eliminate disagreement. It preserved unity by limiting its destructive reach. Quiet preservation, not dramatic triumph, sustained the nation during its most vulnerable moments.

God's hand was seen not in silencing voices, but in restraining hearts.
"Except the LORD build the house, they labour in vain that build it."
— *Psalm 127:1*
Providence often works this way—unnoticed, uncelebrated, yet essential—keeping what might easily have been lost.

---

11. Closing Scripture & Prayer Prompt
Read aloud:
"Now the God of patience and consolation grant you to be likeminded one toward another."
— *Romans 15:5*
Prayer Prompt:
"Lord, teach us to guard unity with humility, patience, and love."

SECTION V - CIVIL WAR & NATIONAL TESTING

Judgment, Humility, and Mercy in a Divided Land

"Every kingdom divided against itself is brought to desolation."
— **Matthew 12:25**

Section Purpose

This section examines one of the darkest chapters in American history—not as a tale of heroes and villains, but as a season of **national testing**.

Here, providence is not seen primarily in deliverance from enemies, but in:

- **Exposure of national sin**
- **Humbling of pride**
- **Calls to repentance**
- **Preservation through mercy rather than triumph**

This is not a section about victory.

It is a section about **cost**.

Lessons in This Section

- **Lesson 22:** A Nation Divided
- **Lesson 23:** Lincoln's Humility Before God
- **Lesson 24:** Turning Points No One Expected
- **Lesson 25:** Preservation, Not Destruction

Guiding Truth

God sometimes allows division and suffering to reveal sin, humble a people, and redirect a nation toward repentance.

(Optional Closing Line for Print or Teaching)

"Providence does not always spare a nation from pain—but it never wastes suffering."

Teaching Orientation (Leader Use)

As you enter this section, remind the class:

- Suffering is not always a sign of abandonment
- Judgment and mercy often walk together
- National pride can invite national correction

Encourage the class to:

- Listen carefully
- Avoid triumphalism
- Approach the material with humility and prayer

Lesson 22 — A Nation Divided

Series Title

God's Providence in American History: From the Pilgrims to the Present

Theme Verse

"Every kingdom divided against itself is brought to desolation."
— *Matthew 12:25*

Lesson Aim (For the Teacher)

To show how deep moral, spiritual, and social divisions weakened the nation long before the first shots were fired, demonstrating that **division is often the fruit of unresolved sin and ignored warnings**.

This lesson emphasizes **exposure before judgment**, not political blame.

Time Flow (Minimum 40 Minutes)

- Opening Scripture & Prayer – 4 minutes
- Biblical Framework – 10 minutes
- Historical Reality & Providential Observations – 18 minutes
- Discussion – 5 minutes
- Application & Closing Reflection – 3 minutes

---

1. Opening Scripture Reading

Read aloud together:

"If ye bite and devour one another, take heed that ye be not consumed one of another."
— *Galatians 5:15*

---

2. Core Truth Statement

Division weakens what strength cannot protect.

When unity is neglected, collapse becomes possible—even among those who share history, faith, and heritage.

---

3. Biblical Pattern: Division as Warning

Key Scriptures

"Where there is no vision, the people perish."
— *Proverbs 29:18*

"Pride goeth before destruction."
— *Proverbs 16:18*

"Sin is a reproach to any people."
— *Proverbs 14:34*

Teaching Point (Scripture-Anchored)

Scripture consistently shows that division is often **preceded by pride, moral compromise, and ignored correction**, serving as a warning before judgment falls.
(1 Kings 12:1–19; Hosea 10:1–2)
God exposes fractures before allowing collapse.

---

4. The Long Road to Division

The Civil War did not arise suddenly, nor did it emerge from a single decision or failure.
It was the culmination of **decades of unresolved tension**—tensions that were managed, delayed, and negotiated, but never fully resolved.
Beneath outward stability, pressure steadily increased.
The conflict grew from several interwoven realities:

- **Moral contradiction**
  The nation affirmed liberty while tolerating slavery.
  This contradiction strained conscience, Scripture, and national identity.
  Appeals to unity often avoided addressing the deeper moral fracture.
- **Economic interests**
  Regional economies became increasingly dependent on opposing systems of labor and production.
  What benefited one region threatened another, hardening positions over time.
- **Regional identity**
  Loyalty to state, culture, and local tradition frequently outweighed loyalty to national unity.
  Shared victory in the Revolution did not produce shared moral agreement in peace.
- **Political compromise**
  Repeated agreements postponed open conflict but failed to resolve the root injustice.
  Each compromise bought time—but also deepened mistrust.

"They have healed also the hurt of the daughter of my people slightly, saying, Peace, peace; when there is no peace."
— *Jeremiah 6:14*
Avoiding conflict did not remove sin—it **postponed reckoning**.
The nation increasingly relied on delay rather than repentance, procedure rather than transformation.
Scripture warns of this pattern:
"Because sentence against an evil work is not executed speedily, therefore the heart of the sons of men is fully set in them to do evil."
— *Ecclesiastes 8:11*
Time did not heal the wound.
It allowed it to deepen.
What began as tension became division.
Division hardened into hostility.
Hostility made conflict inevitable.
Providence, in this season, did not immediately restrain the consequences.
Instead, it allowed the truth to surface—slowly, painfully, unmistakably.
"Be sure your sin will find you out."
— *Numbers 32:23*
The long road to division reveals a sobering truth:
Unaddressed sin does not disappear. It matures.
God's providence sometimes delays judgment to allow repentance.
When repentance is refused, delay becomes preparation—not for peace, but for correction.
The war that followed was not merely political or economic.
It was the tragic unveiling of a moral failure left unresolved for too long.

---

5. Moral Tension at the Core
At the heart of division lay a deep moral contradiction:
- A nation founded on liberty
- A society tolerating bondage

This contradiction strained:
- Conscience
- Unity
- Moral authority

God often allows contradictions to surface before correcting them.

.

6. Providence Through Exposure

Providential Example #1 — Failed Compromises

Not all compromise heals.

In this period, repeated compromises were attempted with the hope of preserving unity and avoiding conflict. For a time, these agreements appeared successful. They delayed confrontation. They postponed crisis. They gave the appearance of stability.

But they did not heal the division.

Instead, each temporary solution allowed deeper issues to remain unresolved. Underlying moral disagreements were deferred rather than addressed. Tensions were quieted, not reconciled. Over time, frustration hardened, and bitterness increased.

Scripture speaks directly to this kind of false peace:

"They have healed also the hurt of the daughter of my people slightly, saying, Peace, peace; when there is no peace."

— *Jeremiah 6:14*

This verse does not condemn peace.

It condemns **superficial peace**.

Providence here did not appear as immediate resolution.

It appeared as **exposure**.

By allowing compromises to fail, God revealed that unity built on avoidance could not endure. Temporary agreements masked deeper wounds—but only for a season. Eventually, the inadequacy of these solutions became undeniable.

This exposure served a purpose.

It clarified that some divisions could not be healed through half-measures. Moral questions demanded moral clarity. Postponement was no longer sufficient. What had been buried beneath procedure and negotiation surfaced into full view.

Providence sometimes works this way.

God allows provisional solutions to run their course so that their limitations are made clear. When false peace collapses, it forces recognition of reality. The failure itself becomes a teacher.

This was not cruelty—it was mercy through truth.

Had these compromises succeeded indefinitely, injustice and division would have remained hidden beneath surface calm. Instead, exposure made clear that healing required more than delay—it required confrontation with truth.

Providence did not create the conflict.

It **refused to allow illusion to endure**.

Theological Reflection (Optional Closing Sentence)

When peace is declared without repentance or resolution, God may allow it to fail so truth can no longer be ignored.

Providential Example #2 — Hardened Positions

As unresolved issues persisted, dialogue gradually changed in character.

What had once been cautious disagreement hardened into fixed positions. Words grew sharper. Motives were questioned. Trust—once strained—began to erode. Fear increasingly shaped decisions, replacing patience and good faith.

This was not sudden.

It developed slowly, over time, as repeated warnings went unheeded and opportunities for correction were resisted. Appeals were made. Counsel was offered. Compromise was attempted. Yet hearts grew increasingly resistant to reconsideration.

Scripture describes this progression with clarity:

"He, that being often reproved hardeneth his neck, shall suddenly be destroyed, and that without remedy."

— *Proverbs 29:1*

This verse does not condemn conviction.

It warns against **resistance to correction**.

Providence here was revealed through **exposure of the heart**.

As positions hardened, it became clear that the issue was no longer merely disagreement over policy or process. Moral convictions had crystallized. Fear of loss overshadowed willingness to listen. The space for persuasion narrowed.

God often allows such hardening to become visible.

When patience is repeatedly rejected, restraint eventually gives way to clarity. Hardened positions expose the depth of division that delay can conceal. What was once manageable becomes unmistakable.

This exposure served a purpose.

It stripped away the illusion that time alone could heal the conflict. It revealed that neutrality was no longer sustainable. The refusal to yield to correction intensified division, making the stakes unavoidable.

Providence does not always soften hearts.

Sometimes it **reveals hardness**, so that responsibility is no longer hidden behind uncertainty.

When correction is resisted, God may allow consequences to unfold, not to create division—but to expose it.

The hardening did not surprise God.
It confirmed what had been forming unseen.

Theological Reflection (Optional Closing Sentence)
When correction is persistently resisted, God may allow hardness to surface so truth can no longer be deferred.

Providential Example #3 — Loss of Shared Moral Language
As division deepened, something more fundamental than political disagreement was lost.
A shared moral language began to fracture.
Words that once carried common meaning no longer did. Appeals to conscience increasingly fell on divided understandings of right and wrong. Concepts once assumed—justice, obligation, accountability—were interpreted through competing moral frameworks.
Common ground narrowed.
Dialogue became more difficult not merely because positions differed, but because **foundational assumptions no longer aligned**. Participants spoke past one another, using familiar language to express fundamentally different convictions.
Scripture speaks to this reality with sober clarity:
"Can two walk together, except they be agreed?"
— *Amos 3:3*
This verse does not demand uniform opinion.
It highlights the necessity of **shared direction**.
Providence here was seen in **exposure, not resolution**.
God allowed the loss of shared moral language to become unmistakable. What compromise and patience had concealed was now revealed: unity without shared truth is fragile and temporary. Without common moral reference points, disagreement cannot be meaningfully reconciled.
This exposure mattered.
It made clear that procedural unity cannot outlast moral divergence. Institutions can restrain conflict only for a time. When moral agreement fractures, cohesion weakens regardless of structure.
Providence sometimes works by allowing such losses to surface.
God does not force unity where truth is no longer shared. Instead, He allows the consequences of divergence to become visible, so responsibility is no longer hidden behind ambiguity.
This was not sudden abandonment.
It was gradual exposure.

The loss of shared moral language did not cause division—it revealed how far division had already progressed. Unity had depended on shared truth. When that truth fractured, unity followed.

Providence was seen not in preventing this outcome, but in **making it unmistakably clear**.

Theological Reflection (Optional Closing Sentence)

When shared truth is lost, unity becomes a matter of restraint rather than agreement—and restraint cannot endure indefinitely.

---

7. Judgment Begins with Exposure

Important clarification:

- Division itself was not the final judgment
- It was a warning stage
- A call to repentance largely unheeded

Before God disciplines openly, He often exposes inward fracture. Scripture consistently shows that judgment does not begin with destruction—it begins with revelation.

"For the time is come that judgment must begin at the house of God."

— **1 Peter 4:17**

In the years leading to the Civil War, division intensified not because truth was unclear, but because it was increasingly resisted. Compromise delayed confrontation, but it did not resolve contradiction. What had long been tolerated was now being revealed.

Exposure looked like:

- Hardened rhetoric replacing reasoned dialogue
- Moral contradictions becoming unavoidable
- Trust eroding between regions and institutions
- Appeals to convenience replacing appeals to conscience

This stage was merciful—even though it was painful.

God's pattern throughout Scripture is consistent:

- He exposes sin before He corrects it
- He reveals fracture before He allows collapse
- He warns before He disciplines

"Because sentence against an evil work is not executed speedily, therefore the heart of the sons of men is fully set in them to do evil."

— **Ecclesiastes 8:11**

Division was not yet judgment—it was the alarm.

The nation still had opportunities:

- To repent

- To realign morally
- To address injustice honestly

But exposure alone does not heal. When warnings are ignored, exposure gives way to correction.

Scripture cautions:

"He, that being often reproved hardeneth his neck, shall suddenly be destroyed, and that without remedy."

— **Proverbs 29:1**

God exposed division not to humiliate, but to invite repentance. The tragedy was not that the nation fractured—the tragedy was that the warning went largely unanswered.

Providence speaks gently before it speaks loudly.

---

8. Discussion Questions (Choose 2–3)

1. Why does God allow division to grow before intervening?
2. How do unresolved sins weaken unity?
3. Why are temporary solutions often ineffective?
4. What warnings can be ignored too long?

---

9. Personal & National Application

Personal

- Are there divisions in my life God is exposing?
- Do I resist correction or receive it?

National

- Moral contradiction weakens unity
- Compromise cannot replace repentance
- Division signals need for humility

"Search me, O God, and know my heart."

— *Psalm 139:23*

---

10. Closing Reflection

The nation did not fall apart overnight.

It unraveled slowly, as warnings were ignored and wounds were left untreated.

Division was not sudden—it was revealed. What had long been present beneath the surface eventually came into view. Scripture reminds us that neglect, not surprise, often precedes collapse:

"Because I have called, and ye refused; I have stretched out my hand, and no man regarded."

— *Proverbs 1:24*

Compromises delayed consequences, but they did not heal the underlying injury. Temporary peace masked deeper fractures:

"They have healed also the hurt of the daughter of my people slightly, saying, Peace, peace; when there is no peace."

— *Jeremiah 6:14*

Providence did not immediately remove the tension. Instead, it allowed exposure. What could no longer be ignored was brought into the open—not to delight in fracture, but to reveal the cost of resisting correction:

"He, that being often reproved hardeneth his neck, shall suddenly be destroyed, and that without remedy."

— *Proverbs 29:1*

Division was not created by a single event. It was uncovered by time. God's patience restrained judgment, but His truth eventually revealed reality:

"For there is nothing covered, that shall not be revealed; neither hid, that shall not be known."

— *Luke 12:2*

Providence sometimes speaks through fracture before judgment—not to hasten destruction, but to expose the seriousness of sin and the urgency of repentance:

"Come, and let us return unto the LORD: for he hath torn, and he will heal us; he hath smitten, and he will bind us up."

— *Hosea 6:1*

What followed was not inevitable destruction, but a moment of reckoning. Whether correction would be received—or resisted—would determine what came next.

God's providence was not absent in the unraveling.

It was warning—spoken patiently, clearly, and at great cost.

---

11. Closing Scripture & Prayer Prompt

Read aloud:

"Turn thou us unto thee, O LORD, and we shall be turned."

— *Lamentations 5:21*

Prayer Prompt:

"Lord, expose what divides us, humble us before correction is required, and teach us to seek Your truth."

Lesson 23 — Lincoln's Humility Before God

Series Title

God's Providence in American History: From the Pilgrims to the Present

Theme Verse

"Righteousness belongeth unto thee, O Lord, but unto us confusion of faces."
— *Daniel 9:7*

Lesson Aim (For the Teacher)

To show how, during the nation's greatest internal conflict, its leader publicly acknowledged God's sovereignty, confessed national sin, and called for humility—demonstrating that **true leadership bows before God, especially in times of judgment.**

This lesson emphasizes **repentance over rhetoric.**

Time Flow (Minimum 40 Minutes)

- Opening Scripture & Prayer – 4 minutes
- Biblical Framework – 10 minutes
- Historical Narrative & Providential Examples – 18 minutes
- Discussion – 5 minutes
- Application & Closing Reflection – 3 minutes

---

1. Opening Scripture Reading

Read aloud together:

"Wherefore doth a living man complain, a man for the punishment of his sins?"
— *Lamentations 3:39*

---

2. Core Truth Statement

In times of national suffering, God honors humility more than confidence and repentance more than explanation.

Judgment invites confession, not justification.

---

3. Biblical Pattern: Leaders Who Humble Themselves

Key Scriptures

"If my people… shall humble themselves, and pray."
— *2 Chronicles 7:14*
"Humble yourselves therefore under the mighty hand of God."
— *1 Peter 5:6*
"The sacrifices of God are a broken spirit."
— *Psalm 51:17*

Teaching Point (Scripture-Anchored)

Scripture shows that when leaders publicly humble themselves before God, they model repentance and invite mercy—even when outcomes remain painful.
(Daniel 9:3–19; Joel 2:12–17)
Humility does not guarantee relief—but it aligns the heart with truth.

---

4. The Context of Lincoln's Words

When Abraham Lincoln spoke during the Civil War, he did so in a nation overwhelmed by suffering and uncertainty.
The war had exacted a staggering cost:

- **Casualties mounted rapidly**
  Battles claimed lives by the tens of thousands.
  Nearly every community felt the loss of sons, fathers, and brothers.
- **Families were devastated**
  Homes across the nation bore grief.
  Mourning was no longer distant—it was personal and constant.
- **Victory was uncertain**
  Neither side could claim a clear path to resolution.
  The war dragged on with no guarantee of success or survival for the nation itself.
- **National grief was widespread**
  The scale of suffering humbled triumphal language.
  Confidence gave way to lament.

In this setting, Lincoln chose an **uncommon posture**.
Rather than framing the conflict as a contest of moral superiority, he acknowledged **shared guilt and accountability before God**.
"Both read the same Bible, and pray to the same God; and each invokes His aid against the other."
— *Second Inaugural Address, 1865* (paraphrased)

Lincoln recognized that:

- National suffering could not be explained by blame alone
- Judgment and mercy might be intertwined
- God's purposes were not subject to partisan certainty

"The LORD is righteous in all his ways, and holy in all his works."
— *Psalm 145:17*

This posture was **instructive**.

It modeled:

- Humility rather than accusation
- Submission rather than presumption
- Reflection rather than triumphalism

"Shall we receive good at the hand of God, and shall we not receive evil?"
— *Job 2:10*

Providence, in Lincoln's framing, was not a tool for self-justification.

It was a call to repentance, restraint, and charity.

In a moment when victory language could have inflamed division, Lincoln's words reminded the nation that **suffering may serve correction as well as consequence**.

His example teaches a lasting lesson:

When history is painful and outcomes are unclear, the proper response is not certainty—but reverent humility before God.

---

5. Public Calls to Humility and Prayer

During the darkest years of the Civil War, Abraham Lincoln issued multiple proclamations calling the nation to:

- Prayer and fasting
- National humility before God
- Acknowledgment of divine sovereignty
- Recognition of shared moral responsibility

These proclamations did not frame the conflict as merely political or military. Lincoln consistently interpreted national suffering through a spiritual lens.

Rather than portraying one side as innocent and the other as solely guilty, he spoke as a fellow sinner among sinners—placing himself and the nation under God's judgment.

In one proclamation he urged the people:

"Let us then humble ourselves before the offended Power, confess our national sins, and pray for clemency and forgiveness."

This posture was rare among national leaders—especially in wartime. Lincoln did not claim moral superiority. He claimed accountability.

Scripture affirms this posture:
"Humble yourselves in the sight of the Lord, and he shall lift you up."
— **James 4:10**
Lincoln understood that:

- Military victory could not heal moral fracture
- Political authority could not substitute for repentance
- National survival required spiritual honesty

His calls to prayer were not symbolic gestures. They were public acknowledgments that:

- The nation was not self-sufficient
- Power did not equal righteousness
- Suffering demanded self-examination, not self-justification

Providence was honored not by denial of guilt, but by confession of need.

---

6. Specific Providential Observations
Providential Example #1 — National Confession
As suffering intensified, one response stood out—not defiance, not self-vindication, but **confession.**
Rather than framing national suffering as injustice inflicted by others alone, Lincoln spoke in terms of **collective responsibility**. He acknowledged the possibility of divine judgment. He called the nation to consider its own sins rather than merely its enemies' wrongs.
This posture was remarkable.
In moments of crisis, leaders often appeal to grievance, blame, or moral superiority. Here, however, suffering was reframed spiritually. Hardship was not denied—but it was interpreted through the lens of accountability before God.
Scripture affirms this posture:
"The LORD is righteous in all his ways, and holy in all his works."
— *Psalm 145:17*
This verse does not promise exemption from suffering.
It affirms God's **righteousness within it.**
Providence here was seen in **moral clarity**.
By acknowledging the possibility that suffering reflected divine discipline, the nation was invited to humility rather than outrage. Responsibility replaced self-pity. Repentance was presented as a necessary response, not merely victory.
This reframing mattered deeply.
It reminded the people that national calamity is not always proof of innocence or victimhood. Scripture repeatedly teaches that God deals with nations morally, not merely militarily. When

leaders acknowledge this truth publicly, they help reorient hearts toward reflection rather than retaliation.

Providence often works this way.

God allows suffering to continue long enough for deeper questions to be asked. When those questions turn inward rather than outward, exposure becomes opportunity. Judgment, when acknowledged, becomes a call to repentance rather than despair.

This confession did not end suffering immediately.

But it **gave suffering meaning**.

Providence was seen not in escape, but in the courage to interpret hardship honestly before God.

Theological Reflection (Optional Closing Sentence)

When suffering is met with confession rather than accusation, providence may be at work reshaping a nation's heart.

Providential Example #2 — Restraint in Language

In a time marked by immense suffering and profound uncertainty, the language used by national leadership carried unusual restraint.

Rather than boasting of righteousness or proclaiming moral superiority, Lincoln avoided triumphal claims. He resisted absolving rhetoric that would place blame solely on others or portray the nation as innocent victim. Simplistic explanations were deliberately rejected.

Instead, his words acknowledged **mystery**.

Suffering was not reduced to easy conclusions. Judgment was not claimed as fully understood. Outcomes were not presumed. Submission replaced certainty.

Scripture reflects this posture of humility:

"Who knoweth if he will return and repent, and leave a blessing behind him?"

— *Joel 2:14*

This verse does not deny God's power.

It acknowledges **human limitation** in discerning His purposes.

Providence here was seen in **measured speech**.

In moments of crisis, words often inflame, justify, or harden positions. Here, restraint created space for reflection. By refusing to speak beyond what could be known, leadership modeled humility before God and encouraged the nation to do the same.

This restraint mattered.

Language shapes conscience. When leaders speak carefully, they slow emotional escalation and invite moral seriousness. Acknowledging uncertainty before God reinforces the truth that divine purposes are not subject to human interpretation on demand.

Providence often works quietly through tone.
God's hand may be seen not in grand declarations, but in the refusal to declare what cannot be known. Restraint in language preserves reverence, guards against pride, and keeps hearts open to repentance.
These words did not promise relief.
They invited submission.
Providence was evident not in certainty, but in **reverent caution**.

Theological Reflection (Optional Closing Sentence)
When leaders speak with humility before God, restraint itself may become a means of grace.

Providential Example #3 — Moral Clarity Without Hatred
Moral clarity does not require moral hostility.
In a moment when national wounds ran deep and emotions burned hot, Lincoln condemned injustice without demonizing those involved. Wrong was named. Responsibility was acknowledged. Yet hatred was deliberately avoided.
This balance was not accidental.
Rather than framing the conflict in terms of absolute moral superiority, his language distinguished between **condemning sin** and **destroying the sinner**. Accountability was emphasized, but humanity was not erased.
Scripture captures this posture succinctly:
"But speaking the truth in love, may grow up into him in all things, which is the head, even Christ."
— *Ephesians 4:15*
This verse does not soften truth.
It governs **how truth is spoken**.
Providence here was seen in **measured moral clarity**.
In times of deep division, moral clarity often becomes a justification for cruelty. Truth is weaponized. Language hardens. Reconciliation becomes impossible because the opposing side is stripped of dignity.
That path was resisted.
Condemnation of injustice remained firm, yet language preserved the possibility of repentance rather than annihilation. Moral clarity was held alongside humility, restraint, and compassion.
This mattered profoundly.
When hatred defines moral discourse, peace becomes unattainable even after conflict ends. By avoiding demonization, space was preserved for reconciliation once suffering subsided.
Providence sometimes works by guarding the *tone* of righteousness.

God's purposes are not advanced by hatred, even when truth must be spoken plainly. When humility governs moral clarity, the door to restoration remains open.

These words did not erase guilt.

They refused to erase humanity.

Providence here was not dramatic intervention—it was **moral restraint that protected the future**.

Theological Reflection (Optional Closing Sentence)

When truth is spoken without hatred, reconciliation remains possible—even after judgment.

---

7. Judgment and Mercy Together

Important clarification:

- Humility did not end the war immediately
- Repentance did not remove suffering
- Pain and loss continued

God's mercy did not bypass judgment—it accompanied it.

Scripture consistently teaches that divine discipline and divine mercy are not opposites. They often move together.

"Whom the Lord loveth he chasteneth."

— **Hebrews 12:6**

Lincoln recognized this tension. He did not promise relief in response to humility. Instead, he acknowledged that suffering might continue—and that it might be deserved.

Yet humility accomplished vital spiritual work even while the war raged:

- It clarified moral truth in the midst of propaganda
- It preserved conscience when hatred threatened to dominate
- It restrained triumphalism and despair alike
- It prepared hearts for reconciliation once fighting ceased

God's judgment exposed sin.

God's mercy restrained annihilation.

This combination prevented the nation from interpreting survival as vindication. Victory would not be permission to forget suffering—or its causes.

Scripture reminds us:

"It is of the LORD's mercies that we are not consumed."

— **Lamentations 3:22**

Lincoln's humility modeled a crucial truth:

A nation may survive judgment—but only mercy explains why it is not destroyed.

Providence did not remove the cross.
It ensured the cross was not meaningless.

---

8. Discussion Questions (Choose 2–3)

1. Why is humility difficult during conflict?
2. How does confession change the way suffering is understood?
3. Why is moral clarity important without hatred?
4. What role does leadership play in national repentance?

---

9. Personal & National Application

Personal

- Do I humble myself under God's correction?
- Am I willing to confess rather than explain away?

National

- Repentance precedes healing
- Pride prolongs division
- Mercy flows from humility

"Before honour is humility."
— *Proverbs 15:33*

---

10. Closing Reflection

Lincoln did not promise relief.
He acknowledged responsibility.
At a moment when the nation longed for reassurance, he offered something far more difficult—truth. Rather than assigning blame solely to one side or another, he spoke of shared accountability under a righteous God:
"The LORD is righteous in all his ways, and holy in all his works."
— *Psalm 145:17*
In the midst of bloodshed, Lincoln resisted the temptation to frame suffering as injustice alone. Instead, he recognized that judgment and mercy are not contradictions in God's providence, but companions:
"Shall there be evil in a city, and the LORD hath not done it?"
— *Amos 3:6*
He spoke carefully—without triumph, without condemnation, without certainty of outcome. His language reflected humility before mystery:
"Who knoweth if he will return and repent, and leave a blessing behind him?"
— *Joel 2:14*

Providence was not invoked to justify violence or claim divine favor. It was acknowledged as sovereign, searching, and just—calling the nation not to pride, but to repentance:
"Let us search and try our ways, and turn again to the LORD."
— *Lamentations 3:40*
In doing so, Lincoln modeled a rare posture: moral clarity without hatred, conviction without arrogance, truth spoken in restraint:
"Speak the truth in love."
— *Ephesians 4:15*
Providence often speaks most clearly through broken hearts, not bold claims.
Through confession rather than certainty.
Through humility rather than triumph.
In that moment, leadership did not promise escape from suffering—it pointed the nation toward the only place where healing could begin: submission before God.
"The sacrifices of God are a broken spirit: a broken and a contrite heart, O God, thou wilt not despise."
— *Psalm 51:17*

---

11. Closing Scripture & Prayer Prompt
Read aloud:
"Let us search and try our ways, and turn again to the LORD."
— *Lamentations 3:40*
Prayer Prompt:
"Lord, teach us humility in times of suffering, and lead us toward repentance and mercy."

Lesson 24 — Turning Points No One Expected

Series Title

God's Providence in American History: From the Pilgrims to the Present

Theme Verse

"There is no wisdom nor understanding nor counsel against the LORD."
— *Proverbs 21:30*

Lesson Aim (For the Teacher)

To show how God redirected the course of the Civil War through unexpected developments—revealing that **human plans, confidence, and timelines are never final when God is at work.**

This lesson emphasizes **divine interruption**, not human control.

Time Flow (Minimum 40 Minutes)

- Opening Scripture & Prayer – 4 minutes
- Biblical Framework – 10 minutes
- Historical Narrative & Providential Observations – 18 minutes
- Discussion – 5 minutes
- Application & Closing Reflection – 3 minutes

---

1. Opening Scripture Reading

Read aloud together:

"The steps of a good man are ordered by the LORD."
— *Psalm 37:23*

---

2. Core Truth Statement

God often changes the direction of events at moments when outcomes seem settled.

Providence is not bound by momentum.

---

3. Biblical Pattern: God Interrupts Human Expectations

Key Scriptures

"For my thoughts are not your thoughts, neither are your ways my ways."
— *Isaiah 55:8*

"He disappointeth the devices of the crafty."
— *Job 5:12*

"The LORD maketh poor, and maketh rich: he bringeth low, and lifteth up."
— *1 Samuel 2:7*

Teaching Point (Scripture-Anchored)

Throughout Scripture, God brings decisive change not always through strength, but through **unexpected timing, reversal, and restraint**—revealing His sovereignty over human plans.
(Genesis 50:20; Daniel 4:35)

---

4. The War Before the Turning Points

In the early stages of the Civil War, confidence was widespread.
Leaders, commentators, and citizens on both sides expected the conflict to be brief.
There was a prevailing belief that resolve, resources, or early victories would quickly decide the outcome.

- **Confidence existed on both sides**
  Each believed its cause was just and its strength sufficient.
  Moral certainty often accompanied strategic optimism.
- **Predictions of quick resolution were common**
  The war was expected to end within months, not years.
  Few anticipated the scale of sacrifice that lay ahead.
- **Strategies assumed clear outcomes**
  Military plans were built on assumptions of decisive engagements and swift collapse of resistance.
  Little allowance was made for prolonged attrition or unforeseen complexity.

Yet reality unfolded differently.
The war grew **longer, bloodier, and more uncertain** than anyone had predicted.
Battles failed to bring final resolution.
Victories proved temporary.
Losses mounted without closure.

"There are many devices in a man's heart; nevertheless the counsel of the LORD, that shall stand."
— *Proverbs 19:21*

Human confidence proved fragile.
Assumptions gave way to exhaustion.
Certainty gave way to doubt.
The illusion of control dissolved under the weight of sustained suffering.
"Boast not thyself of to morrow; for thou knowest not what a day may bring forth."
— *Proverbs 27:1*
Providence, in this phase of the war, did not reward confidence.
It exposed its limits.
Only when expectations collapsed did the nation begin to reckon with deeper truths:
that strength alone does not guarantee outcomes,
that righteousness cannot be assumed,
and that human plans are always subject to God's sovereign purposes.
The turning points that followed would not arise from confidence—but from humility, endurance, and costly resolve.

---

5. Unexpected Developments That Changed the War
Providential Example #1 — Shifts in Momentum
Throughout the conflict, moments arose when the direction of events appeared settled.
Strategies were devised. Outcomes were anticipated. Confidence hardened into assumption.
From a human perspective, momentum seemed firmly established—sometimes favoring one side, sometimes the other.
Then, unexpectedly, momentum shifted.
Plans failed where success was anticipated. Resources dwindled faster than expected. Morale—once strong—collapsed with little warning. What had appeared inevitable suddenly became uncertain.
Scripture consistently warns against such confidence:
"Boast not thyself of to morrow; for thou knowest not what a day may bring forth."
— *Proverbs 27:1*
This verse does not deny planning.
It denies **certainty apart from God**.
Providence here was seen in **disruption**.
God did not merely strengthen one side or weaken another. He unsettled assumptions.
Human calculations proved unreliable. Predictability dissolved. Certainty evaporated.
These shifts mattered.
Wars are often decided not by a single decisive blow, but by cumulative changes in morale, supply, timing, and endurance. When momentum repeatedly reverses, it exposes the fragility of human forecasting.

Providence often works in this way.
Rather than overturning events dramatically, God allows the future to remain unstable.
Confidence is tempered. Pride is checked. Leaders are reminded that tomorrow is not guaranteed—even when today seems secure.
Momentum, so often treated as destiny, proved temporary.
What seemed fixed was not.
What appeared inevitable was not assured.
Providence revealed itself not by announcing outcomes, but by **reminding all parties of their uncertainty**. Plans were made—and undone. Confidence rose—and collapsed. Expectations were reshaped repeatedly.
God did not promise clarity.
He preserved **humility**.

Theological Reflection (Optional Closing Sentence)
When certainty collapses and outcomes remain unsettled, providence may be at work restraining human pride.

Providential Example #2 — Leadership Changes and Decisions
At critical points in the conflict, outcomes were shaped not only by battles, but by **decisions made far from the battlefield**.
Leadership changes occurred. Strategies were revised. Priorities shifted in response to pressures, losses, and political realities. In some cases, decisions intended to strengthen a position produced unintended consequences instead.
No leader acted with full visibility.
Plans were formed based on limited information. Judgments were made under strain. Choices that appeared reasonable at the moment sometimes redirected the course of the war in unexpected ways—opening opportunities where none were anticipated, or closing paths once thought secure.
Scripture describes this dynamic clearly:
"A man's heart deviseth his way: but the LORD directeth his steps."
— *Proverbs 16:9*
This verse does not deny human agency.
It affirms **divine direction beyond human foresight**.
Providence here was seen in **the outcome of decisions**, not their perfection.
God did not suspend human judgment. Leaders still planned, debated, and chose. Yet the results of those decisions often unfolded in ways no one intended or predicted. Strategic

redirection sometimes exposed weakness rather than strength. Adjustments meant to stabilize situations sometimes accelerated change.

These developments mattered.

Wars often turn not on isolated acts of heroism, but on cumulative decisions—when to advance, when to delay, where to commit resources, whom to trust. When outcomes consistently diverge from intention, it becomes clear that control is limited.

Providence often works through ordinary decision-making.

God does not need to announce His purposes in advance. He governs results quietly, allowing human choices to proceed while directing history toward outcomes unseen by those making them.

Leadership remained accountable.

Decisions remained real.

But outcomes were not fully theirs to command.

Providence was evident not in flawless strategy, but in **directed consequence**.

Theological Reflection (Optional Closing Sentence)

When decisions produce outcomes no one intended, God may be guiding history beyond human sight.

Providential Example #3 — Emancipation as Moral Turning Point

As the conflict dragged on, one development altered its character more profoundly than any battlefield maneuver.

The Emancipation Proclamation reframed the war morally.

What had begun primarily as a struggle to preserve the Union now openly confronted the injustice at its core. The conflict was no longer defined solely by political separation or national survival—it was tied unmistakably to moral accountability.

This shift was costly.

The proclamation did not shorten the war. It intensified it. Opposition hardened. Sacrifice increased. The path forward became more difficult rather than less. Yet the moral direction of the conflict was clarified.

Scripture speaks directly to such moments of moral obligation:

"Open thy mouth for the dumb in the cause of all such as are appointed to destruction."

— *Proverbs 31:8*

This verse does not promise safety.

It calls for **courage on behalf of the voiceless**.

Providence here was seen in **moral redirection**, not relief.

The decision altered international perception, undermining foreign sympathy for the opposing cause. It changed the meaning of sacrifice for those already suffering. And it raised the moral stakes of the war, ensuring that its outcome would not merely preserve a nation, but address a profound injustice.

This mattered deeply.

Providence sometimes advances righteousness by **deepening difficulty**, not easing it. God's purposes are not always aligned with immediate success or comfort. At times, moral clarity increases the cost before it brings resolution.

The proclamation was not universally welcomed.

It was contested. It was debated. It was resisted.

Yet it marked a decisive turning point—one that reshaped the conflict's purpose and legacy. What had been ambiguous became explicit. Neutrality became untenable.

Providence did not remove suffering.

It **gave suffering moral meaning**.

By confronting injustice directly, the war was no longer merely about survival—it became about responsibility before God. The cost increased, but so did clarity.

Providence here was not seen in ease, but in **alignment with righteousness**, even when that alignment demanded greater sacrifice.

Theological Reflection (Optional Closing Sentence)

When righteousness is advanced at great cost, providence may be guiding history toward justice rather than comfort.

---

6. Providence Through Prolonged Suffering

Important clarification:

- Turning points did not end suffering
- Loss increased before resolution
- Pain intensified rather than eased

One of the most difficult truths revealed in Scripture—and in history—is that God's providence does not always shorten suffering. At times, it allows hardship to deepen even as His purposes advance.

The turning points of the Civil War did not immediately bring relief. In many cases:

- Casualties rose after pivotal decisions
- Grief multiplied even as direction became clearer
- Hope grew slowly, overshadowed by continued loss

This pattern is deeply biblical.

"No chastening for the present seemeth to be joyous, but grievous: nevertheless afterward it yieldeth the peaceable fruit of righteousness."
— **Hebrews 12:11**
God's work often unfolds beneath pain rather than apart from it. Suffering does not mean providence has ceased. It may mean correction is still underway.
Scripture reminds us that present anguish does not negate eternal purpose:
"For I reckon that the sufferings of this present time are not worthy to be compared with the glory which shall be revealed."
— **Romans 8:18**
Providence through prolonged suffering accomplishes what swift deliverance cannot:

- It humbles pride deeply
- It exposes false hopes
- It refines motives
- It prevents triumphalism

God was not only shaping outcomes—He was shaping hearts. The cost was high, but the lesson was enduring.

---

7. God's Timing, Not Human Control

Turning points reveal truths that prosperity often hides:

- Human plans are provisional
- Confidence must be restrained
- Dependence remains essential

Throughout the conflict, leaders acted, planned, and adjusted—but none controlled outcomes fully. What seemed decisive one moment often proved uncertain the next.
Scripture speaks plainly to this reality:
"It is not of him that willeth, nor of him that runneth, but of God that sheweth mercy."
— **Romans 9:16**
Turning points expose the illusion of control. They remind nations—and individuals—that resolve does not guarantee results, and effort does not ensure success.
God's timing differs from human expectation:

- He delays when speed would breed pride
- He intervenes when certainty collapses
- He resolves matters only when humility has done its work

"The steps of a good man are ordered by the LORD."
— **Psalm 37:23**
The lesson of unexpected turning points is not strategic brilliance—it is surrendered dependence.

Providence does not follow human schedules. It follows divine wisdom.
And when outcomes finally shift, Scripture leaves no doubt where credit belongs:
"Not unto us, O LORD, not unto us, but unto thy name give glory."
— **Psalm 115:1**

---

8. Discussion Questions (Choose 2–3)

1. Why does God sometimes allow suffering to increase before change comes?
2. How do unexpected events test faith?
3. What dangers arise when confidence replaces humility?
4. How can we recognize providence in reversal?

---

9. Personal & National Application

Personal

- Do I trust God when plans are disrupted?
- Am I patient with His timing?

National

- Moral clarity can require sacrifice
- Turning points often carry cost
- God's purposes outlast momentum

"Be still, and know that I am God."
— *Psalm 46:10*

---

10. Closing Reflection

The war did not turn because plans succeeded.
It turned because certainty failed.
Strategies collapsed. Assumptions proved fragile. Confidence gave way to confusion. At critical moments, what leaders expected to happen simply did not—and in that disruption, providence became visible:
"There are many devices in a man's heart; nevertheless the counsel of the LORD, that shall stand."
— *Proverbs 19:21*
Victory did not arrive along a predictable path. Human calculation reached its limits, and outcomes unfolded beyond control:
"For my thoughts are not your thoughts, neither are your ways my ways, saith the LORD."
— *Isaiah 55:8*

Providence intervened not by rewarding flawless planning, but by redirecting events when certainty disappeared. When strength was insufficient and foresight failed, preservation continued:

"The race is not to the swift, nor the battle to the strong."

— *Ecclesiastes 9:11*

Moments that should have ended the cause instead opened unexpected doors. What appeared to be delay became opportunity. What seemed like weakness became survival:

"When I am weak, then am I strong."

— *2 Corinthians 12:10*

Providence often reveals itself not when the way forward is clear, but when the expected path vanishes entirely:

"Trust in the LORD with all thine heart; and lean not unto thine own understanding."

— *Proverbs 3:5*

The turning of the war reminds us that God does not merely bless human plans—He governs outcomes. When certainty fails, His purposes do not:

"The LORD bringeth the counsel of the heathen to nought: he maketh the devices of the people of none effect."

— *Psalm 33:10*

Providence became visible not in mastery, but in interruption.

Not in confidence, but in collapse.

And through that collapse, preservation quietly continued.

---

11. Closing Scripture & Prayer Prompt

Read aloud:

"Commit thy way unto the LORD; trust also in him."

— *Psalm 37:5*

Prayer Prompt:

"Lord, help us trust You when outcomes change and plans are overturned."

Lesson 25 — Preservation, Not Destruction

Series Title

God's Providence in American History: From the Pilgrims to the Present

Theme Verse

"For the Lord will not cast off for ever."

— *Lamentations 3:31*

Lesson Aim (For the Teacher)

To show how, despite unimaginable loss and suffering, God preserved the nation from total destruction—revealing that **His judgments are tempered with mercy and oriented toward restoration.**

This lesson emphasizes **restraint after judgment**, not victory through force.

Time Flow (Minimum 40 Minutes)

- Opening Scripture & Prayer – 4 minutes
- Biblical Framework – 10 minutes
- Historical Narrative & Providential Observations – 18 minutes
- Discussion – 5 minutes
- Application & Closing Reflection – 3 minutes

---

1. Opening Scripture Reading

Read aloud together:

"It is of the LORD's mercies that we are not consumed."

— *Lamentations 3:22*

---

2. Core Truth Statement

God's judgment aims at correction, not annihilation.

Even in discipline, God preserves what He intends to restore.

---

3. Biblical Pattern: Judgment Tempered by Mercy

Key Scriptures

"Though he cause grief, yet will he have compassion."
— *Lamentations 3:32*

"For whom the Lord loveth he chasteneth."
— *Hebrews 12:6*

"He will not always chide: neither will he keep his anger for ever."
— *Psalm 103:9*

Teaching Point (Scripture-Anchored)

Throughout Scripture, God's judgment is never arbitrary; it is restrained, purposeful, and ultimately directed toward repentance and restoration.
(Isaiah 57:16; Hosea 6:1)
God disciplines in order to heal.

---

4. The Cost of the Civil War

By the end of the Civil War, the cost had become almost unimaginable.
What began as a political crisis had unfolded into a national tragedy measured not only in battles, but in broken lives.

- **Hundreds of thousands had died**
  The number of dead exceeded all previous American conflicts combined.
  Losses were not abstract statistics—they were names, faces, and empty places at family tables.
- **Families were shattered**
  Widows, orphans, and grieving parents filled towns and countryside alike.
  The war reached far beyond the battlefield into homes and churches.
- **Cities and economies were devastated**
  Infrastructure lay in ruins.
  Livelihoods were destroyed, and recovery would take generations.
- **Grief touched nearly every home**
  No region remained untouched.
  Mourning became a shared national experience.

"Righteousness belongeth unto thee, but unto us confusion of faces."
— *Daniel 9:7*

The nation stood **deeply wounded—but not destroyed.**
That preservation was not evidence of righteousness.
It was evidence of restraint.

"For the LORD will not cast off for ever:
But though he cause grief, yet will he have compassion according to the multitude of his mercies."
— *Lamentations 3:31–32*

Providence in this season did not spare the nation from pain.
It spared the nation from annihilation.
Judgment came—but it was bounded.
Suffering was severe—but it was not final.
The survival of the nation itself testified that mercy remained present even in discipline.

"It is of the LORD's mercies that we are not consumed, because his compassions fail not."
— *Lamentations 3:22*

The cost of the Civil War stands as a sober reminder:
sin carries consequences,
delay does not eliminate reckoning,
and God's patience, though great, is not indifference.
Yet even in the aftermath of immense loss, providence preserved space for repentance, rebuilding, and renewed responsibility.
The nation would never be the same.
But it would continue.
And in that continuation lay both warning and hope.

---

5. Providential Restraints After the War

Providential Example #1 — The War Ended Without Total Collapse

When the war finally ended, the nation stood exhausted and scarred.
Cities lay damaged. Families were broken. Trust was fragile. The cost in lives and resources had been staggering. From a human perspective, the conditions for **total collapse** were present.
Yet collapse did not come.
Despite devastation, the nation remained intact. Government continued to function. Civil authority was maintained. The land did not descend into widespread anarchy or fragmentation.
This outcome was not inevitable.
History records many nations that, after prolonged civil conflict, dissolved into chaos—power vacuums filled by violence, regions breaking away, institutions failing under the weight of loss and resentment. That path was possible here.
It did not occur.
Scripture captures the significance of such restraint:

"If it had not been the LORD who was on our side, now may Israel say…"
— *Psalm 124:1*
This verse does not deny danger.
It acknowledges **preservation in the face of it.**
Providence here was seen in **structural restraint.**
God did not erase the consequences of war. Wounds remained. Grief endured. Reconstruction would take years. Yet the basic framework of national life held together. Authority was not abandoned. Order was not swept away by vengeance or despair.
This restraint mattered profoundly.
Preservation of structure allowed healing to begin. It prevented suffering from multiplying unchecked. It ensured that loss, however great, did not become permanent ruin.
Providence often works this way after judgment.
God restrains the aftermath so that correction does not become annihilation. He preserves enough stability for repentance, rebuilding, and reconciliation to remain possible.
The war ended with devastation—but not disintegration.
Providence was seen not in undoing the cost, but in **preventing collapse from becoming complete**.

Theological Reflection (Optional Closing Sentence)
When destruction stops short of collapse, restraint itself may be the work of God's mercy.

Providential Example #2 — Calls for Healing and Mercy
As the war came to its conclusion, the nation faced a critical crossroads.
The wounds were deep. Loss was widespread. Grief and anger lingered on both sides. In such moments, history often records cycles of retaliation—revenge justified by suffering, punishment demanded by pain.
That path was possible.
Yet a different tone began to emerge.
Instead of calls for widespread retribution, language of **reconciliation** surfaced. Appeals were made for charity rather than vengeance. Restraint was encouraged at a moment when emotion could easily have overruled wisdom.
This shift was not guaranteed.
After prolonged conflict, mercy often feels undeserved. Forgiveness appears premature. Yet Scripture consistently teaches that healing cannot begin where mercy is absent.
Jesus' words speak directly to this moment:
"Blessed are the merciful: for they shall obtain mercy."
— *Matthew 5:7*

This blessing does not deny justice.

It governs **how justice is pursued.**

Providence here was seen in **the softening of tone.**

God did not erase pain or pretend suffering had not occurred. Instead, He restrained the impulse toward collective punishment. Words of mercy redirected hearts away from bitterness and toward the difficult work of restoration.

This restraint mattered profoundly.

Healing requires more than the cessation of violence. It requires a change in spirit. When mercy is spoken aloud by leaders and echoed by communities, it creates space for repentance, rebuilding, and renewed trust.

Providence often works through language.

Words shape memory. Tone shapes future response. By encouraging mercy rather than revenge, the nation was guided toward healing rather than prolonged division.

Mercy did not remove consequences.

It **opened the door to recovery.**

Providence here was not dramatic intervention—it was the quiet redirection of hearts toward compassion when cruelty might have prevailed.

Theological Reflection (Optional Closing Sentence)

When mercy is chosen at the moment vengeance seems justified, providence may be guiding a nation toward healing.

Providential Example #3 — Space for Repentance and Reform

The war did more than devastate the nation—it **exposed it.**

Long-standing sins were brought into the open. Moral contradictions that had been tolerated for generations could no longer be ignored. The cost of avoidance had become undeniable, written in suffering and loss.

This exposure was painful.

Yet providence did not end with exposure alone. The aftermath of the war created **space**—space for reflection, repentance, and reform. Judgment did not close the door to the future; it prepared the way for correction.

Scripture speaks to this pattern clearly:

"Come, and let us return unto the LORD: for he hath torn, and he will heal us; he hath smitten, and he will bind us up."

— *Hosea 6:1*

This verse does not deny discipline.

It reveals **God's purpose within it.**

Providence here was seen in **opportunity after judgment**.
God did not allow the nation to be consumed. He restrained destruction enough to leave room for response. Reflection replaced denial. Moral reckoning became unavoidable. The question was no longer whether change was needed—but whether it would be embraced.
This mattered profoundly.
Judgment without opportunity leads to despair. Mercy without truth leads to repetition of sin. Providence, however, often brings both—exposure followed by space to respond rightly.
The war forced the nation to confront what it had postponed. But the restraint that followed ensured that confrontation did not end in annihilation. Instead, it opened the possibility of reform grounded in humility.
Providence often works this way.
God allows sin to bear fruit so it cannot be denied, yet restrains the outcome so repentance remains possible. Discipline is not His final word—**restoration is**.
The nation was wounded.
But it was not abandoned.
Providence preserved enough stability, enough conscience, and enough time for correction to begin.
Judgment prepared the way—not for despair—but for change.

Theological Reflection (Optional Closing Sentence)
When judgment leaves room for repentance, restraint itself may be an act of mercy.

---

6. Mercy Did Not Erase Consequences
Important clarification:

- Suffering remained
- Healing took generations
- Wounds did not vanish overnight

God's mercy does not cancel reality. Scripture never teaches that forgiveness removes all earthly consequences. Instead, it teaches that mercy restrains destruction while allowing correction to accomplish its work.
"Be not deceived; God is not mocked: for whatsoever a man soweth, that shall he also reap."
— **Galatians 6:7**
After the Civil War:

- Lives had been lost permanently
- Families were fractured
- Economic devastation lingered
- Social wounds remained raw

Mercy did not rewind history. It did not undo death or erase grief. The consequences of national sin were real, lasting, and costly.

Yet mercy accomplished something equally real: it set limits.

"For whom the Lord loveth he chasteneth."

— **Hebrews 12:6**

God's discipline corrected without annihilating. Judgment came—but it was measured. The nation was broken, but not erased.

Scripture reminds us that mercy and discipline often walk together:

"The LORD will not cast off for ever:
But though he cause grief, yet will he have compassion."

— **Lamentations 3:31–32**

Mercy did not spare pain.

It spared extinction.

---

7. Why Preservation Matters

If destruction had been total:

- No rebuilding would have been possible
- No repentance could have followed
- No restoration could have occurred

Total collapse would have ended the story. Preservation kept it open.

God's providence is often seen not in what He immediately heals, but in what He refuses to destroy.

"For I know the thoughts that I think toward you, saith the LORD, thoughts of peace, and not of evil, to give you an expected end."

— **Jeremiah 29:11**

Preservation matters because:

- It allows time for repentance
- It leaves space for correction
- It makes restoration possible—even if slow

Scripture repeatedly shows that God's redemptive work requires continuity. Destruction ends opportunity. Preservation sustains it.

"The LORD is gracious, and full of compassion; slow to anger, and of great mercy."

— **Psalm 145:8**

In preserving the nation after immense suffering, God demonstrated a consistent biblical pattern:

- Judgment exposes and humbles
- Mercy restrains and sustains

- Time allows transformation

Providence did not declare the nation righteous.

It declared the future *possible.*

God preserved the present not because it was worthy—but because He was merciful.

---

8. Discussion Questions (Choose 2–3)

1. Why does God temper judgment with mercy?
2. How does restraint create room for repentance?
3. Why is destruction never God's final goal?
4. How can suffering lead to restoration?

---

9. Personal & National Application

Personal

- Do I recognize mercy in seasons of correction?
- Am I willing to learn from discipline?

National

- Healing requires humility
- Mercy enables rebuilding
- Judgment is not abandonment

"Return, ye backsliding children."

— *Jeremiah 3:22*

---

10. Closing Reflection

The Civil War broke the nation—but it did not end it.

The conflict exposed sin, tore communities apart, and left wounds that would last for generations. Providence did not spare the nation from pain, nor did it soften the cost of judgment:

"For whom the Lord loveth he chasteneth, and scourgeth every son whom he receiveth."

— *Hebrews 12:6*

God's hand was not seen in the avoidance of suffering, but in the limits placed upon it. Though devastation was widespread, total annihilation did not occur. Structure endured. A future remained possible:

"It is of the LORD's mercies that we are not consumed, because his compassions fail not."

— *Lamentations 3:22*

Judgment passed—but it was restrained. The nation was not erased. Governance continued. Order, though shaken, was not destroyed:

"For the LORD will not cast off for ever."
— *Lamentations 3:31*
Providence does not always appear as rescue. Sometimes it appears as survival—when destruction could have gone further, deeper, and beyond recovery:
"Except the LORD had been on our side… then the waters had overwhelmed us."
— *Psalm 124:1, 4*
Mercy did not mean innocence. Healing did not mean forgetting. The scars remained as testimony that sin carries consequence:
"Be sure your sin will find you out."
— *Numbers 32:23*
Yet mercy remained alongside judgment—not to erase responsibility, but to allow repentance, rebuilding, and restraint:
"The LORD is merciful and gracious, slow to anger, and plenteous in mercy."
— *Psalm 103:8*
Providence in the Civil War was not sentimental.
It was severe—but measured.
It was just—but restrained.
God did not prevent the breaking—but He prevented the ending.
Judgment passed—but mercy remained.

---

11. Closing Scripture & Prayer Prompt
Read aloud:
"Turn thou us unto thee, O LORD, and we shall be turned."
— *Lamentations 5:21*
Prayer Prompt:
"Lord, teach us to receive correction with humility and to walk forward in mercy and repentance."

SECTION VI - MODERN MIRACLES & PRESERVATION

Restraint, Protection, and God's Unseen Hand

"Except the LORD keep the city, the watchman waketh but in vain."
— **Psalm 127:1**

Section Purpose

This section examines modern history with **careful humility**.

Unlike earlier centuries, recent events come with:

- Extensive documentation
- Competing interpretations
- Heightened emotional memory

Here, providence is not claimed lightly or declared boldly. Instead, we look for **patterns of restraint, protection, and preservation**—moments where outcomes could have been far worse, yet were limited.

This is not a section about declaring certainty.

It is a section about **recognizing mercy**.

Lessons in This Section

- **Lesson 26:** World War I & the Unseen Restraint
- **Lesson 27:** World War II Turning Points
- **Lesson 28:** Israel and America
- **Lesson 29:** The Cold War That Never Turned Hot
- **Lesson 30:** Technological Protection & Providence
- **Lesson 31:** September 11 Survivals
- **Lesson 32:** America at a Crossroads

Guiding Truth

God's providence is often revealed not by what happens—but by what is restrained from happening.

(Optional Closing Line for Print or Teaching)

"Mercy is sometimes most visible in what never occurred."

Teaching Orientation (Leader Use)

As you enter this section, remind the class:

- Not every event can be labeled a miracle
- God's hand may be seen in restraint as much as rescue
- Humility honors God more than certainty

Encourage the class to:

- Weigh evidence carefully
- Avoid speculation
- Recognize mercy without presumption

Lesson 26 — World War I & the Unseen Restraint

Series Title

God's Providence in American History: From the Pilgrims to the Present

Theme Verse

"Surely the wrath of man shall praise thee: the remainder of wrath shalt thou restrain."
— *Psalm 76:10*

Lesson Aim (For the Teacher)

To show how, even amid unprecedented global violence, God restrained total destruction—revealing His providence through **limits placed on human wrath** rather than through triumph or celebration.

This lesson emphasizes **restraint amid chaos**, not victory.

Time Flow (Minimum 40 Minutes)

- Opening Scripture & Prayer – 4 minutes
- Biblical Framework – 10 minutes
- Historical Narrative & Providential Observations – 18 minutes
- Discussion – 5 minutes
- Application & Closing Reflection – 3 minutes

---

1. Opening Scripture Reading

Read aloud together:

"He maketh wars to cease unto the end of the earth."
— *Psalm 46:9*

---

2. Core Truth Statement

God's providence is sometimes revealed not in preventing conflict, but in restraining its reach and duration.

Mercy may appear as limitation rather than deliverance.

---

3. Biblical Pattern: God Restrains Human Wrath

Key Scriptures

"The LORD sitteth upon the flood; yea, the LORD sitteth King for ever."
— *Psalm 29:10*
"Hitherto shalt thou come, but no further."
— *Job 38:11*
"When the enemy shall come in like a flood, the Spirit of the LORD shall lift up a standard against him."
— *Isaiah 59:19*

Teaching Point (Scripture-Anchored)

Scripture repeatedly affirms that while God may permit human conflict, **He also sets boundaries**—preventing destruction from exceeding His sovereign purposes.
(Genesis 6:3; Nahum 1:7)

---

4. The Nature of World War I

World War I marked a decisive shift in the nature of human conflict.
For the first time, war was waged on an **industrial scale**, combining modern technology with unprecedented mobilization.

- **Industrial-scale warfare**
  Factories, railways, and entire economies were devoted to sustaining combat.
  Warfare became systematic, continuous, and impersonal.
- **Trench combat and mass casualties**
  Soldiers endured months and years in muddy trenches under constant threat.
  Battles produced staggering losses for minimal territorial gain.
- **Chemical weapons**
  Poison gas introduced a new and terrifying dimension to combat.
  Suffering extended beyond the battlefield, haunting survivors long after fighting ceased.
- **Global involvement**
  Nations from multiple continents were drawn into the conflict.
  What began as a regional crisis became a worldwide catastrophe.

Human ingenuity, once a source of progress, was now harnessed for destruction.
"Their feet run to evil, and they make haste to shed innocent blood."
— *Isaiah 59:7*
The war revealed how technological advancement can outpace moral restraint.
Innovation multiplied humanity's capacity to destroy faster than wisdom multiplied its capacity to restrain.

"Knowledge puffeth up, but charity edifieth."
— *1 Corinthians 8:1*
Providence, in this context, did not prevent the conflict.
Instead, it revealed the sobering truth that progress without moral grounding magnifies harm.
World War I stands as a warning:
when human power expands without corresponding humility, the consequences are devastating.
Yet even in this dark chapter, destruction was not limitless.
Restraints remained.
Civilization endured.
Providence did not eliminate suffering—but it prevented complete collapse, leaving room for recovery, reflection, and correction.

---

5. Where Unchecked Destruction Was Possible
Without restraint, World War I could have descended into far greater devastation than it already did.
The conflict introduced unprecedented tools of destruction:

- Chemical weapons capable of mass civilian casualties
- Industrial-scale artillery that leveled entire regions
- Mechanized warfare that multiplied death beyond prior imagination

Human capacity for destruction expanded faster than moral restraint.
And yet—limits appeared.

- Chemical warfare, though horrifying, did not escalate unchecked across every front
- Entire population centers were not systematically obliterated
- Civilian annihilation, while grievous, did not reach its full potential

These restraints were not the result of human virtue alone. Fear, revulsion, hesitation, logistical limits, and conscience all played roles—but Scripture reminds us that restraint itself is often providential.
"Surely the wrath of man shall praise thee: the remainder of wrath shalt thou restrain."
— **Psalm 76:10**
God's restraint is often invisible because it operates by *withholding*, not intervening visibly. We notice what happens—but rarely what does not.
Providence in this war was not seen primarily in protection from suffering, but in limitation of annihilation. The absence of total destruction was itself a mercy.
God's unseen hand does not always stop the blow.
Sometimes it shortens its reach.

6. Providential Observations of Restraint

Providential Example #1 — Containment of Chemical Warfare

The introduction of chemical weapons marked one of the most horrifying developments in modern warfare.

Their effects were devastating. Their potential for mass annihilation was undeniable. Once unleashed, such weapons could have transformed warfare into continuous, unchecked destruction.

That escalation was possible.

Yet it did not fully occur.

Though chemical weapons were introduced, their use was **not continuous**. Their expansion was limited. Global annihilation was avoided. Public revulsion—shared even among combatant nations—created moral pressure that restrained wider deployment.

This restraint was significant.

History shows that once a new weapon proves effective, its unchecked use often follows. Here, however, a line was drawn—imperfectly, painfully, but decisively enough to prevent total collapse into indiscriminate destruction.

Scripture speaks to God's restraining hand in moments of extreme temptation:

"There hath no temptation taken you but such as is common to man: but God is faithful, who will not suffer you to be tempted above that ye are able; but will with the temptation also make a way to escape."

— *1 Corinthians 10:13*

This verse does not deny the presence of evil.

It affirms **limits placed upon it**.

Providence here was seen in **containment**.

God did not remove the reality of human cruelty. He restrained its reach. The capacity for escalation existed, but it was curbed—through conscience, public outcry, and shared recognition of horror.

This restraint mattered profoundly.

Had chemical warfare expanded without limit, the scale of devastation could have altered civilization itself. Instead, even amid conflict, a boundary held. Humanity recoiled from its own capacity for destruction.

Providence often works this way in modern history.

Rather than erasing evil, God restrains it. He limits what could otherwise spiral beyond recovery. He allows consequences to warn without allowing annihilation to consume.

Restraint did not make the use of such weapons acceptable.

It prevented them from becoming **normative**.

Providence here was not deliverance from suffering—it was **limitation of catastrophe**.

Theological Reflection (Optional Closing Sentence)
When destruction stops short of its full potential, restraint itself may testify to God's mercy.

Providential Example #2 — Preservation of Civil Order
Periods of upheaval place immense strain on societies.
Institutions are tested. Trust erodes. Fear spreads. In such moments, history often records total collapse—lawlessness replacing order, authority dissolving into chaos, and recovery becoming impossible.
That outcome was possible.
Yet despite widespread disruption, **civil order did not universally collapse**.
Governments continued to function. Basic structures endured. Law, though strained, remained operative. Communities retained enough cohesion to prevent descent into unchecked disorder. Even amid devastation, recovery remained conceivable.
Scripture affirms the importance of such restraint:
"For God is not the author of confusion, but of peace."
— *1 Corinthians 14:33*
This verse does not promise ease.
It reveals **God's character as a preserver of order**.
Providence here was seen in **continuity amid disruption**.
God did not remove conflict or hardship. But He restrained chaos from becoming absolute.
Authority did not vanish entirely. Institutions did not universally fail. Social bonds, though stressed, were not severed beyond repair.
This restraint mattered deeply.
Order is the soil in which healing can grow. Without it, suffering multiplies and reform becomes impossible. By preserving structure—even imperfectly—God allowed the possibility of restoration rather than permanent ruin.
Providence often works quietly in this way.
Rather than dramatic intervention, God sustains the framework of society just enough to prevent collapse. Confusion is limited. Peace, though fragile, remains attainable.
Order endured—not because humanity deserved it, but because God restrained disintegration.
Providence here was not triumph.
It was **preservation**.

Theological Reflection (Optional Closing Sentence)
When order endures amid chaos, restraint itself may be evidence of God's sustaining hand.

Providential Example #3 — War Ended Without Total Collapse

The war reached a conclusion—but not the worst imaginable one.

Destruction was immense. Loss was staggering. Entire regions were scarred, and millions of lives were altered forever. Yet the conflict **ended before total annihilation**. Civilization itself was not destroyed. The structures necessary for life, governance, and rebuilding remained.

That outcome was not guaranteed.

The capacity for escalation existed. The tools of destruction had advanced. The will to continue fighting could have persisted far beyond reason. History offers many examples where war consumed societies so completely that recovery became impossible.

That did not happen here.

Scripture speaks directly to this kind of restraint:

"For the LORD will not cast off for ever."

— *Lamentations 3:31*

This verse does not deny judgment.

It declares **that judgment has limits**.

Providence here was seen in **final restraint**.

God did not prevent suffering. He did not erase consequences. But He set a boundary beyond which destruction would not pass. The war concluded before civilization itself collapsed. Enough remained to allow rebuilding, reconciliation, and renewal.

This restraint mattered profoundly.

Recovery requires more than peace—it requires survivability. When a society is left with no structure, no memory, and no continuity, healing becomes impossible. Here, restraint preserved the future.

Providence often works this way at the end of great trials.

God allows correction to run its course, but He does not abandon entirely. Judgment gives way to mercy—not because sin was insignificant, but because destruction was not His final purpose.

The war ended with devastation.

But it also ended with **possibility**.

Providence was seen not in sparing the nation from pain, but in **preventing pain from becoming permanent annihilation**.

Theological Reflection (Optional Closing Sentence)

When judgment stops short of destruction, mercy may already be at work.

7. Judgment and Mercy Together

Important clarification:

- The war involved immense suffering
- God does not delight in destruction
- Pain does not negate mercy

World War I stands as a reminder that judgment and mercy are not opposites in Scripture—they often unfold together.

The war exposed:

- Human pride
- National ambition
- Confidence in technology and power

It shattered illusions of progress and moral superiority.

Yet within judgment, mercy remained present—not by erasing suffering, but by restraining total collapse.

Scripture speaks directly to this tension:

"In wrath remember mercy."

— **Habakkuk 3:2**

God's mercy does not deny wrath.

It *limits* it.

The war ended before:

- Entire civilizations were erased
- Global order collapsed completely
- Humanity destroyed itself with the tools it had created

This restraint did not excuse sin.

It created space for reflection.

"The LORD is merciful and gracious, slow to anger, and plenteous in mercy."

— **Psalm 103:8**

Providence in World War I was not triumphant.

It was sobering.

Judgment humbled the nations.

Mercy preserved the future.

God allowed the world to see what unchecked human power could do—without allowing it to do everything it could.

That restraint was not accidental.

It was providential.

---

8. Discussion Questions (Choose 2–3)

1. Why does God sometimes restrain evil rather than remove it?
2. How can restraint itself be an act of mercy?
3. What dangers arise when humans assume control over destruction?
4. How does this lesson shape how we view modern conflict?

---

9. Personal & National Application

Personal

- Do I recognize God's mercy in what does *not* happen?
- Am I grateful for unseen protection?

National

- Technological power requires moral restraint
- Peace depends on humility
- God's limits preserve the future

"Unless the LORD had been my help…"
— *Psalm 94:17*

---

10. Closing Reflection

World War I revealed humanity's capacity for devastation on an industrial scale.

For the first time, war harnessed modern technology to destroy life faster and farther than previous generations had imagined.

The conflict exposed what Scripture has long declared about the human heart:

"The heart is deceitful above all things, and desperately wicked: who can know it?"
— *Jeremiah 17:9*

Nations marched with confidence, convinced the war would be brief. Instead, it consumed millions, reshaped borders, and left scars that stretched across continents. Providence did not prevent suffering. Judgment was permitted:

"When thy judgments are in the earth, the inhabitants of the world will learn righteousness."
— *Isaiah 26:9*

Yet even amid unprecedented destruction, restraint remained.

Though new weapons were introduced, their use was not limitless. Though chaos spread, civilization did not collapse entirely. Though hatred intensified, the war did not end in total annihilation of nations:

"For the LORD will not cast off for ever."
— *Lamentations 3:31*

Providence appeared not in sparing humanity from pain, but in placing boundaries upon how far destruction would go:

"Thus far shalt thou come, but no farther."

— *Job 38:11*

The war ended—not because humanity found wisdom, but because exhaustion, limitation, and restraint intervened. God allowed mankind to see the consequences of pride and ambition, yet preserved the world from complete ruin:

"Except the LORD had been on our side… then had they swallowed us up quick."

— *Psalm 124:1, 3*

World War I stands as a sober reminder that providence does not always stop suffering—but it often restrains annihilation. Judgment was real. Mercy remained.

The lesson is not triumph.

It is warning.

"Righteousness exalteth a nation: but sin is a reproach to any people."

— *Proverbs 14:34*

Providence preserved humanity not because it deserved preservation—but because God's purposes were not yet finished.

---

11. Closing Scripture & Prayer Prompt

Read aloud:

"The LORD is good, a strong hold in the day of trouble."

— *Nahum 1:7*

Prayer Prompt:

"Lord, thank You for the mercy You show through restraint, and help us trust You even when we cannot see Your hand."

Lesson 27 — World War II Turning Points

Series Title
God's Providence in American History: From the Pilgrims to the Present
Theme Verse
"The LORD bringeth the counsel of the heathen to nought: he maketh the devices of the people of none effect."
— *Psalm 33:10*

Lesson Aim (For the Teacher)
To show how the course of World War II changed through a series of unexpected turning points—revealing providence through **timing, restraint, and intervention against overwhelming evil**, rather than through human certainty or moral pride.
This lesson emphasizes **interruption of evil**, not glorification of war.

Time Flow (Minimum 40 Minutes)
- Opening Scripture & Prayer – 4 minutes
- Biblical Framework – 10 minutes
- Historical Narrative & Providential Observations – 18 minutes
- Discussion – 5 minutes
- Application & Closing Reflection – 3 minutes

---

1. Opening Scripture Reading
Read aloud together:
"When the wicked are multiplied, transgression increaseth: but the righteous shall see their fall."
— *Proverbs 29:16*

---

2. Core Truth Statement
God's providence may be seen when evil advances unchecked—until it is suddenly restrained.
Turning points often arrive when defeat appears certain.

3. Biblical Pattern: God Interrupts the Advance of Evil

Key Scriptures

"He disappointeth the devices of the crafty."
— *Job 5:12*

"For the LORD is a God of judgment."
— *Isaiah 30:18*

"The rod of the wicked shall not rest upon the lot of the righteous."
— *Psalm 125:3*

Teaching Point (Scripture-Anchored)

Scripture shows that God allows evil to rise only to a point, then restrains it—often suddenly and decisively—so that destruction does not become total.
(Genesis 18:25; Daniel 4:35)

---

4. The World on the Brink

By the late 1930s, the world stood at a dangerous precipice.
Events unfolded with alarming speed, creating the widespread sense that history itself was slipping out of control.

- **Totalitarian regimes expanded rapidly**
  Governments built on absolute power consolidated authority through fear, propaganda, and force.
  Individual conscience was crushed beneath the weight of the state.
- **Democracies appeared weak**
  Free nations hesitated, divided by internal debate and haunted by the memory of previous war.
  Moral clarity often lagged behind events.
- **Entire nations fell in quick succession**
  Military campaigns overwhelmed countries in weeks rather than years.
  Resistance collapsed faster than observers believed possible.
- **The scale of brutality shocked the world**
  Civilians became deliberate targets.
  Genocide, forced labor, and systematic cruelty revealed depths of evil previously unseen.

Humanly speaking, **evil seemed unstoppable**.

"When the wicked are multiplied, transgression increaseth."
— *Proverbs 29:16*

Power appeared absolute.
Opposition appeared futile.
The capacity for destruction outpaced the ability to resist.
"The way of the wicked is as darkness: they know not at what they stumble."
— *Proverbs 4:19*
In this moment, providence was not obvious.
Deliverance was not immediate.
The world entered a season where restraint seemed absent and darkness ascendant.
Yet Scripture reminds us:
"Though his excellency mount up to the heavens… yet he shall perish for ever."
— *Job 20:6–7*
The rise of unchecked power did not mean divine absence.
It marked the approaching limit of human arrogance.
World War II would reveal that even when evil appears invincible, it is never sovereign.
Its advance has boundaries known to God alone.
Providence often waits until human strength is fully exposed—before it intervenes.

---

5. Unexpected Turning Points
Providential Example #1 — Survival Against Improbability
At several critical moments, the outcome appeared settled.
Forces were surrounded. Resources were depleted. Conditions were extreme. From a human standpoint, destruction seemed inevitable. Collapse was not merely possible—it was expected.
Yet survival occurred.
Lives were preserved under circumstances where endurance alone appeared unlikely. Forces escaped situations that should have resulted in defeat. What seemed certain loss became narrow escape.
Scripture gives voice to this kind of astonished survival:
"If it had not been the LORD who was on our side, now may Israel say…"
— *Psalm 124:1*
This verse is not a declaration of strength.
It is a confession of **dependence**.
Providence here was seen in **continuance when ending was assumed**.
God did not guarantee safety. He did not eliminate danger. But He intervened—or restrained—just enough that destruction did not have the final word. Survival itself became testimony.
This mattered deeply.

History often turns not on overwhelming victory, but on moments where defeat was avoided by the narrowest margin. When survival occurs repeatedly against expectation, it suggests restraint beyond human planning.

Providence often works in these margins.

God preserves not by removing risk, but by preventing final collapse. He allows pressure to build, danger to threaten, and outcomes to appear sealed—then preserves life where loss would have ended the story.

Such survival humbles.

It strips away illusion of control. It replaces confidence with gratitude. It turns attention away from human capability and toward divine mercy.

Survival was not celebrated as triumph.

It was recognized as **providence**.

The turning point was not brilliance or power—it was the simple fact that what should have ended did not.

Theological Reflection (Optional Closing Sentence)

When survival itself defies expectation, providence may be the only honest explanation.

Providential Example #2 — Reversals in Momentum

Unexpected Turning Points — Reversals in Momentum

At several points, momentum appeared firmly established.

Confidence grew. Plans solidified. Assumptions hardened into expectation. From a strategic perspective, outcomes seemed increasingly predictable.

Then momentum reversed.

Advantage dissolved rapidly. Overconfidence collapsed. Strategies built on assumed superiority failed under conditions they could not control. What had looked inevitable only days or weeks earlier suddenly became uncertain.

Scripture warns repeatedly of this pattern:

"Pride goeth before destruction, and an haughty spirit before a fall."

— *Proverbs 16:18*

This verse does not condemn strength.

It condemns **certainty divorced from humility**.

Providence here was seen in **the interruption of presumption**.

God did not merely strengthen the weaker side or weaken the stronger. He disrupted confidence itself. Aggressive certainty was humbled. Assumptions were exposed as fragile. Plans unraveled at moments when success seemed assured.

This mattered deeply.

Momentum often carries psychological power. Once confidence hardens, leaders take greater risks, dismiss caution, and overlook warning signs. When momentum collapses suddenly, it reveals how dependent outcomes are on factors beyond human control.

Providence often works through reversal.

God allows confidence to rise—then reminds humanity of its limits. He humbles aggressive certainty not always through defeat, but through unexpected change. Advantage evaporates. Control proves illusory.

These reversals were not random.

They occurred at moments when certainty had replaced vigilance. The collapse of momentum forced reassessment, restraint, and renewed humility.

Providence did not eliminate conflict.

It **checked pride**.

Turning points like these do not merely alter outcomes—they reshape attitudes. They remind all involved that success is not self-sustaining and that tomorrow is never guaranteed.

Momentum reversed.

Humility was reintroduced.

Theological Reflection (Optional Closing Sentence)

When confidence collapses without warning, God may be reminding humanity that certainty belongs to Him alone.

Providential Example #3 — Exposure of Evil

As the war progressed, another turning point emerged—one not measured in territory or numbers, but in **truth**.

Atrocities were revealed.

False narratives collapsed.

Actions once hidden were brought into public view.

What had been denied, minimized, or concealed could no longer be ignored. Moral ambiguity narrowed. Claims of innocence weakened. The reality of evil became unmistakable.

Scripture speaks directly to this unveiling:

"For there is nothing covered, that shall not be revealed; neither hid, that shall not be known."
— *Luke 12:2*

This verse does not promise immediate justice.

It promises **inevitable exposure**.

Providence here was seen in **revelation**.

God did not allow evil to remain permanently concealed. Over time, truth surfaced—sometimes through testimony, sometimes through consequence, sometimes through undeniable evidence. Lies lost credibility. Deception collapsed under its own weight.

This mattered profoundly.

Wars often thrive on propaganda and distortion. When evil remains hidden, accountability is delayed and repentance resisted. Exposure changes the moral landscape. What was once debatable becomes undeniable. What was excused becomes condemned.

Providence often works through light.

God allows darkness to operate for a season—but not forever. When exposure comes, it clarifies responsibility and removes the refuge of ignorance. Moral clarity emerges not because hearts are softened, but because truth can no longer be denied.

This exposure did not immediately end suffering.

But it **ended illusion**.

Once evil was revealed, neutrality became impossible. Silence became complicity. The moral cost of denial increased.

Providence here did not create righteousness.

It **unmasked unrighteousness**.

The turning point was not victory—it was truth.

Theological Reflection (Optional Closing Sentence)

When hidden evil is exposed, providence may be preparing the ground for accountability and repentance.

---

6. Providence Without Triumph

Important clarification:

- Victory did not erase suffering
- Innocent lives were lost
- Outcomes carried heavy and lasting cost

World War II is often remembered through its turning points—battles won, regimes defeated, territory reclaimed. Yet Scripture cautions us against confusing the restraint of evil with the absence of pain.

God's providence does not always appear as triumph. Often, it appears as *limitation.*

The defeat of totalitarian evil did not undo:

- The horrors of genocide
- The devastation of cities
- The trauma carried by survivors

Even righteous outcomes were accompanied by grievous loss.

Scripture reminds us that God's holiness does not prevent Him from allowing suffering—but it does prevent evil from reigning unchecked.

"Thou art of purer eyes than to behold evil, and canst not look on iniquity."

— **Habakkuk 1:13**

Yet at the same time:

"Surely the wrath of man shall praise thee: the remainder of wrath shalt thou restrain."

— **Psalm 76:10**

God did not approve evil—but He restrained it.

He did not celebrate suffering—but He limited destruction.

Providence in World War II was not clean, simple, or celebratory. It was costly, sobering, and morally clarifying. Evil was confronted—not because humanity suddenly became righteous, but because God did not allow darkness to prevail indefinitely.

Restraint, not triumph, marked God's hand.

---

7. Why Turning Points Matter

Turning points matter because they expose truths that power often conceals.

They demonstrate that:

- Human power is limited
- Evil is not sovereign
- God's purposes cannot be overrun

Totalitarian regimes appeared unstoppable at various moments. Entire nations fell quickly. Democracies seemed fragile. Hope dimmed.

And yet—evil did not have the final word.

"The LORD reigneth; let the earth rejoice."

— **Psalm 97:1**

Turning points reveal that history does not ultimately bend according to:

- Military dominance
- Ideological certainty
- Technological superiority

It bends according to divine authority.

Scripture reminds us:

"He doeth according to his will in the army of heaven, and among the inhabitants of the earth."

— **Daniel 4:35**

The defeat of evil regimes was not inevitable.

It was permitted.

God's providence ensured that:

- Tyranny did not become permanent
- Darkness did not become destiny
- Destruction did not consume the future

Turning points matter because they remind us that even when evil advances rapidly, it remains *bounded.*

History moves not by strength alone—
but by the sovereign will of God

---

8. Discussion Questions (Choose 2–3)

1. Why does God sometimes allow evil to advance before restraining it?
2. How do turning points challenge human pride?
3. Why must we avoid triumphalism after victory?
4. How does recognizing restraint deepen gratitude?

---

9. Personal & National Application

Personal

- Do I trust God when evil appears unchecked?
- Can I recognize His hand without demanding certainty?

National

- Power must be exercised humbly
- Victory demands responsibility
- Gratitude guards against pride

"Not unto us, O LORD, not unto us."
— *Psalm 115:1*

---

10. Closing Reflection

World War II did not end because humanity suddenly became righteous.

The conflict laid bare both extraordinary courage and unimaginable cruelty. It confirmed what Scripture declares about fallen humanity when power is unchecked:

"There is none righteous, no, not one."
— *Romans 3:10*

Evil advanced with efficiency, ideology hardened hearts, and destruction spread across continents. Providence did not erase human responsibility, nor did it excuse wickedness. Judgment was permitted:

"Shall there be evil in a city, and the LORD hath not done it?"
— *Amos 3:6*

Yet the war ended—not because mankind mastered itself, but because evil was restrained.

Key moments occurred that no single leader, army, or strategy fully controlled. Decisions hesitated. Timelines shifted. Outcomes changed unexpectedly:
"He disappointeth the devices of the crafty, so that their hands cannot perform their enterprise."
— *Job 5:12*
Providence appeared not in human perfection, but in interruption.
Plans collapsed. Momentum reversed. What seemed inevitable was halted:
"Thus far shalt thou come, but no farther."
— *Job 38:11*
The restraint of evil was not clean or painless. The cost was immense. Yet total annihilation did not occur. Civilization endured. A future remained possible:
"For the LORD will not cast off for ever."
— *Lamentations 3:31*
Providence does not mean God approves of all that happens.
It means nothing escapes His authority:
"Surely the wrath of man shall praise thee: the remainder of wrath shalt thou restrain."
— *Psalm 76:10*
World War II stands as a warning and a witness. Evil can rise far—but it does not rule forever. Human strength fails, but God's restraint remains.
"The LORD reigneth; let the earth rejoice."
— *Psalm 97:1*
Providence ended the war not with perfection—but with interruption.

---

11. Closing Scripture & Prayer Prompt
Read aloud:
"The LORD is known by the judgment which he executeth."
— *Psalm 9:16*
Prayer Prompt:
"Lord, thank You for restraining evil, for revealing truth, and for reminding us that You alone rule history."

Lesson 28 — Israel and America

Series Title

God's Providence in American History: From the Pilgrims to the Present

Theme Verse

"And I will bless them that bless thee, and curse him that curseth thee."
— *Genesis 12:3*

Lesson Aim (For the Teacher)

To show how God's unchanging covenant with Israel remains active in history, and how nations—including America—have experienced blessing or restraint in relation to their posture toward God's purposes for Israel.
This lesson emphasizes **covenant faithfulness**, not national favoritism.

Time Flow (Minimum 40 Minutes)

- Opening Scripture & Prayer – 4 minutes
- Biblical Framework – 12 minutes
- Historical Narrative & Providential Observations – 16 minutes
- Discussion – 5 minutes
- Application & Closing Reflection – 3 minutes

---

1. Opening Scripture Reading

Read aloud together:
"For the gifts and calling of God are without repentance."
— *Romans 11:29*

---

2. Core Truth Statement

God's covenant with Israel is permanent, and His faithfulness to that covenant shapes the course of nations.

God does not forget His promises—even across centuries.

3. Biblical Foundation: God's Covenant with Israel

Key Scriptures

"I will establish my covenant between me and thee."
— *Genesis 17:7*

"He hath remembered his covenant for ever."
— *Psalm 105:8*

"Blindness in part is happened to Israel… until the fulness of the Gentiles be come in."
— *Romans 11:25*

Teaching Point (Scripture-Anchored)

Scripture affirms that God's covenant with Israel is **unconditional, ongoing, and not replaced**, even during periods of discipline.
(Jeremiah 31:35–37; Zechariah 2:8)
God's faithfulness to Israel reflects His faithfulness to all His promises.

---

4. Historical Context: Israel's Return to the World Stage

In the modern era, Israel's return to nationhood marked one of the most unexpected developments in world history.
After nearly two millennia of dispersion, the Jewish people re-emerged as a sovereign nation—an outcome few believed possible.

- **Israel re-emerged after centuries of dispersion**
  For generations, the Jewish people lived without a homeland, scattered across nations and cultures.
  History recorded their survival—but not their restoration.
- **This return followed immense suffering**
  The trauma of the Holocaust devastated European Jewry and shocked the conscience of the world.
  Loss was immeasurable, and recovery seemed unimaginable.
- **Events unfolded rapidly and unexpectedly**
  Diplomatic decisions, international votes, and military outcomes converged within a brief window of time.
  What had been debated for decades resolved in months.

Humanly speaking, **restoration appeared improbable**.
Nations do not typically re-form after centuries of absence.
Peoples displaced for generations do not suddenly reclaim sovereignty.
"Shall a nation be born at once?"
— *Isaiah 66:8*

Yet it occurred.
The emergence of Israel was not the result of a single cause or actor.
It involved political maneuvering, global fatigue from war, moral reckoning, and historical convergence.
"For the LORD hath chosen Zion; he hath desired it for his habitation."
— *Psalm 132:13*
Providence in this moment does not eliminate complexity.
It does not simplify suffering.
It does not assign moral perfection.
Instead, it reveals that **God remains active in history over long spans of time**.
What seemed impossible in one generation became reality in another.
What appeared forgotten remained remembered.
"The counsel of the LORD standeth for ever, the thoughts of his heart to all generations."
— *Psalm 33:11*
Israel's return to the world stage reminds us that providence operates on a timeline far longer than human expectation.
History may pause.
Promises may seem delayed.
But God's purposes do not expire.

---

5. America's Historical Posture
Historically, America has maintained a notable posture toward Israel that, while imperfect and inconsistent, has been directionally significant.
Across decades, this posture has included:

- Support for Israel's right to exist as a nation
- Diplomatic recognition at critical moments
- Military, humanitarian, and economic assistance
- Advocacy for Israel's security amid regional hostility

This posture was neither unanimous nor uninterrupted. Policies shifted. Leaders differed. Motivations varied. Yet taken as a whole, America's stance leaned toward recognition rather than rejection.
Scripture reminds us that God often evaluates direction more than flawlessness.
"Happy is that people, whose God is the LORD."
— **Psalm 144:15**
Providence is rarely seen in unbroken consistency. It is seen in repeated alignment—especially when alignment carries cost or controversy.
America's posture toward Israel was not always convenient:

- It invited criticism
- It complicated foreign relations
- It required moral clarity in complex circumstances

Yet support persisted, even when politically difficult.

Scripture establishes a foundational principle regarding God's purposes:

"For the LORD hath chosen Zion; he hath desired it for his habitation."

— **Psalm 132:13**

This does **not** mean:

- That Israel's actions are beyond critique
- That political decisions are automatically righteous
- That nations receive unconditional favor

It means that God's redemptive purposes involving Israel are ongoing—and nations are wise to treat those purposes with reverence rather than dismissal.

Providence is therefore observed not in claiming moral superiority, but in choosing restraint, recognition, and respect toward what God has declared significant.

"The LORD shall count, when he writeth up the people, that this man was born there."

— **Psalm 87:6**

America's historical posture does not prove righteousness.

It demonstrates awareness.

Providence is not measured by perfection—but by orientation.

Nations that acknowledge God's purposes, even imperfectly, place themselves within the stream of His restraint rather than outside it.

---

6. Providential Observations (With Restraint)

Providential Example #1 — Survival Against Odds

Across decades of hostility, one reality has remained striking: **survival**.

Israel's continued existence has repeatedly defied expectations. Military analysts, political observers, and adversaries alike have forecast collapse, disappearance, or absorption. Threats have been persistent. Pressure has been constant. The margin for error has often appeared impossibly thin.

Yet survival has endured.

Despite repeated conflicts and sustained hostility, Israel has persisted as a people and a nation. Outcomes that were widely predicted to be temporary proved lasting. Scenarios that seemed unsustainable continued.

Scripture speaks directly to this kind of preservation:

"Behold, he that keepeth Israel shall neither slumber nor sleep."

— *Psalm 121:4*

This verse does not promise peace without conflict.
It affirms **unceasing vigilance**.
Providence here was seen not in the absence of danger, but in **continuance despite it**.
God did not remove opposition. He did not guarantee ease. But He preserved life where extinction was often expected. Survival itself became the testimony—not as triumph, but as endurance.
This matters biblically.
Throughout Scripture, Israel's existence is repeatedly threatened, yet preserved. The pattern is not one of uninterrupted blessing, but of divine keeping through discipline, exile, opposition, and return. Survival does not imply perfection; it points to preservation.
Providence often works this way.
God's hand may be seen not in dominance, but in persistence. Not in victory without loss, but in survival where loss should have ended the story.
This observation is not a claim of moral superiority.
It is an acknowledgment of **preservation amid improbability**.
Survival itself—continued existence against sustained pressure—invites reflection rather than presumption. Scripture calls such moments reminders of God's watchfulness, not grounds for pride.
Providence here was not loud.
It was **steady**.

Theological Reflection (Optional Closing Sentence)
When survival endures where disappearance is repeatedly predicted, preservation itself may point beyond human explanation.

Providential Example #2 — Blessing Through Alignment
Throughout history, Scripture records a consistent principle: God's purposes move forward regardless of human resistance, and blessing flows toward those who align themselves respectfully with what He is doing.
This principle appears clearly in God's words to Abraham:
"I will bless them that bless thee, and curse him that curseth thee."
— *Genesis 12:3*
And later reaffirmed:
"Blessed is he that blesseth thee."
— *Numbers 24:9*
These passages do not describe a political transaction.
They reveal a **directional reality**.

Alignment with God's purposes carries consequence.

Across modern history, nations that aligned respectfully with Israel—recognizing its right to exist and acting with restraint rather than hostility—often experienced relative stability. Catastrophic reversal was avoided. Long-term relationships proved more durable than predicted.

This does not mean those nations were morally superior.

It does not mean they were free from hardship.

It does not guarantee prosperity.

Providence here is **not mechanical**.

God's blessing does not function like a contract or bargaining chip. Scripture never reduces divine favor to political loyalty. Rather, it reveals that opposition to God's declared purposes carries consequence, while alignment tends toward preservation.

This distinction matters deeply.

When blessing is treated transactionally, it breeds presumption. When it is understood directionally, it encourages humility. God's purposes move forward whether nations cooperate or resist. The question is not whether God's will succeeds—but whether resistance places a nation in its path.

Providence here was seen in **avoidance of collapse**, not exemption from trial.

Nations that acted with restraint rather than hostility often avoided severe reversal. Stability endured not because of perfection, but because alignment placed them within the current of God's unfolding purposes rather than against it.

Providence often works this way.

God does not promise ease to those who align with Him—but He does warn against opposition to what He has declared. Blessing flows along the path of obedience, not entitlement.

This observation calls for sobriety, not pride.

Alignment is not leverage.

It is humility before God's purposes.

Theological Reflection (Optional Closing Sentence)
When nations align with what God is doing rather than resisting it, preservation may follow—even without guarantees.

Providential Example #3 — Restraint Rather Than Favoritism
Any discussion of providence must be carefully guarded against misunderstanding.
Scripture is clear: **God does not operate through favoritism.**
Support does not equal righteousness.
Blessing does not imply moral approval.
Preservation does not remove accountability.
Providence is not a declaration of innocence.
The Bible states this plainly:
"Then Peter opened his mouth, and said, Of a truth I perceive that God is no respecter of persons."
— *Acts 10:34*
This verse eliminates any notion of entitlement.
God's dealings with nations—and with people—are governed by justice, holiness, and purpose, not partiality. No nation is exempt from discipline. No people are immune to correction. No alignment guarantees exemption from God's moral standards.
Providence here must be understood as **restraint**, not reward.
God may restrain destruction without endorsing behavior. He may preserve life without approving conduct. He may limit judgment without denying accountability. Scripture repeatedly shows God disciplining those He preserves.
This distinction matters deeply.
When providence is mistaken for favoritism, humility gives way to presumption. Moral self-examination stops. Correction is resisted. History shows that this misunderstanding often precedes decline.
Providence works through **alignment with God's purposes**, not entitlement to His favor. Alignment invites preservation—but it does not cancel responsibility. God's justice remains active even where His restraint is evident. Blessing, when present, should produce repentance, not pride.
Scripture consistently affirms this balance.
God is patient—but impartial.
Merciful—but just.
Preserving—but correcting.
Providence is not God taking sides blindly.

It is God advancing His purposes while holding all accountable.

Theological Reflection (Optional Closing Sentence)
When preservation leads to humility rather than presumption, providence has been rightly understood.

---

7. Avoiding Common Errors

Any discussion of God's providence among nations must be handled with care.
Scripture records God's active involvement in history—but it also draws **clear boundaries**.
When those boundaries are ignored, providence is easily distorted into entitlement, nationalism, or theological confusion.
This lesson deliberately avoids several common errors.
First, it avoids **declaring any nation "chosen."**
The Bible uses covenant language precisely and sparingly. God's covenant promises are not transferable by admiration, influence, or political alignment. Scripture does not authorize the labeling of modern nations as "chosen" in the covenantal sense.
Second, it avoids **assuming automatic blessing.**
Providence is not a guarantee of ongoing favor. Scripture repeatedly shows that preservation does not cancel discipline. Blessing does not remove accountability. God's patience is often misread as approval—but the Bible warns against this error.
Third, it avoids **confusing policy with covenant.**
Political decisions, alliances, or sympathies do not create biblical standing before God. Scripture alone defines covenant relationship, and covenant is always grounded in God's sovereign choosing—not human declaration.
The Bible is explicit on this point:
"The LORD hath chosen Zion; he hath desired it for his habitation."
— *Psalm 132:13*
This verse does not describe a pattern to be repeated.
It declares a **specific, divine act**.
God's covenant with Israel is unique in Scripture—rooted in promise, lineage, and redemptive purpose. No other nation is described this way. No modern people may claim this status without departing from biblical authority.
Providence must therefore be understood **without covenant inflation**.
God governs all nations.
He restrains evil.
He advances His purposes.
But covenant identity remains defined by Scripture alone.

This distinction protects humility.

When nations confuse providence with chosenness, pride follows. When blessing is assumed rather than received with gratitude, repentance fades. Scripture warns repeatedly that presumption invites correction.

Providence is not covenant.

Alignment is not election.

Preservation is not entitlement.

Understanding this rightly allows providence to be appreciated **without distortion**.

Theological Reflection (Optional Closing Sentence)

When providence is interpreted through Scripture rather than sentiment, humility replaces presumption.

---

8. Discussion Questions (Choose 2–3)

1. Why is God's covenant with Israel still relevant today?
2. How can nations align with God's purposes without presumption?
3. What dangers arise when Scripture is oversimplified?
4. How does God's faithfulness to Israel strengthen our trust in Him?

---

9. Personal & National Application

Personal

- Do I trust God to keep His promises over time?
- Do I submit my views to Scripture?

National

- Blessing follows humility
- Alignment requires discernment
- God's purposes transcend politics

"The counsel of the LORD standeth for ever."

— *Psalm 33:11*

10. Closing Reflection

Israel's story reminds us that history is not random.

It unfolds under the watchful governance of a God who remembers, preserves, and fulfills His Word—often across centuries rather than moments:

"God is not a man, that he should lie; neither the son of man, that he should repent: hath he said, and shall he not do it?"

— *Numbers 23:19*

Empires have risen and fallen around Israel. Threats have come from every direction. Exile, dispersion, and opposition have marked her history. Yet preservation has endured—not because of strength, numbers, or political favor, but because of divine faithfulness:

"He that keepeth Israel shall neither slumber nor sleep."

— *Psalm 121:4*

Providence in Israel's history does not deny discipline. Scripture records judgment, correction, and long seasons of suffering:

"You only have I known of all the families of the earth: therefore I will punish you for all your iniquities."

— *Amos 3:2*

Yet judgment was never abandonment. God's promises were not canceled by human failure:

"For the gifts and calling of God are without repentance."

— *Romans 11:29*

Israel's survival across generations stands as testimony that God works on a scale beyond headlines and human attention spans. Providence is often invisible in a single lifetime, yet unmistakable across centuries:

"One generation shall praise thy works to another, and shall declare thy mighty acts."

— *Psalm 145:4*

This lesson guards us against shallow conclusions. God's purposes are not rushed. His faithfulness is not hurried. What appears delayed to man is deliberate in heaven:

"The Lord is not slack concerning his promise… but is longsuffering."

— *2 Peter 3:9*

Israel's story calls us to humility. It reminds us that God governs history with memory, intention, and covenant faithfulness. Providence is not measured by immediacy—but by fulfillment.

"The counsel of the LORD standeth for ever, the thoughts of his heart to all generations."

— *Psalm 33:11*

Providence is measured not in moments—but in centuries.

---

11. Closing Scripture & Prayer Prompt

Read aloud:

"Pray for the peace of Jerusalem."

— *Psalm 122:6*

Prayer Prompt:

"Lord, teach us to honor Your covenant faithfulness and to walk humbly before Your purposes."

Lesson 29 — The Cold War That Never Turned Hot

Series Title

God's Providence in American History: From the Pilgrims to the Present

Theme Verse

"Hitherto shalt thou come, but no further: and here shall thy proud waves be stayed."
— *Job 38:11*

Lesson Aim (For the Teacher)

To show how God restrained global destruction during decades of unprecedented tension, illustrating that **His providence may be most clearly seen in disasters that never occurred**.

This lesson emphasizes **restraint over resolution.**

Time Flow (Minimum 40 Minutes)

- Opening Scripture & Prayer – 4 minutes
- Biblical Framework – 10 minutes
- Historical Narrative & Providential Observations – 18 minutes
- Discussion – 5 minutes
- Application & Closing Reflection – 3 minutes

---

1. Opening Scripture Reading

Read aloud together:

"The LORD reigneth; let the earth rejoice."
— *Psalm 97:1*

---

2. Core Truth Statement

God's providence is often revealed not in what happens, but in what is restrained from happening.

When destruction is possible at any moment, restraint itself becomes mercy.

---

3. Biblical Pattern: God Sets Limits on Human Power

Key Scriptures

"He removeth kings, and setteth up kings."
— *Daniel 2:21*

"The king's heart is in the hand of the LORD."
— *Proverbs 21:1*

"Except the LORD keep the city, the watchman waketh but in vain."
— *Psalm 127:1*

Teaching Point (Scripture-Anchored)

Scripture affirms that even the most powerful rulers and systems operate **within boundaries established by God**, whether they acknowledge Him or not.
(Isaiah 10:5–7; Romans 13:1)

---

4. The Unique Danger of the Cold War

The Cold War introduced a form of danger unlike any previous conflict in human history.
For the first time, humanity possessed the ability to destroy itself **instantaneously**.

- **Nuclear weapons made instant annihilation possible**
  The destructive power of atomic and thermonuclear weapons far exceeded all prior forms of warfare.
  Entire cities could be erased in moments.
- **Miscommunication could have ended civilization**
  Decisions were often made under intense pressure and incomplete information.
  A single error—technological or human—had the potential to trigger irreversible catastrophe.
- **Fear shaped global policy**
  Nations planned not merely for victory, but for survival.
  Deterrence replaced diplomacy, and restraint became a strategic necessity.
- **Entire generations lived under threat**
  Children practiced emergency drills.
  Societies adapted psychologically to the possibility of sudden destruction.

Never before had humanity possessed such **destructive capability** without corresponding moral certainty.

"Except the LORD keep the city, the watchman waketh but in vain."
— *Psalm 127:1*

The Cold War revealed a sobering reality:
human power had outpaced human wisdom.

"There is no wisdom nor understanding nor counsel against the LORD."
— *Proverbs 21:30*
Providence during this era did not appear through triumph or decisive victory.
It appeared through **restraint**.
Missiles were not launched.
Warnings were questioned.
Systems failed without escalating.
"In quietness and in confidence shall be your strength."
— *Isaiah 30:15*
The absence of catastrophe was itself remarkable.
The Cold War stands as a testament to a difficult truth:
when humanity holds the power of total destruction, survival depends not on strength—but on restraint.
Providence did not eliminate danger.
It limited its reach.

This section intentionally examines a sustained pattern of restraint across the Cold War rather than isolating one event, emphasizing what did not occur despite continual opportunity for catastrophe.

---

5. Where Total Destruction Was Avoided
Providential Example #1 — Crises That Did Not Escalate
At several moments in modern history, the margin between survival and catastrophe was frighteningly thin.
Crises arose suddenly. Information was incomplete. Decisions had to be made under intense pressure, often within minutes. The tools available for response carried irreversible consequences.
A single misstep could have ended civilization as it was known.
Yet escalation did not occur.
At critical moments:

- Decisions were delayed rather than rushed
- Launches were aborted
- Communication replaced immediate reaction
- Restraint prevailed over impulse

These pauses mattered.
Scripture speaks to the strength found in restraint rather than reaction:

"In quietness and in confidence shall be your strength."
— *Isaiah 30:15*
This verse does not praise passivity.
It praises **measured response under pressure**.
Providence here was seen in **delay**.
God did not remove the danger. He did not prevent the existence of destructive capability. But He restrained action long enough for reason, verification, and communication to intervene.
This restraint was decisive.
History records moments when alarms were triggered falsely, intelligence was misinterpreted, or assumptions proved wrong only moments before irreversible action might have been taken. The fact that escalation stopped—sometimes seconds before catastrophe—cannot be dismissed lightly.
Providence often works through **hesitation**.
When reaction is delayed, consequences can be avoided. When confidence replaces panic, destruction may be restrained. God's hand may be seen not in dramatic rescue, but in the quiet interruption of impulse.
Restraint mattered more than dominance.
Victory would have meant nothing in the face of annihilation. Strength was shown not by force, but by the refusal to unleash it. Leadership was tested not by aggression, but by the ability to pause.
Providence here was not loud.
It was **measured silence** where chaos could have erupted.
Total destruction was avoided—not because danger was absent, but because restraint prevailed.

Theological Reflection (Optional Closing Sentence)
When catastrophe is avoided by restraint rather than power, providence may be seen in what was never unleashed.

Providential Example #2 — Human Limitations and Conscience
In moments of extreme danger, the greatest restraint did not come from technology—but from **people**.
Despite immense pressure to act quickly, individuals hesitated. Procedures required confirmation. Systems designed for speed were slowed by human judgment. Automation was interrupted by conscience.
This interruption mattered.

At critical moments, decisions that could not be reversed were delayed by ordinary people who sensed the gravity of what was at stake. They questioned assumptions. They sought verification. They resisted the momentum of fear-driven response.

Scripture repeatedly shows God working through such moments:

"And who knoweth whether thou art come to the kingdom for such a time as this?"

— *Esther 4:14*

And again:

"What doth the LORD require of thee, but to do justly, and to love mercy, and to walk humbly with thy God?"

— *Micah 6:8*

These passages do not describe dramatic intervention.

They describe **moral courage exercised at decisive moments**.

Providence here was seen in **human restraint**.

God did not remove the systems capable of destruction. He allowed them to exist—and then ensured they were not absolute. Human conscience interrupted automation. Moral judgment slowed processes designed for rapid response.

This restraint was not accidental.

Systems fail. Data misleads. Alarms trigger falsely. In such environments, unthinking obedience could have ended everything. Instead, hesitation created space for truth to surface.

Providence often works through **limitation**.

God places boundaries not only on evil, but on human systems. He ensures that conscience has a seat at the table. Ordinary people—unknown to history at the time—became instruments of preservation simply by refusing to act without certainty.

This matters deeply.

It reminds us that God does not always save through power. He often saves through restraint. He does not always act through leaders alone, but through individuals willing to pause, question, and choose wisely under pressure.

Extraordinary destruction was restrained by ordinary conscience.

Providence here was not visible in force.

It was visible in **hesitation that saved the world**.

Theological Reflection (Optional Closing Sentence)

When conscience interrupts automation, providence may be working through ordinary faithfulness at extraordinary moments.

Providential Example #3 — Collapse Without Catastrophe

The Cold War concluded—but not in the way many had feared.

For decades, the world lived under the shadow of nuclear exchange. Entire generations expected that the conflict would end in fire, devastation, and irreversible loss. The capacity for annihilation existed. The hostility was real. The ideological divide was entrenched.

Yet catastrophe did not occur.

The era ended:

- Without nuclear exchange
- Without global annihilation
- Without civilization-destroying war

Instead, the conflict closed through **internal collapse rather than external destruction.**

This outcome was not inevitable.

History offers few examples where prolonged, deeply polarized conflicts involving such destructive capability ended without violent resolution. The tools for catastrophe were in place. The opportunity existed. The expectation was widespread.

That expectation was not fulfilled.

Scripture speaks to the mercy found in such restraint:

"For the LORD will not cast off for ever."

— *Lamentations 3:31*

This verse does not deny judgment.

It declares **that judgment has an end.**

Providence here was seen in **how the era closed.**

God did not eliminate conflict instantly. He did not erase decades of tension or suffering. But He brought the period to an end without unleashing the destruction it had long threatened to produce.

The collapse was systemic, not catastrophic.

Structures failed. Ideologies weakened. Control eroded. Yet the world did not burn. What could have ended civilization instead ended an era.

This mattered profoundly.

The absence of catastrophe preserved the future. It allowed nations to adjust, recover, and redefine relationships without starting from ashes. It ensured that correction did not become annihilation.

Providence often works this way at the close of long trials.

God allows systems to exhaust themselves. He permits collapse without permitting destruction. He ends eras not always with spectacle, but with restraint.

The Cold War did not end because humanity became perfect.

It ended because destruction was **held back.**
Providence here was not dramatic intervention.
It was **merciful conclusion.**

Theological Reflection (Optional Closing Sentence)
When a long season of threat ends without catastrophe, restraint itself may testify to God's preserving mercy.

---

6. Restraint Does Not Mean Innocence

Important clarification:

- Suffering occurred globally
- Proxy wars claimed millions of lives
- Fear shaped entire generations

The Cold War was not peaceful—it was restrained.
Across decades:

- Nations lived under constant threat
- Entire regions suffered through proxy conflicts
- Innocent civilians bore the cost of ideological struggle
- Fear became a daily reality rather than a distant possibility

Restraint does not imply moral innocence. It does not absolve nations of responsibility for suffering caused indirectly or deliberately.
Scripture makes this distinction clear:
God's protection does not deny human guilt—it limits human destruction.
"God is our refuge and strength, a very present help in trouble."
— **Psalm 46:1**
The restraint of nuclear war did not erase pain.
It prevented *annihilation.*
At multiple moments in Cold War history:

- Launch decisions were delayed
- Alarms proved false
- Human judgment interrupted automation
- Conscience overruled protocol

These moments of hesitation were not random. They reveal a biblical pattern:
God often restrains evil by restraining *reaction.*
"Surely the wrath of man shall praise thee: the remainder of wrath shalt thou restrain."
— **Psalm 76:10**

Providence did not make the era righteous.
It made survival possible.

---

7. Why This Matters Spiritually

he Cold War teaches enduring spiritual lessons:

- Human power has limits
- Fear is not sovereign
- God's boundaries still hold

For the first time in history, humanity possessed the ability to destroy itself completely—and did not.

This restraint confronts a common illusion:
That power determines destiny.
Scripture counters that illusion directly:
"Be still, and know that I am God."
— **Psalm 46:10**
Silence after restraint is not emptiness.
It is mercy.
The absence of catastrophe invites reflection rather than pride.
It calls for gratitude rather than explanation.
It demands humility rather than self-congratulation.
"The LORD reigneth."
— **Psalm 97:1**
God's sovereignty does not disappear in moments of tension—it becomes more apparent in what does *not* occur.
The Cold War ended not with global collapse, but with gradual unraveling—leaving space for repentance, rebuilding, and reorientation.
Providence closed the era without fire.
That restraint speaks louder than any explosion.

---

8. Discussion Questions (Choose 2–3)

1. Why does God sometimes restrain disaster rather than remove threat?
2. How does recognizing restraint change our understanding of history?
3. What dangers arise when humanity trusts technology over humility?
4. How should gratitude shape memory of near-catastrophe?

---

9. Personal & National Application

Personal

- Do I thank God for dangers avoided?
- Am I aware of unseen mercy in my life?

National

- Power must be restrained
- Wisdom must guide capability
- Gratitude guards humility

"The LORD is good."
— *Psalm 34:8*

---

10. Closing Reflection

The Cold War was defined not primarily by what happened,
but by what never did.

For decades, nations stood armed with the power to destroy civilization many times over. Suspicion ruled, fear escalated, and moments of crisis brought humanity to the edge of irreversible disaster. Scripture warns of such pride and power:

"There is no king saved by the multitude of an host: a mighty man is not delivered by much strength."
— *Psalm 33:16*

Providence did not remove the threat. Weapons were built. Plans were made. Yet destruction was restrained. Again and again, catastrophe was delayed—sometimes by hesitation, sometimes by conscience, sometimes by systems designed to slow reaction:

"The discretion of a man deferreth his anger; and it is his glory to pass over a transgression."
— *Proverbs 19:11*

History records moments when a single decision could have unleashed devastation beyond recovery. That restraint was not accidental. Scripture reminds us that God governs even the hearts of rulers:

"The king's heart is in the hand of the LORD… he turneth it whithersoever he will."
— *Proverbs 21:1*

Providence appeared not in victory, but in mercy. Not in triumph, but in limitation. Humanity was capable of annihilation—yet annihilation did not come:

"Thus far shalt thou come, but no farther."
— *Job 38:11*

The Cold War ended not with a final battle, but with collapse from within and a path opened for change. God allowed tension to reveal human limits, while restraining destruction that would have ended history itself:
"For the LORD will not cast off for ever."
— *Lamentations 3:31*
Providence is sometimes loud—but often it is silent.
It works through delay.
It works through restraint.
It works through mercy undeserved.
"Surely the wrath of man shall praise thee: the remainder of wrath shalt thou restrain."
— *Psalm 76:10*
The Cold War stands as a sobering testimony: humanity was capable of unleashing destruction—but God held it back.
Providence did not erase danger.
It restrained it.

---

11. Closing Scripture & Prayer Prompt
Read aloud:
"The LORD hath done great things for us; whereof we are glad."
— *Psalm 126:3*
Prayer Prompt:
"Lord, thank You for mercy we often overlook, and help us live humbly before You."

Lesson 30 — Technological Protection & Providence

Series Title

God's Providence in American History: From the Pilgrims to the Present

Theme Verse

"Though they be wise, and many, yet shall they be cut down."
— *Nahum 1:12*

Lesson Aim (For the Teacher)

To show how, in an age of increasing technological power, God's providence is revealed through **limitations, safeguards, and restraint**—reminding us that technology may assist, but **God alone preserves**.

This lesson emphasizes **dependence over confidence**.

Time Flow (Minimum 40 Minutes)

- Opening Scripture & Prayer – 4 minutes
- Biblical Framework – 10 minutes
- Historical Narrative & Providential Observations – 18 minutes
- Discussion – 5 minutes
- Application & Closing Reflection – 3 minutes

---

1. Opening Scripture Reading

Read aloud together:

"The horse is prepared against the day of battle: but safety is of the LORD."
— *Proverbs 21:31*

---

2. Core Truth Statement

Technology can extend human ability—but it cannot replace God's protection.

Confidence in systems without humility invites failure.

---

3. Biblical Pattern: Tools Without Trust Fail

Key Scriptures

"Some trust in chariots, and some in horses: but we will remember the name of the LORD."
— *Psalm 20:7*

"Except the LORD keep the city, the watchman waketh but in vain."
— *Psalm 127:1*

"Cursed be the man that trusteth in man."
— *Jeremiah 17:5*

Teaching Point (Scripture-Anchored)

Scripture teaches that tools are neutral, but **trust misplaced in tools becomes dangerous** when reliance shifts from God to human systems.
(Isaiah 31:1; 2 Chronicles 16:12)

---

4. The Rise of Technological Safeguards

As the dangers of modern warfare and global systems became apparent, nations sought ways to reduce the risk of catastrophic error.
In response to growing awareness of human fallibility, **technological safeguards** were introduced.

- **Early warning systems were developed**
  Radar, satellite monitoring, and detection networks were created to identify threats as early as possible.
  These systems were intended to provide time for verification rather than immediate reaction.
- **Communication networks expanded**
  Direct lines between leadership were established to reduce misunderstanding.
  Rapid communication replaced silence and delay, allowing clarification during moments of crisis.
- **Safety protocols were established**
  Multiple layers of authorization were required before irreversible actions could be taken.
  Procedures were designed to slow decision-making when emotions or uncertainty ran high.
- **Redundancies were built into critical systems**
  Fail-safes, backups, and cross-checks acknowledged that machines and humans both fail.
  No single signal was meant to carry final authority.

These advances **reduced risk—but did not eliminate it.**

"There is a way which seemeth right unto a man, but the end thereof are the ways of death."
— *Proverbs 14:12*
Technology can warn.
Technology can delay.
Technology can assist.
But it cannot replace wisdom.
"Except the LORD keep the city, the watchman waketh but in vain."
— *Psalm 127:1*
Providence in the modern era often appears through layers of restraint rather than dramatic intervention.
Safeguards reflect an unspoken recognition of human limitation.
Yet Scripture reminds us that **ultimate security does not rest in systems**.
"Put not your trust in princes, nor in the son of man, in whom there is no help."
— *Psalm 146:3*
The rise of technological safeguards reveals both human ingenuity and human vulnerability.
They stand as tools—useful, necessary, and limited.
Protection, in the final measure, remains the work of God.

---

5. Where Technology Failed—and Was Restrained
Providential Example #1 — System Failures That Did Not Escalate
False Alarms and Human Discernment
As technological systems advanced, early-warning networks were designed to detect threats faster than human senses could. Sensors monitored skies and seas. Computers analyzed signals. Alerts were meant to prompt immediate response.
Yet technology proved fallible.
Historical Illustration
In September 1983, during the height of the Cold War, a Soviet early-warning satellite system falsely reported the launch of multiple U.S. nuclear missiles. According to established protocol, this alert could have triggered rapid escalation toward nuclear retaliation.
The warning was not real.
The system had misinterpreted reflected sunlight as missile launches.
Rather than following automation without question, the officer on duty questioned the alert.
He judged the data inconsistent with reality and delayed reporting it as a confirmed attack.
Further verification revealed the error.
From a technical standpoint, catastrophe was possible.
From a human standpoint, judgment intervened.
From a providential standpoint, escalation was restrained.

Scripture commends such discernment:
"A prudent man foreseeth the evil, and hideth himself: but the simple pass on, and are punished."
— Proverbs 22:3
This example does not glorify technology.
Nor does it praise human brilliance.
It highlights restraint.
God did not prevent systems from failing.
He prevented failure from becoming final.
Providence appeared not in perfect design, but in the interruption of automated momentum.
Human responsibility—willing to pause, verify, and question—became the means by which destruction was restrained.
Technology failed.
Disaster did not follow.
Providence worked through discernment.

Theological Reflection (Optional Closing Sentence)
When vigilance restrains what automation would unleash, providence may be working through human discernment.

Providential Example #2 — Limits on Automation
Authority Intentionally Restrained
As technology increased in speed and capability, so did the temptation to remove human hesitation from decision-making. Automation promised efficiency. Systems were designed to respond faster than conscience could deliberate.
Yet even at the height of technological power, limits were deliberately retained.
Historical Illustration
Throughout the Cold War—and continuing into the present—nuclear launch systems were intentionally designed to require human authorization at multiple levels. Automation could detect threats, calculate trajectories, and issue warnings. It could not act alone.
Safeguards included:

- Multiple human confirmations
- Separate authorization codes
- Physical distance between decision-makers
- Built-in delays requiring verification and review

These limits were not technical weaknesses.
They were moral acknowledgments.

Scripture affirms the wisdom of such restraint:
"To every thing there is a season, and a time to every purpose under the heaven."
— Ecclesiastes 3:1
Providence here was seen in delay.
God often restrains destruction not by removing capability, but by inserting time—time to reflect, time to verify, time for conscience to speak. Speed without wisdom multiplies error.
Hesitation, in some moments, is mercy.
Automation advanced.
Authority remained human.
Responsibility could not be delegated to machines.
Providence was seen not in flawless systems, but in limits that forced judgment.

Theological Reflection (Optional Closing Sentence)
When time is built into decision-making, restraint itself may be an act of God's mercy.

Providential Example #3 — Collapse Without Technological Disaster
Failure Moderated, Not Exploited
As complex technological systems aged, strain became unavoidable. Infrastructure grew interconnected. Maintenance lagged. Errors accumulated. Predictions of sudden collapse became common.
Yet collapse did not come all at once.
Historical Illustration
At multiple points in modern history, technological systems faced the possibility of cascading failure. One widely recognized example was the approach of the year 2000 (Y2K), when experts warned that computer date errors could disrupt power grids, banking systems, transportation, and communications worldwide.
Failures were possible.
Catastrophe was anticipated.
Yet systems did not collapse suddenly. Disruptions were limited. Essential functions continued. Time remained for correction, transition, and repair.
Scripture speaks to this sustaining restraint:
"He upholdeth all things by the word of his power."
— Hebrews 1:3
This verse does not promise uninterrupted success.
It describes continual sustaining.
Providence here was seen in what did not happen.

God did not make systems indestructible.
He restrained collapse from becoming total.
Gradual failure allows time—for repentance, reform, and rebuilding. Sudden catastrophe leaves none. Providence often favors endurance over appearance.
Technology weakened.
Order endured.
The future remained possible.
Providence sustained what human design could not secure.

---

6. Technology as Stewardship, Not Savior

Important clarification:

- Technology is a tool
- Wisdom must govern its use
- Dependence must remain spiritual

Throughout modern history, technological advancement has brought undeniable benefits:

- Early-warning systems
- Medical breakthroughs
- Safer transportation
- Improved communication
- Redundant safety mechanisms

These developments have saved lives and reduced risk. Yet Scripture warns that increased capability does not automatically produce increased wisdom.
"Knowledge puffeth up, but charity edifieth."
— 1 Corinthians 8:1
Technology magnifies human intent—both good and evil. Without moral restraint, increased capability becomes increased danger.
History repeatedly demonstrates that:

- Tools cannot govern conscience
- Systems cannot replace judgment
- Automation cannot remove accountability

God entrusts humanity with stewardship, not sovereignty.
"Moreover it is required in stewards, that a man be found faithful."
— 1 Corinthians 4:2
Providence is not diminished by technology. It operates through it—by limiting failure, restraining escalation, and preserving oversight.
But technology must remain *servant*, never *savior*.
When confidence shifts from God to systems, Scripture warns that pride is near.

"Except the LORD keep the city, the watchman waketh but in vain."
— **Psalm 127:1**

---

7. Why Providence Still Matters

Technology cannot:

- Govern morality
- Replace conscience
- Prevent pride

No system—however advanced—can address the deepest human problems. It may delay consequences, but it cannot redeem hearts.

Only God:

- Sets moral boundaries
- Preserves life beyond human planning
- Sustains order when systems fail

"The LORD reigneth; he is clothed with majesty."
— **Psalm 93:1**

Modern society is tempted to believe that risk has been mastered—that enough innovation can secure the future. Scripture challenges this assumption.

"Trust in the LORD with all thine heart; and lean not unto thine own understanding."
— **Proverbs 3:5**

Providence still matters because:

- Human error remains
- Pride persists
- Judgment requires wisdom beyond data

Technology may warn.
Technology may delay.
Technology may assist.
But protection belongs to God alone.

"He upholdeth all things by the word of his power."
— **Hebrews 1:3**

Providence does not disappear in modernity.
It becomes easier to overlook.
And the greatest danger is not technological failure—
but forgetting the One who restrains it.

8. Discussion Questions (Choose 2–3)

1. Why is trust in technology tempting?
2. How does humility protect us in a high-tech world?
3. What dangers arise when systems replace conscience?
4. How can we practice technological stewardship?

9. Personal & National Application

Personal

- Where do I place my trust?
- Do I depend on systems more than God?

National

- Wisdom must guide power
- Safeguards must include humility
- Gratitude guards against pride

"Trust in the LORD with all thine heart."
— *Proverbs 3:5*

10. Closing Reflection

Technology may warn.
Technology may delay.
Technology may assist.
But protection belongs to God alone.

Modern systems can detect threats, analyze data, and slow reaction—but they cannot guarantee wisdom, restraint, or mercy. Scripture reminds us that tools are never the ultimate safeguard:

"There is no wisdom nor understanding nor counsel against the LORD."
— *Proverbs 21:30*

Throughout history, humanity has trusted in its inventions—walls, weapons, systems, and safeguards—yet Scripture consistently warns against misplaced confidence:

"Some trust in chariots, and some in horses: but we will remember the name of the LORD our God."
— *Psalm 20:7*

Technology can fail. Sensors can misread. Systems can malfunction. Decisions still rest in human hands—and human hearts remain fallen:

"Except the LORD keep the city, the watchman waketh but in vain."
— *Psalm 127:1*

Providence has not vanished in the modern age. It has become easier to overlook. The more advanced our tools become, the more subtle God's restraint appears—often working through delays, hesitations, corrections, and conscience:

"Man's goings are of the LORD; how can a man then understand his own way?"

— *Proverbs 20:24*

Protection does not ultimately come from machines, protocols, or automation. It comes from a God who upholds all things—even systems humanity barely understands:

"And he is before all things, and by him all things consist."

— *Colossians 1:17*

Providence in a technological age does not shout.

It restrains.

It interrupts.

It limits catastrophe.

"Thus far shalt thou come, but no farther."

— *Job 38:11*

The lesson is not to reject technology—but to remember its limits. Tools are servants, not saviors. Protection remains the work of God alone.

"The LORD shall preserve thee from all evil: he shall preserve thy soul."

— *Psalm 121:7*

Providence does not disappear with progress.

It becomes quieter—and more easily ignored.

---

11. Closing Scripture & Prayer Prompt

Read aloud:

"My help cometh from the LORD."

— *Psalm 121:2*

Prayer Prompt:

"Lord, help us use technology wisely while trusting You fully."

Lesson 31 — September 11 Survivals

Series Title

God's Providence in American History: From the Pilgrims to the Present

Theme Verse

"A thousand shall fall at thy side, and ten thousand at thy right hand; but it shall not come nigh thee."

— *Psalm 91:7*

Lesson Aim (For the Teacher)

To show how, even in one of the darkest days in American history, God's providence was evident through **unexpected survivals, delayed arrivals, interrupted routines, and preserved lives**—while carefully avoiding claims that explain suffering or minimize loss. This lesson emphasizes **mercy amid tragedy**, not answers to why tragedy occurred.

Time Flow (Minimum 40 Minutes)

- Opening Scripture & Prayer – 4 minutes
- Biblical Framework – 10 minutes
- Historical Narrative & Providential Observations – 18 minutes
- Discussion – 5 minutes
- Application & Closing Reflection – 3 minutes

---

1. Opening Scripture Reading

Read aloud together:

"It is of the LORD's mercies that we are not consumed."

— *Lamentations 3:22*

---

2. Core Truth Statement

God's mercy is sometimes revealed not by preventing tragedy, but by preserving life within it.

Providence does not always explain—but it does preserve.

---

3. Biblical Pattern: God Preserves Amid Calamity

Key Scriptures

"The name of the LORD is a strong tower."
— *Proverbs 18:10*

"God is our refuge and strength, a very present help in trouble."
— *Psalm 46:1*

"Though I walk through the valley of the shadow of death, I will fear no evil."
— *Psalm 23:4*

Teaching Point (Scripture-Anchored)

Scripture shows that God's protection does not always remove danger—but **He remains present and active within it**, preserving according to His purposes.
(Daniel 3:24–27; Acts 27:22–24)

---

4. The Day of the Attacks

September 11, 2001, stands as one of the most painful days in American history.
The events of that morning unfolded with suddenness and shock, leaving the nation stunned and grieving.

- **Thousands lost their lives**
  Ordinary people—workers, responders, travelers—were caught in extraordinary violence.
  Lives were ended without warning.
- **Families were devastated**
  Homes were emptied in a single morning.
  Grief was immediate, personal, and enduring.
- **The nation was shaken**
  A sense of security collapsed.
  The realization of vulnerability settled deeply into the national conscience.
- **Questions overwhelmed answers**
  Why this happened, how it could have been prevented, and what it meant were questions with no easy resolution.

This lesson does **not** attempt to explain why the attacks occurred.
Scripture cautions against quick conclusions in the face of suffering:
"As for God, his way is perfect."
— *Psalm 18:30*
Instead, this lesson observes **where preservation was evident**.
Within the devastation:

- Lives were spared by delays and interruptions
- Evacuations succeeded where collapse was expected
- Courage and self-sacrifice guided others to safety

"The LORD is nigh unto them that are of a broken heart."
— *Psalm 34:18*

Providence in this moment does not appear as explanation.
It appears as **presence**.
God's hand is seen not in the absence of suffering, but in the restraint of its reach.
"God is our refuge and strength, a very present help in trouble."
— *Psalm 46:1*

September 11 reminds us of a solemn truth:
we live in a fallen world where evil acts occur,
yet we are not abandoned within it.
Providence does not always answer our questions.
Sometimes it simply carries us through the day.

---

5. Providential Observations of Preservation

Providential Example #1 — Delayed Arrivals

In many instances, survival came not through decisive action—but through interruption.
Lives were spared because schedules changed.
Meetings were postponed. Appointments were canceled. Transit was delayed. Ordinary routines were disrupted by circumstances that, at the time, felt inconvenient or frustrating.
People arrived late. Some turned back unexpectedly. Others never reached their intended destination.
From a human perspective, these delays appeared insignificant—minor disruptions in otherwise ordinary days.
Yet those delays placed individuals **outside the moment of destruction**.
Scripture reminds us:
"Man's goings are of the LORD; how can a man then understand his own way?"
— *Proverbs 20:24*

Providence here did not appear as warning or miracle.
It appeared as **timing**.
God did not alter the event itself.
He altered who was present.
Preservation came through rerouting, hesitation, and delay—quiet acts of restraint that changed outcomes without drawing attention to themselves.
This pattern is deeply biblical.

God often preserves life not by removing danger, but by **redirecting paths**. The interruption itself becomes the protection.
What felt like inconvenience became mercy.
What seemed like lost time became preserved life.
Providence did not announce itself.
It simply adjusted timing.
And when the moment of danger passed, many later realized that what they had once resented—a delay, a detour, a disruption—had quietly placed them beyond harm.
God's hand was not seen in dramatic rescue, but in **missed moments**.
Preservation came through interruption.

Teaching Insight (Optional for Adult Class)
You might ask:

- *Why do we often resist delays without considering their purpose?*
- *How does this example challenge our view of "wasted time"?*

Providential Example #2 — Unoccupied Spaces
Providential Observations of Preservation
On that morning, preservation was seen not in escape—but in emptiness.
Some offices were unexpectedly vacant.
Certain floors stood largely unoccupied.
Areas that were normally full of life and routine were quiet.
Renovation projects had displaced workers.
Schedules had shifted.
Early evacuations had already begun.
From a human perspective, these were ordinary circumstances—temporary adjustments, administrative decisions, routine safety responses.
Yet those ordinary absences placed people **outside the path of destruction**.
Scripture reminds us that God's hand is often revealed not only in what He does—but in what He **withholds**:
"Except the LORD had been on our side… then the waters had overwhelmed us."
— *Psalm 124:1, 4*
Providence here was not dramatic.
There was no warning siren from heaven.
No visible intervention.
No sudden change to the event itself.
Instead, God's preservation was seen in **spaces left empty**.

Lives were spared because people were not where they normally would have been. Absence became protection. Vacancy became mercy.

This is a recurring biblical pattern.

God often protects not by shielding those present, but by ensuring that **fewer are present at all**. He governs placement, presence, and timing with quiet authority.

The emptiness of those spaces was not random.

It was unremarkable at the time.

Unnoticed by most.

Uncelebrated afterward.

Yet that absence spared countless lives.

Providence worked silently—through renovation schedules, early evacuations, and altered routines—using ordinary decisions to produce extraordinary preservation.

God did not fill the space with intervention.

He preserved life by leaving the space unfilled.

Absence became mercy.

Teaching Insight (Optional for Adult Class)

You might ask:

- *Why do we struggle to recognize God's hand in what is missing rather than what is present?*
- *How does this example reshape our understanding of protection?*
- *Where might God be working through absence in our own lives?*

Providential Example #3 — Survival in Escape

Preservation was also seen **within** the danger itself.

Some survived not because they were absent—but because **a path remained**.

Stairwells stayed passable.

Exit routes remained open longer than expected.

Structural failure did not occur all at once.

Warnings were heard and heeded.

Voices called out.

Directions were given.

Moments of clarity broke through panic.

And in the midst of fear, courage emerged.

Some chose to guide others rather than flee alone.

Some returned to help.

Some remained steady long enough to lead the way.

Scripture speaks tenderly of this kind of deliverance:

"He delivereth the poor in his affliction, and openeth their ears in oppression."
— *Psalm 72:12*
Providence here was not the removal of danger.
It was the **preservation of possibility**.
God did not erase chaos.
He sustained order within it.
Escape was not guaranteed.
Paths narrowed.
Time was limited.
Yet enough remained intact for many to survive.
This too reflects a biblical pattern.
God often delivers **through** affliction, not merely *from* it. He provides just enough clarity, strength, and direction for escape—without eliminating the cost or the urgency of obedience.
Preservation did not come easily.
It came through motion, choice, and courage.
The paths held long enough.
The warnings reached ears willing to listen.
The courage of some preserved the lives of many.
Providence did not calm the moment.
It sustained escape **within** it.
And when the moment passed, survival stood as quiet testimony—not to human control, but to God's restraining mercy amid chaos.

Section Summary (Optional for Book or Class)
Taken together, these three examples reveal how preservation often works:
- **Timing** diverted people away from danger
- **Absence** reduced loss before it occurred
- **Sustained escape** preserved life amid chaos

Providence did not eliminate suffering.
It limited destruction.

Teaching Reflection (Optional)

You might ask:

- *Why does God sometimes preserve through endurance rather than removal?*
- *How do human courage and divine providence work together?*
- *What responsibility do we have when God preserves a path for others?*

---

6. What This Lesson Does *Not* Claim

Important clarification:

- Survivors were not "more righteous"
- Loss does not imply judgment on victims
- God's purposes are not fully known

Scripture is clear that human suffering cannot be neatly categorized or morally ranked. Survival does not equal virtue, and loss does not equal condemnation.

Jesus Himself rejected simplistic explanations for tragedy:

"Suppose ye that these Galilaeans were sinners above all the Galilaeans, because they suffered such things?

I tell you, Nay."

— **Luke 13:2–3**

This lesson does not claim:

- That those who lived were favored above those who died
- That victims were being judged
- That tragedy can be fully explained from human perspective

Instead, it acknowledges the limits of human understanding.

"The secret things belong unto the LORD our God."

— **Deuteronomy 29:29**

God's providence does not always explain *why* some are spared and others are not. Scripture never requires believers to assign meaning where God has not revealed it.

"Shall not the Judge of all the earth do right?"

— **Genesis 18:25**

Faith does not demand answers in moments when Scripture offers silence.

Sometimes silence is not avoidance—it is reverence.

Silence can be faithful.

---

7. God's Presence in Grief

Providence does not erase pain.

It does not minimize loss.

It does not rush healing.

Instead, it appears in quieter ways.

Providence:

- Walks with the broken
- Comforts the grieving
- Strengthens those who serve others

"The LORD is nigh unto them that are of a broken heart."

— **Psalm 34:18**

In the aftermath of September 11:

- First responders ran toward danger
- Ordinary people helped strangers
- Compassion rose amid chaos
- Courage appeared where fear might have ruled

These acts did not undo loss—but they revealed God's nearness in suffering.

"Blessed are they that mourn: for they shall be comforted."

— **Matthew 5:4**

Scripture does not promise exemption from grief.

It promises presence within it.

"When thou passest through the waters, I will be with thee."

— **Isaiah 43:2**

Providence was not displayed in explanation.

It was displayed in preservation, compassion, endurance, and mercy.

God was not absent on that day.

He was present—among the grieving, the wounded, and the helpers.

And He remains present still.

---

8. Discussion Questions (Choose 2–3)

1. Why must we speak carefully about tragedy?
2. How can preservation be recognized without explaining suffering?
3. What dangers arise from over-interpreting events?
4. How does God's presence comfort even without answers?

---

9. Personal & National Application

Personal

- Am I grateful for life preserved?
- Do I trust God without demanding explanation?

National

- Tragedy invites humility
- Memory requires reverence
- Mercy deserves gratitude

"Teach us to number our days."
— *Psalm 90:12*

---

10. Closing Reflection

September 11 revealed humanity's vulnerability in stark and unforgettable ways.

Strength failed. Systems were overwhelmed. Certainty vanished in a single morning. Scripture reminds us how fragile human security truly is:

"Boast not thyself of to morrow; for thou knowest not what a day may bring forth."
— *Proverbs 27:1*

The devastation was real, the loss immeasurable, and the questions overwhelming. Providence did not come with immediate explanations. God did not reveal all His purposes. Silence followed the shock:

"Be still, and know that I am God."
— *Psalm 46:10*

Yet within the devastation, mercy quietly moved.

Lives were preserved through delays no one planned. Routines were interrupted. Meetings were postponed. Decisions were changed at the last moment. Spaces stood empty that should have been full:

"Man's goings are of the LORD; how can a man then understand his own way?"
— *Proverbs 20:24*

Providence did not appear as prevention—but as preservation. Not all were spared, but many were. Not all danger was removed, but destruction was restrained:

"The LORD is merciful and gracious, slow to anger, and plenteous in mercy."
— *Psalm 103:8*

In stairwells, in moments of courage, in warnings heeded and help offered, God's hand was present—not loudly, not dramatically, but faithfully:

"He delivereth the poor in his affliction, and openeth their ears in oppression."
— *Job 36:15*

September 11 reminds us that providence does not always answer *why*.
Often, it answers *how far*.
"Thus far shalt thou come, but no farther."
— *Job 38:11*
The day exposed human weakness—but it also revealed divine restraint. God allowed grief, but He did not abandon the world to chaos:
"For the LORD will not cast off for ever."
— *Lamentations 3:31*
Providence was present—not in explanation, but in preservation.
Not in removing sorrow, but in limiting devastation.
Not in certainty, but in mercy that quietly endured.
"The LORD shall preserve thee from all evil: he shall preserve thy soul."
— *Psalm 121:7*
In moments when answers are withheld, preservation itself becomes testimony.

---

11. Closing Scripture & Prayer Prompt
Read aloud:
"The LORD is nigh unto them that are of a broken heart."
— *Psalm 34:18*
Prayer Prompt:
"Lord, comfort the grieving, strengthen the living, and help us walk humbly before You."

Lesson 32 — America at a Crossroads

Series Title

God's Providence in American History: From the Pilgrims to the Present

Theme Verse

"If my people, which are called by my name, shall humble themselves, and pray, and seek my face, and turn from their wicked ways; then will I hear from heaven, and will forgive their sin, and will heal their land."

— *2 Chronicles 7:14*

Lesson Aim (For the Teacher)

To help the class understand that providence is not only something to be recognized in the past, but something that **calls for present response**. This lesson emphasizes that **blessing, restraint, or correction depends on humility and repentance—not heritage or history**. This lesson emphasizes **responsibility before God**, not prediction of outcomes.

Time Flow (Minimum 40 Minutes)

- Opening Scripture & Prayer – 4 minutes
- Biblical Framework – 12 minutes
- Historical Reflection & Present Application – 16 minutes
- Discussion – 5 minutes
- Closing Exhortation & Prayer – 3 minutes

---

1. Opening Scripture Reading

Read aloud together:

"Righteousness exalteth a nation: but sin is a reproach to any people."

— *Proverbs 14:34*

---

2. Core Truth Statement

Nations do not drift accidentally—they move according to spiritual direction.

God's providence responds to humility or pride, repentance or resistance.

---

3. Biblical Pattern: Crossroads Moments

Key Scriptures

"I have set before you life and death, blessing and cursing."
— *Deuteronomy 30:19*
"Choose you this day whom ye will serve."
— *Joshua 24:15*
"The LORD shall judge the people."
— *Psalm 7:8*

Teaching Point (Scripture-Anchored)

Scripture reveals that nations repeatedly arrive at moments of decision where **direction matters more than momentum**. God does not force obedience—but He responds to choice.
(Jeremiah 18:7–10; Amos 4:12)

---

4. Looking Back: Patterns Repeated

As we look back across the span of this series—from early settlers to modern history—certain patterns emerge with striking consistency.
Though circumstances change, cultures shift, and technology advances, **God's dealings with nations remain steady**.
Throughout these lessons we have observed:

- **Deliverance following humility**
  When individuals and nations acknowledged dependence on God, help often came in unexpected ways.
  Not always immediate—but timely.

"Humble yourselves therefore under the mighty hand of God, that he may exalt you in due time."
— *1 Peter 5:6*

- **Restraint following prayer**
  Moments of collective prayer were frequently followed by the limitation of destruction rather than its escalation.
  Danger remained—but its reach was curbed.

"Call unto me, and I will answer thee."
— *Jeremiah 33:3*

- **Correction following pride**
  When confidence hardened into presumption, consequences followed.
  History repeatedly warns that unchecked pride invites collapse.

"Pride goeth before destruction, and an haughty spirit before a fall."
— *Proverbs 16:18*

- **Preservation following repentance**
  Where repentance occurred—personally or collectively—space was made for renewal, rebuilding, and restraint.
  Judgment did not have the final word.

"If my people… shall humble themselves, and pray, and seek my face, and turn from their wicked ways."
— *2 Chronicles 7:14*

These patterns reveal an essential truth:

Providence is consistent—even when circumstances change.

God's hand is not reactive.

It is purposeful.

"The counsel of the LORD standeth for ever, the thoughts of his heart to all generations."
— *Psalm 33:11*

History does not repeat itself by accident.

It echoes spiritual realities.

The same God who preserved life in storms, restrained destruction in war, and sustained hope in tragedy remains active today.

The lesson of history is not prediction—it is discernment.

Those who learn from providence gain wisdom.

Those who ignore it repeat the cost.

"Whoso is wise, and will observe these things, even they shall understand the lovingkindness of the LORD."
— *Psalm 107:43*

---

5. The Present Moment

Today's challenges include:

- Moral confusion
- Cultural division
- Loss of shared truth
- Confidence in systems rather than God

These conditions are not unique to our time. Scripture repeatedly shows societies reaching moments where clarity fades and confidence shifts from God to human wisdom.

"There is a way which seemeth right unto a man, but the end thereof are the ways of death."
— **Proverbs 14:12**

What makes the present moment significant is not novelty—but responsibility. History demonstrates that decline is rarely sudden. It comes through gradual neglect of truth, erosion of conscience, and substitution of convenience for conviction.

The danger is not disagreement alone.

It is confusion without humility.

"Professing themselves to be wise, they became fools."

— **Romans 1:22**

This moment does not demand panic.

It demands discernment.

Providence places generations at crossroads—not to predict outcomes, but to test responses.

---

6. What Providence Does *Not* Guarantee

Important clarification:

- No nation is promised permanence
- History does not secure the future
- Blessing is never automatic

Scripture is clear: past favor does not guarantee future protection. God's dealings with nations are moral, not sentimental.

"Be not highminded, but fear."

— **Romans 11:20**

Remembering God's mercy without continuing humility leads not to gratitude—but to presumption.

Israel learned this truth repeatedly:

- Deliverance was followed by forgetfulness
- Blessing gave way to pride
- Protection was withdrawn when warning was ignored

"Because thou sayest, I am rich… and knowest not that thou art wretched."

— **Revelation 3:17**

Providence does not guarantee:

- That liberty will remain without stewardship
- That institutions will endure without virtue
- That blessing will continue without obedience

Memory without humility becomes pride.

Pride invites correction.

---

7. What God Still Requires

Scripture is clear and unchanged:

- Humility precedes healing
- Repentance precedes restoration
- Prayer precedes guidance

"He hath shewed thee, O man, what is good; and what doth the LORD require of thee."
— **Micah 6:8**

God does not require:

- Political certainty
- Cultural dominance
- Historical nostalgia

He requires hearts aligned with truth.

"If my people, which are called by my name, shall humble themselves, and pray."
— **2 Chronicles 7:14**

Providence does not force outcomes.

It invites response.

The question before the nation is not whether God has acted in the past—but whether humility, repentance, and obedience will mark the present.

History shows what God can preserve.

Scripture reveals what God requires.

The future remains open—

but the path forward is not unclear.

---

8. Discussion Questions (Choose 2–3)

1. What does humility look like for a nation today?
2. Why is repentance difficult in times of prosperity?
3. How does history warn against presumption?
4. What responsibility belongs to God's people specifically?

---

9. Personal & National Application

Personal

- Am I responsive to God's correction?
- Do I seek God more than solutions?

National

- Healing requires humility
- Direction matters more than power

- God remains sovereign

"Serve the LORD with fear."
— *Psalm 2:11*

---

10. Closing Reflection

America's history reveals moments of mercy, restraint, and correction—often woven together in ways only visible with time. Blessing was not constant, discipline was not absent, and preservation was never automatic. Scripture teaches us that God's dealings with nations are purposeful and responsive:

"Righteousness exalteth a nation: but sin is a reproach to any people."
— *Proverbs 14:34*

History shows seasons when mercy was extended beyond expectation, moments when judgment was restrained, and periods when correction was permitted for the sake of humility:

"Whom the LORD loveth he correcteth."
— *Proverbs 3:12*

Providence does not guarantee outcomes. It responds to posture.
When humility was present, mercy followed.
When repentance was sought, restraint appeared.
When pride hardened hearts, correction was allowed:

"If my people, which are called by my name, shall humble themselves, and pray, and seek my face, and turn from their wicked ways; then will I hear from heaven."
— *2 Chronicles 7:14*

The future is not written. No nation possesses a permanent claim on blessing. Scripture is clear that God's patience has purpose, but it is not endless:

"The LORD is longsuffering, and great in mercy… but he will not at all acquit the wicked."
— *Numbers 14:18*

What history makes unmistakable is this pattern:
God responds not to power, not to prosperity, not to heritage—but to the posture of the heart:

"To this man will I look, even to him that is poor and of a contrite spirit, and trembleth at my word."
— *Isaiah 66:2*

Providence is not mechanical.
It is moral.
It is patient—but purposeful.
America's story, like all national stories, stands as both testimony and warning. Preservation was given—but responsibility followed. Mercy was extended—but accountability remained:

"Unto whomsoever much is given, of him shall be much required."
— *Luke 12:48*
The lesson of providence is not confidence in the past—but humility in the present. History does not promise the future. It instructs it.
"Blessed is the nation whose God is the LORD."
— *Psalm 33:12*
Providence responds to the posture of the heart.

---

11. Closing Scripture & Prayer Prompt
Read aloud together:
"Now therefore fear the LORD, and serve him in sincerity and in truth."
— *Joshua 24:14*
Prayer Prompt:
"Lord, turn our hearts toward You, teach us humility, and guide us according to Your truth."

CONCLUSION

Providence Remembered — Responsibility Renewed

"So teach us to number our days, that we may apply our hearts unto wisdom."
— **Psalm 90:12**

What We Have Seen

Across centuries of American history, a consistent pattern emerges—not of perfection, but of providence.

We have seen:

- Deliverance where success was unlikely
- Preservation amid weakness and division
- Restraint when destruction was possible
- Mercy following judgment

God's hand is not always dramatic.
It is often quiet, patient, and corrective.
Providence does not mean God approved every decision.
It means God remained sovereign even when people failed.
"Known unto God are all his works from the beginning of the world."
— Acts 15:18

What History Does Not Guarantee

History is a teacher—but it is not a protector.
Past blessing does not secure future favor.
Former humility does not replace present obedience.
Memory without repentance becomes pride.
Scripture warns:
"Be not highminded, but fear."
— Romans 11:20
Providence remembered without humility becomes presumption.

The Responsibility of God's People

Throughout Scripture, responsibility is placed not on nations in general—but on **God's people within them**.

"If my people, which are called by my name, shall humble themselves, and pray…"

— 2 Chronicles 7:14

Revival has never begun with institutions.

It has always begun with repentant hearts.

History does not call us to political solutions first—but to spiritual ones:

- Humility before God
- Prayer instead of presumption
- Obedience over confidence

Providence Going Forward

The future is not fixed—but God is faithful.

Providence does not promise ease.

It promises presence.

Whether through blessing or correction, restraint or renewal, God remains active in the affairs of men.

"The counsel of the LORD standeth for ever, the thoughts of his heart to all generations."

— Psalm 33:11

A Closing Charge

Let history do its work.

Let it humble us.

Let it warn us.

Let it teach gratitude.

And above all, let it turn our hearts again toward the Lord.

"Now therefore fear the LORD, and serve him in sincerity and in truth."

— Joshua 24:14

APPENDIX A - Teacher's Guide

Guidance for Teaching

God's Providence in American History: From the Pilgrims to the Present

---

"The servant of the Lord must not strive; but be gentle unto all men, apt to teach, patient."
— *2 Timothy 2:24*

Purpose of This Guide

This appendix exists to support teachers—not to script them.

The lessons in this curriculum are intentionally written to be:

- Scripture-anchored
- Historically careful
- Spiritually restrained
- Suitable for mixed-age adult settings

This guide provides **teaching orientation, pacing advice, and guardrails** to help instructors teach with confidence, humility, and clarity.

---

1. Teaching Philosophy

Scripture First, History Second

History is the **illustration**, not the authority.

- Scripture interprets history
- History never reinterprets Scripture
- Avoid forcing conclusions Scripture does not make

If a historical claim becomes uncertain, return to biblical principle.

"Thy word is a lamp unto my feet."
— *Psalm 119:105*

Providence Is Observed, Not Declared

Teachers should **point to patterns**, not pronounce verdicts.

Use language such as:

- "This appears to show…"
- "We can observe restraint here…"
- "This aligns with the biblical pattern of…"

Avoid language such as:

- "This proves God did…"
- "This guarantees blessing…"
- "This explains why tragedy happened…"

Humility honors God more than certainty.

---

2. Recommended Class Structure (40 Minutes)

Each lesson is designed to fit a **40-minute window**:

- **Opening Scripture & Prayer** – 3–5 minutes
- **Biblical Framework** – 10–12 minutes
- **Historical Narrative** – 15–18 minutes
- **Discussion & Application** – 5–7 minutes

If time is short:

- Never skip Scripture
- Condense historical examples
- Preserve application and reflection

---

3. Handling Sensitive Topics

This curriculum intentionally addresses:

- War
- National failure
- Slavery
- Tragedy
- Modern events

Teaching Guardrails

- Do not assign motives to God
- Do not equate survival with righteousness
- Do not equate suffering with judgment
- Do not turn lessons into political debates

When emotions arise:

- Slow the pace
- Return to Scripture
- Acknowledge pain without explanation

"Be swift to hear, slow to speak."
— *James 1:19*

---

4. Discussion Leadership Tips

Discussion questions are **optional**, not mandatory.

Best Practices:

- Choose 2–3 questions per lesson
- Redirect debates to Scripture

- Allow silence—it often signals reflection
- Affirm humility over certainty

If discussion drifts:

"Let's return to the biblical principle we just read."

---

5. Mixed-Age Teaching Considerations

This curriculum works best when:

- Complex ideas are explained simply
- Vocabulary is clear, not academic
- Scripture is read aloud regularly

For younger adults:

- Emphasize patterns and principles

For older adults:

- Emphasize memory, gratitude, and reflection

Avoid assuming:

- Political alignment
- Uniform historical knowledge
- Shared emotional reactions

---

6. Using Historical Sources Wisely

This study draws from:

- Primary historical documents
- Widely recognized historians
- Respected Christian researchers

Teachers should:

- Paraphrase rather than quote extensively
- Avoid "name-dropping" as authority
- Emphasize documented events, not speculation

History supports the lesson—it does not carry it.

---

7. When Questions Arise You Cannot Answer

Say so.

Phrases that preserve trust:

- "Scripture does not tell us."
- "History does not give a clear answer."
- "We can observe, but not conclude."

"The secret things belong unto the LORD."
— *Deuteronomy 29:29*
Unanswered questions often deepen faith.

---

8. The Teacher's Role

You are not asked to:

- Defend a nation
- Prove a thesis
- Resolve every tension

You are asked to:

- Open Scripture
- Teach with humility
- Encourage reflection
- Point hearts toward God

"Who then is Paul, and who is Apollos, but ministers by whom ye believed?"
— *1 Corinthians 3:5*

---

9. Recommended Opening Prayer (Optional)

"Lord, teach us through Your Word, guide us by Your truth, and help us see history with humility and gratitude. Guard our hearts from pride, and turn us toward wisdom. Amen."

---

10. Recommended Closing Prayer (Optional)

"Father, thank You for Your mercy, restraint, and faithfulness. Help us remember rightly, respond humbly, and walk obediently before You. Amen."

Final Encouragement to Teachers

This study is not about proving America's greatness.
It is about **recognizing God's faithfulness.**
Teach patiently.
Speak carefully.
Trust the Word.
"So then neither is he that planteth any thing, neither he that watereth; but God that giveth the increase."
— *1 Corinthians 3:7*

TIMELINE WALL CHART

God's Providence in American History

From the Pilgrims to the Present

"Known unto God are all his works from the beginning of the world."

— *Acts 15:18*

SECTION I — FOUNDATIONS BEFORE AMERICA (1500s–1620)

Preparing a People

1517–1600s — Reformation & Scripture Access

- Bible translated into common language
- Literacy spreads among ordinary people
- Conscience elevated over coercion

📖 *John 8:32; Psalm 119:130*

Providence Theme: Truth prepares liberty

1608–1619 — Pilgrims' Flight from Persecution

- Escape religious oppression
- Preservation despite poverty and exile

📖 *Psalm 34:19*

Providence Theme: God preserves seekers of truth

1620 — Mayflower Voyage & Compact

- Atlantic storms survived
- Covenant-based self-government formed

📖 *Psalm 107:23–30*

Providence Theme: Unity forged in crisis

SECTION II — SURVIVAL & COVENANT (1620–1700)

Preservation Against Odds

1620–1621 — First Winter at Plymouth

- Nearly half perish
- Colony survives against expectation

📖 *Deuteronomy 8:2–4*

Providence Theme: Sustenance in weakness

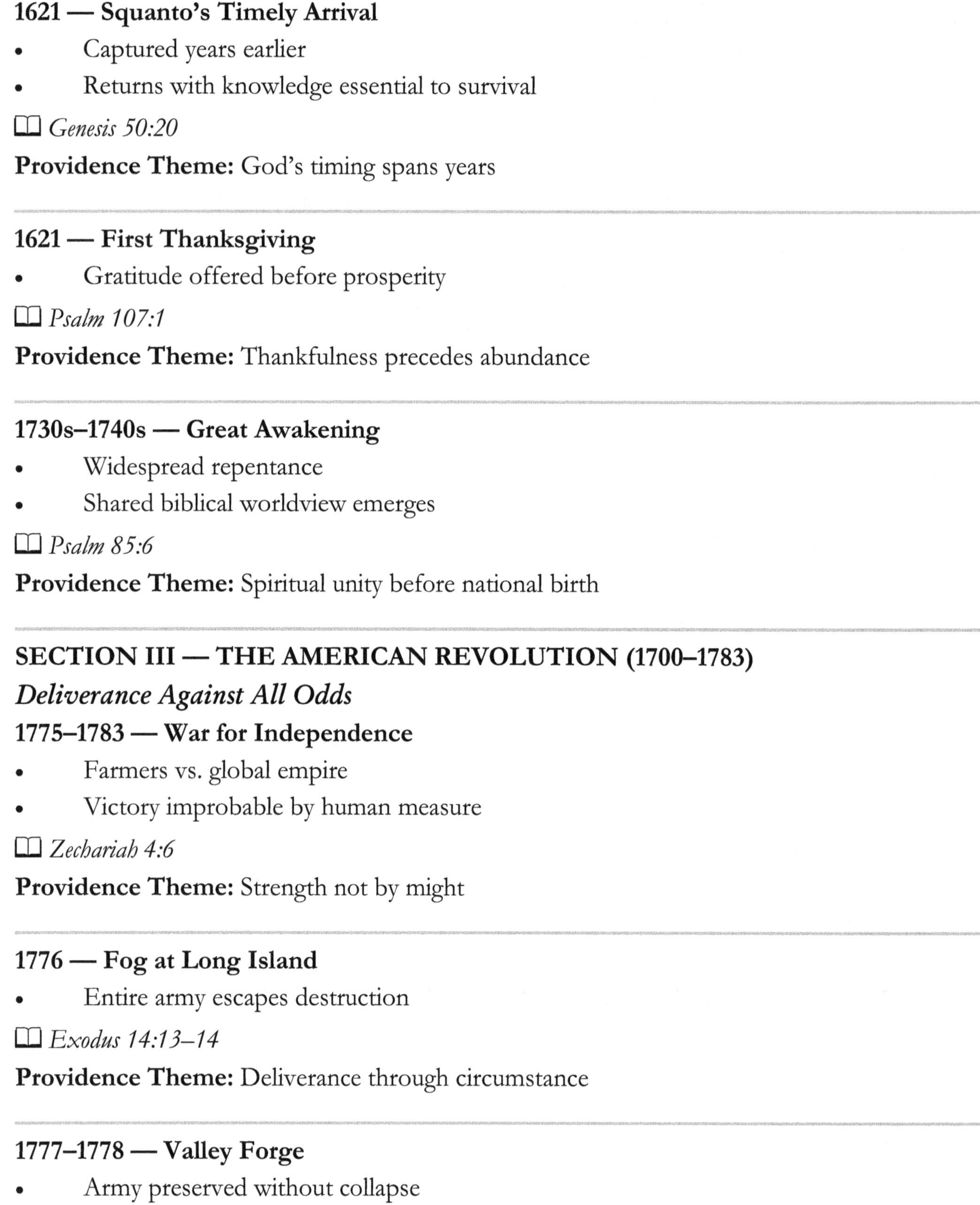

1621 — Squanto's Timely Arrival

- Captured years earlier
- Returns with knowledge essential to survival

🕮 *Genesis 50:20*

Providence Theme: God's timing spans years

1621 — First Thanksgiving

- Gratitude offered before prosperity

🕮 *Psalm 107:1*

Providence Theme: Thankfulness precedes abundance

1730s–1740s — Great Awakening

- Widespread repentance
- Shared biblical worldview emerges

🕮 *Psalm 85:6*

Providence Theme: Spiritual unity before national birth

SECTION III — THE AMERICAN REVOLUTION (1700–1783)

Deliverance Against All Odds

1775–1783 — War for Independence

- Farmers vs. global empire
- Victory improbable by human measure

🕮 *Zechariah 4:6*

Providence Theme: Strength not by might

1776 — Fog at Long Island

- Entire army escapes destruction

🕮 *Exodus 14:13–14*

Providence Theme: Deliverance through circumstance

1777–1778 — Valley Forge

- Army preserved without collapse

🕮 *Psalm 66:10–12*

Providence Theme: Endurance through testing

1781 — Yorktown Victory

- Critical timing of allied forces

📖 *Psalm 44:3*

Providence Theme: Victory through divine timing

SECTION IV — CONSTITUTION & EARLY REPUBLIC (1787–1820)

Wisdom After Victory

1787 — Constitutional Convention

- Prayer for wisdom
- Compromise without collapse

📖 *James 1:5*

Providence Theme: Counsel over chaos

1789 — Washington's Inauguration

- Public acknowledgment of God

📖 *Psalm 127:1*

Providence Theme: Humility in leadership

1790s–1800s — Early National Revivals

- Moral restraint strengthened

📖 *Proverbs 14:34*

Providence Theme: Righteousness sustains liberty

SECTION V — CIVIL WAR & NATIONAL TESTING (1861–1865)

Judgment Tempered with Mercy

1861–1865 — Civil War

- Nation divided
- Immense suffering

📖 *Matthew 12:25*

Providence Theme: Exposure before healing

1863 — National Calls to Prayer

- Public humility before God

📖 *Daniel 9:7*

Providence Theme: Repentance in judgment

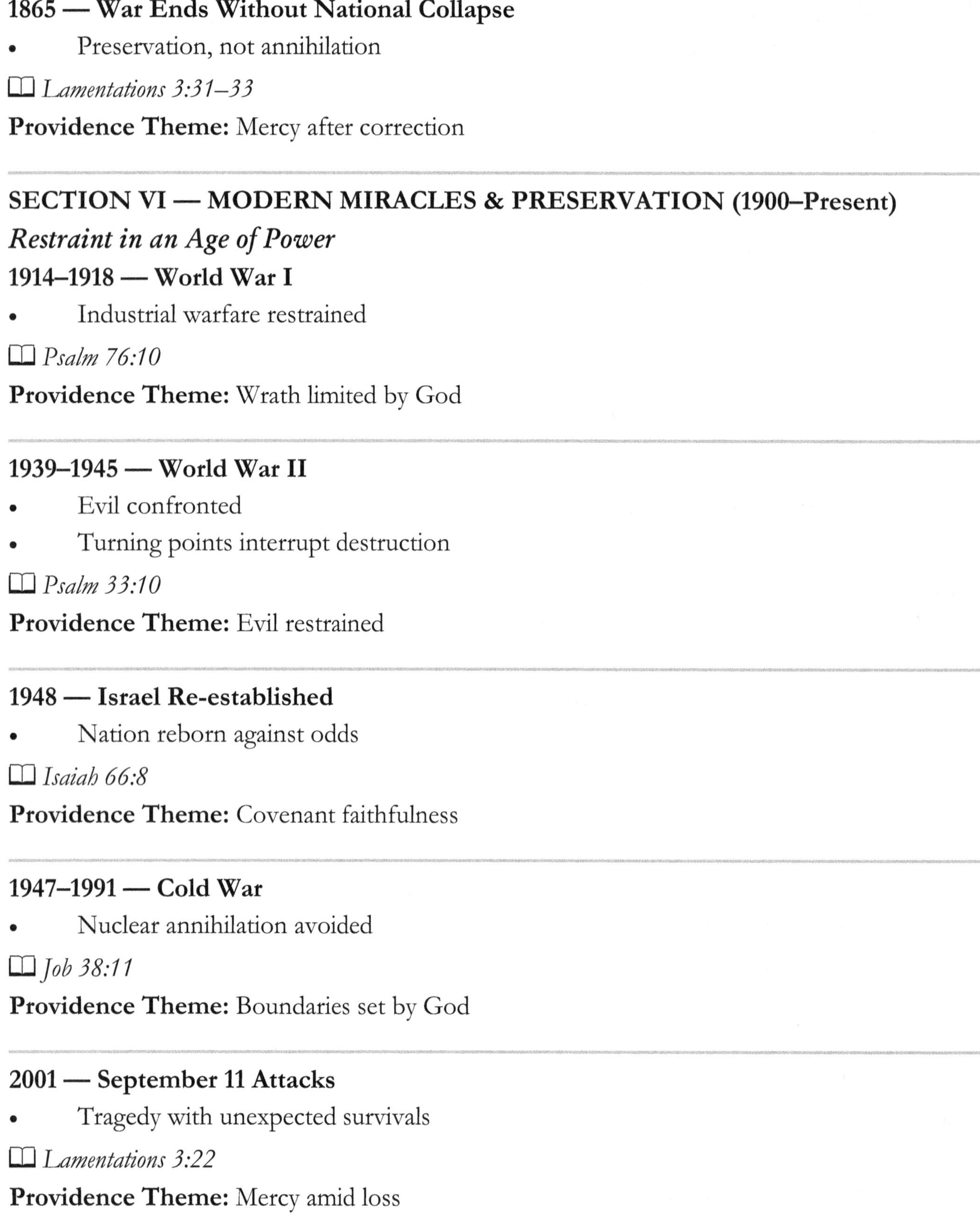

1865 — War Ends Without National Collapse

- Preservation, not annihilation

🕮 *Lamentations 3:31–33*

Providence Theme: Mercy after correction

SECTION VI — MODERN MIRACLES & PRESERVATION (1900–Present)

Restraint in an Age of Power

1914–1918 — World War I

- Industrial warfare restrained

🕮 *Psalm 76:10*

Providence Theme: Wrath limited by God

1939–1945 — World War II

- Evil confronted
- Turning points interrupt destruction

🕮 *Psalm 33:10*

Providence Theme: Evil restrained

1948 — Israel Re-established

- Nation reborn against odds

🕮 *Isaiah 66:8*

Providence Theme: Covenant faithfulness

1947–1991 — Cold War

- Nuclear annihilation avoided

🕮 *Job 38:11*

Providence Theme: Boundaries set by God

2001 — September 11 Attacks

- Tragedy with unexpected survivals

🕮 *Lamentations 3:22*

Providence Theme: Mercy amid loss

Present — America at a Crossroads

- Moral and spiritual decision point

📖 *2 Chronicles 7:14*

Providence Theme: Responsibility before God

FOOTER (For the Wall Chart)

Key Pattern Across History:

Humility → Mercy

Pride → Correction

Repentance → Preservation

"The counsel of the LORD standeth for ever."

— *Psalm 33:11*

A FINAL PASTORAL EXHORTATION

Remembering God's Hand — Responding with Our Hearts

"Only take heed to thyself, and keep thy soul diligently, lest thou forget the things which thine eyes have seen."
— *Deuteronomy 4:9*

A Word Before We Part

As this study comes to a close, it is important to pause—not to summarize facts, but to **listen.**
History speaks.
Scripture interprets.
And conscience responds.
This series was never intended to make us proud of a nation, confident in outcomes, or certain about the future. It was written to help us **remember God rightly**—and to respond **humbly**.

What Providence Has Shown Us

Across centuries, one truth has emerged repeatedly:
God is faithful—even when people are not.
We have seen:

- Deliverance when success was unlikely
- Preservation amid weakness
- Restraint when destruction was possible
- Mercy following judgment

Providence has not meant perfection.
It has meant **patience**.
"The LORD is merciful and gracious, slow to anger, and plenteous in mercy."
— *Psalm 103:8*

What History Cannot Do

History can teach—but it cannot save.
Memory can warn—but it cannot transform.
Heritage can inspire—but it cannot substitute for obedience.
Scripture reminds us:
"Say not thou, It is through the LORD that this is come upon us."
— *Deuteronomy 9:4*
Past blessing never guarantees future favor.

The Call Is Always Personal

Throughout Scripture, when nations stood at crossroads, God spoke not first to governments—but to **His people**.

"If my people, which are called by my name…"

— *2 Chronicles 7:14*

Revival has never begun with legislation.

It has always begun with **repentance**.

This study ends where responsibility begins: **with the heart**.

A Word About the Times We Live In

Every generation feels unique—and in some ways, it is.

But spiritually, the patterns repeat.

- Confidence grows
- Dependence fades
- Correction follows
- Mercy invites return

"There is no new thing under the sun."

— *Ecclesiastes 1:9*

What changes is not God's character—but our response.

How Then Shall We Live?

Not in fear.

Not in pride.

Not in nostalgia.

But in:

- Humility before God
- Gratitude for mercy
- Obedience in daily life
- Faithfulness where we stand

"To do justly, and to love mercy, and to walk humbly with thy God."

— *Micah 6:8*

A Quiet Hope

Providence does not promise ease—but it promises **presence**.

God has not abandoned His authority over nations, nor His care for individuals. He still:

- Hears prayer
- Resists pride
- Honors humility
- Extends mercy

"The LORD reigneth."

— *Psalm 97:1*

That truth has outlasted empires—and it will outlast us.

A Final Appeal

Remember what you have seen.

Teach it faithfully.

Live it quietly.

And when history presses hard, let Scripture guide your steps.

"Now therefore fear the LORD, and serve him in sincerity and in truth."

— *Joshua 24:14*

Closing Prayer (Optional for Reading Aloud)

"Lord, teach us to remember rightly, to walk humbly, and to trust You fully. Guard our hearts from pride, awaken us to repentance, and help us live faithfully in the time You have given us. Amen."

End of Study

May God grant wisdom to remember,
humility to respond,
and faithfulness to endure.

STUDENT TIMELINE

God's Providence in American History

From the Pilgrims to the Present

"Blessed is the nation whose God is the LORD."

— *Psalm 33:12*

FOUNDATIONS BEFORE AMERICA (1500s–1620)

Preparing a People

- **Reformation Era** — Bible translated; truth spreads

📖 *John 8:32*

- **Pilgrims Flee Persecution** — Preserved in exile

📖 *Psalm 34:19*

- **1620 – Mayflower Voyage** — Storms survived; covenant formed

📖 *Psalm 107:23–30*

Providence Pattern: Truth prepares liberty

SURVIVAL & COVENANT (1620–1700)

Preservation Against Odds

- **First Winter at Plymouth** — Colony survives severe loss

📖 *Deuteronomy 8:2–4*

- **Squanto's Timely Help** — God's timing over years

📖 *Genesis 50:20*

- **First Thanksgiving (1621)** — Gratitude before prosperity

📖 *Psalm 107:1*

- **Great Awakening (1730s–40s)** — Spiritual unity emerges

📖 *Psalm 85:6*

Providence Pattern: God sustains the weak

AMERICAN REVOLUTION (1700–1783)

Deliverance Against All Odds

- **War for Independence** — Victory improbable

📖 *Zechariah 4:6*

- **Fog at Long Island (1776)** — Army escapes destruction

📖 *Exodus 14:13–14*

- **Valley Forge (1777–78)** — Army preserved

🕮 *Psalm 66:10–12*

- **Yorktown (1781)** — Victory through timing

🕮 *Psalm 44:3*

Providence Pattern: Not by might, but by God

CONSTITUTION & EARLY REPUBLIC (1787–1820)

Wisdom After Victory

- **Constitutional Convention (1787)** — Prayer for wisdom

🕮 *James 1:5*

- **Washington's Inauguration (1789)** — Public humility

🕮 *Psalm 127:1*

- **Early Revivals** — Moral restraint strengthened

🕮 *Proverbs 14:34*

Providence Pattern: Liberty requires humility

CIVIL WAR & NATIONAL TESTING (1861–1865)

Judgment Tempered with Mercy

- **Nation Divided** — Moral contradiction exposed

🕮 *Matthew 12:25*

- **Calls to Prayer (1863)** — Public humility

🕮 *Daniel 9:7*

- **War Ends** — Nation preserved, not destroyed

🕮 *Lamentations 3:31*

Providence Pattern: Correction without annihilation

MODERN PRESERVATION (1900–Present)

Restraint in an Age of Power

- **World War I** — Destruction restrained

🕮 *Psalm 76:10*

- **World War II** — Evil interrupted

🕮 *Psalm 33:10*

- **Israel Re-established (1948)** — Covenant faithfulness

🕮 *Isaiah 66:8*

- **Cold War** — Nuclear catastrophe avoided

🕮 *Job 38:11*

- **September 11, 2001** — Preservation amid tragedy

🕮 *Lamentations 3:22*

Providence Pattern: Mercy seen in restraint

TODAY — A CROSSROADS

- **Present Generation** — Responsibility before God

🕮 *2 Chronicles 7:14*

KEY PATTERN TO REMEMBER

Humility → Mercy

Pride → Correction

Repentance → Preservation

"The counsel of the LORD standeth for ever."

— *Psalm 33:11*

SOURCES & INFLUENCES

A Note on Authority, History, and Purpose

Primary Authority: Scripture

This book is grounded first and foremost in **the Word of God.**

All historical reflection, interpretation, and application within these pages is intentionally filtered through Scripture, not placed above it.

Scripture quotations throughout this book are taken from the **King James Version.**

The Bible provides the framework for understanding:

- God's sovereignty over nations
- His restraint of evil
- His use of imperfect people
- His patience across generations
- His calls to humility, repentance, and obedience

History is examined here **in light of Scripture**, not the other way around.

Use of Historical Material

This work is **not intended to be an academic textbook**, nor does it attempt to catalog every historical detail or debate. Its purpose is to highlight **patterns of providence**—moments where restraint, preservation, timing, and mercy are evident despite human weakness.

Historical facts, events, and quotations referenced in this book are drawn from **widely accepted historical records**, including:

- Colonial journals and early settlement accounts
- Public documents from America's founding era
- Presidential proclamations, speeches, and correspondence
- Well-established summaries of major American and global conflicts
- Recognized historical timelines and public records

Care has been taken to present events **accurately and responsibly**, while avoiding speculation, sensationalism, or partisan interpretation.

Historical Voices and Influences

While this book does not rely on any single historian or modern author, its understanding of American history reflects the influence of **classical historical voices and primary-source documents**, such as:

- **William Bradford**, *Of Plymouth Plantation*
- **Colonial sermons and proclamations** from the 17th and 18th centuries

- **George Washington**, including his Farewell Address and public correspondence
- **Abraham Lincoln**, especially the Second Inaugural Address
- **Early American historical works**, including those of **George Bancroft**
- Standard historical accounts of the American Revolution, Civil War, World Wars, Cold War, and modern events

These sources provide **context**, not authority. Scripture alone defines truth, morality, and ultimate meaning.

What This Book Does — and Does Not — Claim

This book:

- Does not declare America (or any modern nation) to be "chosen" in the biblical covenant sense uniquely given to the nation of Israel—God's covenant people in the past, present, and future (Genesis 12:1–3; Deuteronomy 7:6–8; Romans 9:4–5).
- Does **not** claim moral perfection for America or its leaders
- Does **not** equate political success with divine approval
- Does **not** assume future blessing based on past mercy

Instead, it seeks to show that:

- God governs nations whether they acknowledge Him or not
- Providence often appears through restraint rather than spectacle
- Preservation is not endorsement
- Blessing does not remove accountability

History is presented as **testimony**, not proof—inviting reflection rather than demanding conclusions.

Purpose of This Work

This book was written to help readers:

- Recognize God's providence without presumption
- Remember mercy without forgetting responsibility
- Learn from history without idolizing it
- Respond to preservation with humility and obedience

The lessons of providence are meant not to produce pride, but **gratitude**—and not confidence in nations, but **dependence on God**.

"Known unto God are all his works from the beginning of the world."
— Acts 15:18

How to Trust Jesus as Your Savior

The most important decision any person will ever make is what they do with Jesus Christ.
Becoming a Christian is not about joining a religion, trying harder, or becoming good enough. It is about **trust** — trusting Jesus.
The Bible tells us that every one of us has fallen short of God's perfect standard. We have all sinned. That sin separates us from God, and left on its own, it leads to death — not only physical death, but eternal separation from the God who made us and loves us.
But God did not leave us there.
In His great love, God sent His Son, Jesus Christ, to do for us what we could never do for ourselves. Jesus lived a perfect life, willingly died on the cross for our sins, was buried, and rose again. His resurrection is God's assurance that sin and death have been defeated.
The Bible speaks of this love in simple and beautiful words:
"For God so loved the world, that He gave His only begotten Son, that whoever believes in Him shall not perish, but have eternal life."
— John 3:16
Becoming a Christian is not a long process — it is a moment of trust. It is the moment when you personally rely on Jesus Christ alone to save you. It is choosing, from the heart, to say something like this:
"Jesus, I know that I cannot save myself. I believe You died for me and rose again. I place my trust in You right now to forgive my sins and give me eternal life."
The words themselves are not what save you. What matters is the posture of your heart — trusting Jesus alone to save you.
That is faith. You do not need to walk an aisle, join a church, or perform good works to be saved. Salvation is God's free gift, received by faith alone.
If you have never trusted Jesus Christ, you can do so right now — wherever you are, in the quiet of your heart. The moment you place your trust in Him, God declares you forgiven, gives you eternal life, and welcomes you as His child.
And if you have already trusted Christ, keep growing. Walk with Him day by day. Read His Word. Learn to rely on His Spirit. Remember — the Christian life begins with grace, and it continues by grace.

Scripture References

📖 **Romans 3:23**
For all have sinned, and come short of the glory of God;

📖 **Romans 6:23**
For the wages of sin is death; but the gift of God is eternal life through Jesus Christ our Lord.

📖 **1 Peter 3:18**
For Christ also hath once suffered for sins, the just for the unjust, that he might bring us to God, being put to death in the flesh, but quickened by the Spirit:

📖 **John 3:16**
For God so loved the world, that he gave his only begotten Son, that whosoever believeth in him should not perish, but have everlasting life.

📖 **Romans 10:9–10, 13**
That if thou shalt confess with thy mouth the Lord Jesus, and shalt believe in thine heart that God hath raised him from the dead, thou shalt be saved.
For with the heart man believeth unto righteousness; and with the mouth confession is made unto salvation.
For whosoever shall call upon the name of the Lord shall be saved.
These verses explain the simple and wonderful truth of salvation by grace through faith in Jesus Christ.

About the Author

Russell McFall is a Bible teacher and author whose lifelong passion is helping people see God's Word as a living story—clear, accessible, and deeply personal. A graduate of Trinity Bible College in Dunedin, Florida, he has spent decades studying Scripture, serving in ministry, teaching young people, and encouraging believers to walk with God in everyday life.

Russell writes with a warm, fatherly voice shaped by years of faith, family, and experience. Whether through devotional reflections or imaginative adventure stories for teens, his desire is the same: to point readers toward the goodness, faithfulness, and redeeming love of God.

Through **Ordained Path Books**, Russell continues to create resources that strengthen hearts, build faith, and draw readers closer to the Savior. His greatest joy is seeing God use simple words to make a lasting impact—one heart, one home, one generation at a time.

He and his wife make their home in the United States, where he keeps writing, keeps teaching, and keeps marveling at the grace of the God who still transforms lives today.

Ordained Path Books

Clean Science Fiction and Inspirational
Writing for Thoughtful Readers

Russell McFall writes both imaginative science-fiction adventures and reflective Christian nonfiction, each shaped by a commitment to clear truth, moral courage, and hope rooted in Scripture.

Fiction Series

- *The Space Cadet Richard Series*
- *The Space Cadet Legacy Series*

Devotional and Reflection Books

- *Remembering God's Help — Stone by Stone*
- *The Bible Unlocked*
- *Attributes of God*
- *This Is My Story, This Is My Song*
- *Lives of Faith*
- *Foundations of Faith*
- *Handling God's Word With Care*
- *God's Providence in American History*

Each book from Ordained Path Books is written with the same purpose—to encourage careful thinking, faithful living, and confidence that light still wins.
Clean Stories. Clear Truth. Courage for Every Generation.

www.ingramcontent.com/pod-product-compliance
Lightning Source LLC
LaVergne TN
LVHW061202120826
845149LV00011B/1876
* 9 7 8 1 9 7 2 7 2 4 1 8 7 *